Schooling for Resilience

Schooling for Resilience

Improving the Life Trajectory
of Black and Latino Boys

Edward Fergus, Pedro Noguera,
and Margary Martin

Harvard Education Press
Cambridge, Massachusetts

Third Printing, 2015

Library of Congress Control Number 2013952616

Paperback ISBN 978-1-61250-674-6
Library Edition ISBN 978-1-61250-675-3

Published by Harvard Education Press,
an imprint of the Harvard Education Publishing Group

Harvard Education Press
8 Story Street
Cambridge, MA 02138

Cover Design: Wilcox Design
Cover Photo: © Purestock/SuperStock/Corbis

The typefaces used in this book are Scala and Myriad Pro.

Contents

1

Single-Sex Schools

An Intervention in Search of a Theory

Over the past ten years, much of the concern over the so-called "achievement gap"—the pervasive disparities in academic achievement between Black[1] and Latino[2] students and their White counterparts—has centered on the performance of boys of color.[3] The reason for concern is not surprising: Black and Latino males are conspicuously overrepresented on most indicators associated with risk and academic failure. While many other groups of students are also more likely to underperform in school—English language learners, students with learning disabilities, students from low-income families—the vast array of negative outcomes associated with Black and Latino males distinguishes them as among the most vulnerable populations.[4]

All of the most important quality-of-life indicators suggest that Black and Latino males face a wide variety of hardships that, generally speaking, impede their abilities to succeed both socially and academically. Black and Latino male teenagers lead the nation in homicides, both as victims and as perpetrators.[5] For the last decade, Black and Latino males have contracted HIV at a faster rate than any other segment of the population and represent the largest percentages of new diagnoses.[6] Even as infants, Black males have the highest probability of dying within the first year of life,[7] and as they grow older they face the unfortunate reality of being the only group in the United States to experience a decline in life expectancy. In the labor market, Black males are generally the least likely to be hired, while Latinos are the most likely to be permanently trapped in low-wage jobs.[8]

Considering the ominous array of social and economic hardships that beset them, compounded by a history of systematic discrimination, it is hardly surprising that many young Black and Latino males fare poorly in education. The challenges and hardships are evident on most indicators of academic performance, from test scores to degree attainment. Nationally, Black males are more likely than any other group to be suspended and expelled from school, and they are more likely to be arrested in a school setting.

Though there is considerable variation based on national origin and the region of the country where they reside, the plight of Latino males tends to mirror that of Black males. Latino males are also vastly overrepresented in the penal system; over half of all inmates in California, for example, are Latino.[9] Latino males drop out of school in higher numbers than any group in American society.[10] College attendance rates for Latino males remain extremely low, while their attrition rates from universities and community colleges are extremely high.[11] Due to discrimination and the inability of many schools to serve the language needs of recent immigrant students, Latinos are often tracked into remedial classes and ESL (English as a Second Language) programs that deny them access to college prep courses. Such practices contribute to failure and alienation and to the high dropout rates that are widespread in school districts throughout the country.[12]

Gradually, as awareness of these patterns and the social costs associated with them has grown, educators, community groups, and policy makers have begun formulating a response. In recent years, several private foundations (e.g., the Ford Foundation, Open Society Foundation, Schott Foundation, and California Endowment, to name just a few) and public officials at the local, state, and federal levels of government have called for urgent measures to address the negative trends associated with Black and Latino males. In August 2011, New York City Mayor

Michael Bloomberg announced that he and billionaire philanthropist George Soros were donating $200 million of their own fortunes and redirecting millions more in public funds to a variety of initiatives that they felt would address the "crisis" confronting Latino and African American males. Similar initiatives have been launched in other communities throughout the country.

While these efforts are an encouraging development, it is too early to know whether they are having an impact on the broad array of problems confronting Black and Latino males, nor is it certain that they will be sustained. Part of what is particularly troubling about many of the initiatives that have been launched in response to this crisis is the lack of clarity about the role of race and gender in the failure of so many boys and young men. Race and gender set this vulnerable population apart, but it is not clear how those factors relate to the underlying causes of the academic and social problems that Black and Latino males face. Elsewhere we have described the current situation as *an intervention in search of a theory*.[13] Good intentions—rather than a clear understanding about the nature of the problems to be solved—are what appear to be guiding many recent initiatives. As we will show in this study of seven single-sex schools, good intentions may not be enough to generate real solutions. To the extent that those seeking to craft solutions lack an understanding of how and why so many Black and Latino males are at risk, and why race, ethnicity, and gender seem to be so clearly implicated in the problems they face, it may turn out that the programs now being designed will not only fail to solve the problem, but may even inadvertently make it worse.

Yet lack of clarity about the causes has not prevented those who seek to help Black and Latino males from taking action. Since 2003, the creation of single-sex schools has been embraced in various parts of the United States as a strategy for ameliorating the risks and hardships commonly associated with the academic performance and social development of these young men. Single-sex schools are by no means new to education, but in recent years most of the new single-sex schools that have been established—public, private, and charter—have been created specifically for this "at-risk" population. As we will show, the effort to protect and support Black and Latino boys through the creation of single-sex schools grows out of a genuine desire on the part of dedicated educators to protect the vulnerable and reverse the tide of failure. However, these educators have not had the benefit of a clear and convincing body of research to guide their efforts. For this reason, despite their extraordinary dedication—and even some evidence of relative success—the intervention strategies they have devised have not always been sufficient to address the complex problems facing these students.

Two specific policy developments have contributed to the proliferation of all-boys schools as a remedy for the academic underperformance of Black and Latino boys and a strategy to alter the life course endemic to this population. The first policy development involved the amendment changes to Title IX in No Child Left Behind (NCLB) in 2002, which allowed for the creation of single-sex classrooms, programs, and schools. The second development involved the subgroup analyses that emerged from the implementation of Adequate Yearly Progress (AYP) measures in the 2001 Elementary Secondary Education Act (ESEA). This provision required an annual public record of academic underperformance of specific subgroups (e.g., economically disadvantaged students, racial groups, students with disabilities, and gender groups).[14] As more and more school districts began compiling and disaggregating data on academic performance of students, the overrepresentation of Black and Latino boys on most indices related to school failure became evident. Increasingly, single-sex schools (and classrooms in some places) have emerged as an intervention embraced by a growing number of educators and community groups. Encouraged by leaders from communities of color, schools districts in cities like Chicago, New York, Houston, and Philadelphia, as well as Columbus, Ohio, and Lexington, Kentucky, have created all-male schools designed specifically to serve Black and Latino boys. In many of these cities, the assumption has been that such schools would be better at reaching this population than traditional public schools, where failure has been widespread and persistent.

As the number of public schools offering single-sex education has grown, the demand for evidence that such schools are in fact better than traditional coeducational schools has also increased. In 1999, only four public schools in the United States offered single-sex education. By 2006 there were 223 public single-sex schools, and by 2011 that number had reached 506.[15] Despite this dramatic increase, there has been a shortage of research supporting the academic benefits of isolating Black and Latino males from their peers, and the small number of studies that have been conducted so far have not found consistent benefits in such schools.[16]

Some of the inconsistencies in the results obtained by single-sex schools may be due to variation in research design and/or variation in the characteristics of the participating schools.[17] For example, Fred Mael, in a meta-analysis of single-sex school research, cites studies measuring different areas of academic achievement, as well as comparisons between parochial and public schools without accounting for differences in enrollment policies. The variation in the design of the small number of studies that do exist has made it difficult to definitively identify positive or negative results of single-sex education. Furthermore, there is an absence of quasi-experimental or experimental research studies of single-sex schools for boys of color—the research design commonly regarded as the "gold standard" for empirical evidence. Nonetheless, despite the absence of clear and compelling evidence, a growing number of policy makers and educators have begun to embrace all-male schools and classrooms as an educational option for Black and Latino males. Advocates view these schools as an intervention that represents hope for solving many of the problems facing this vulnerable population. Yet the question remains whether single-sex schools are a promising intervention or just another of the many experiments carried out in the name of school reform.

In this book we attempt to shed light on both the limits and the possibilities of single-sex schooling for Black and Latino boys. We offer this study not as the final word on the merits of single-sex education, but rather as a careful analysis of seven single-sex schools. It is our hope that by deeply probing the strategies and practices utilized by these schools to meet the academic and social needs of the boys they served, we will be in a better position to understand why some of these schools seem to be succeeding while others are not.

Our study focuses on seven all-male schools that opened between 2003 and 2007. The schools are located in major urban centers in the Midwest, Southwest, Northeast, and Southeast. To our surprise, without ever consulting one another, each school developed core curriculum, created mentoring and rites-of-passage programs, designed professional development for teachers, and implemented counseling and out-of-school-time services that were remarkably similar. As we will show, they viewed these measures as necessary to protect their students from the dangers and hardships present in the neighborhoods where they lived and to increase the likelihood that their efforts to educate boys of color would show success. In this book we explore the assumptions that guided the choices they made in order to understand how these schools sought to protect the boys they served from the risks they were perceived as facing. (Please see appendix 1 for detailed descriptions of each of the schools, including history and community context, student recruitment and demographics, organizational structure, curriculum, school climate, and activities.)

As a byproduct of this analysis we begin to construct a new framework that we hope can be used to create schools that are protective of boys of color. Based on the findings we present from this study, we hypothesize that in order for boys of color to successfully negotiate the structural and cultural obstacles that exist within their communities and society generally, schools must create environments that are deliberately designed to protect them and to promote resilience. These protective factors include strategies, programs, and interventions that are based on an understanding of the ways in which race, ethnicity, and gender shape the identities of the students served. In each of these schools we found deliberate efforts to address the social identities of Black and Latino males through practices that were intended to promote resilience and combat adversity. Knowing how influential and potentially detrimental stereotypes related to race and gender can be to the academic success of these students,[18] we have been particularly atten-

6

tive to whether the efforts undertaken by the schools either reinforced or countered them. We also analyze the way these schools organized and implemented their vision and mission (chapter 2), their approach to teaching and learning (chapter 3), the way they sought to mold the climate and culture (chapter 4), and the approaches they adopted to support the socioemotional development of their students (chapter 5). Our goal has been to understand how these features of the schools were influencing the academic and social development of the boys they serve (chapter 6).

Description of the Study and Schools

The Study

In response to the proliferation of single-sex schools, and aware of the wide gulf between practice and evidence-based theory, we identified a pressing need for an applied-research study that could shed some light on what was happening within single-sex schools. In 2006, with funding from the Bill and Melinda Gates Foundation, we began a three-year longitudinal study of seven single-sex schools located in four school districts in different American cities. The goal of the study was to examine these newly formed single-sex schools (opening in 2003–04 or later) in order to understand how they were developed, what practices they employed, and how their students were responding academically and socially in these contexts. Please note that throughout the book we have used pseudonyms to refer to these schools and to the individuals whom we interviewed.

The three years of data collection made it possible for us to conduct in-depth interviews and focus groups with nearly three hundred students, parents, and school staff. We also collected and analyzed a variety of documents and artifacts (such as brochures, school/district policy manuals, lesson plans, professional development agendas, handouts for parents and students, Web sites, etc.) from each school, and engaged in over three hundred hours of classroom and hallway observations. Additionally, we surveyed nearly 2,500 students at the seven schools. The data was collected via three site visits per year (fall, winter, and spring) with each school. Each site visit involved four to five days of data collection at each school, starting at the beginning of the school day and lasting through dismissal from the afterschool programs. At some sites we were also able to attend parent-teacher meetings and special speaker events.

We began our study by developing a theory-of-change map for each of the seven schools. We did this in order to make explicit the assumptions that were guiding the schools as they implemented their visions. We also found this to be an effective way to understand why and how they rationalized the particular practices and strategies they had implemented. This, in turn, allowed us to map out how each school went about meeting the academic and social needs of their students. By exploring the theoretical basis underlying the development of these schools, we were better able to understand the choices that were made pertaining to the curriculum, instructional practices, the selection of staff, the initiation of programs and community partnerships, and the organizational structure of the schools. We understood that it was insufficient to simply describe the strategies implemented in these schools, since this would not make it possible to capture the underlying assumptions guiding the approach taken to meet the needs of a vulnerable population. We hypothesized that by exposing and examining these assumptions we might better understand how they perceived their students and the nature of the risks they faced, a point we will return to shortly. We also closely examined how the educators thought about addressing the contextual factors that influenced the development of their male students in positive as well as negative ways. Our goal was to make the theory of change guiding the operation of these schools explicit so that we could unearth and make sense of the particular strategies utilized to promote resilience and to create protective schools.

Over the course of the three years we spent in these schools, we witnessed a variety of practices and rituals that were adopted to build community and reinforce core values. Some of these practices were sustained, while others were abandoned when they proved to be ineffective. At each school we sought to understand how the goal of creating a learning climate where male students of color would succeed was pursued. An administrator at Kennedy College Preparatory Academy explained the intent behind the practices his school had adopted by stating, "What we're doing here is intended to save the boys from what society is doing to them." Saving boys was a goal we heard expressed repeatedly during the three years we carried out our research, and we wanted to understand how it was being done.

It is important to note that the notion that these schools are "saving" boys of color constitutes a significant departure from the national discourse on school reform. While moral imperatives abound in much of the rhetoric about school reform (e.g., characterizing it as "the civil rights issue of the twenty-first century"), many national school reform efforts have been based on a variety of narrowly focused policy initiatives such as high-stakes testing, implementation of common core standards, teacher accountability, and using data to monitor academic performance. There are also a number of educational practices that have been embraced to promote higher achievement, such as personalization, the use of technology, and a host of practices associated with "No Excuses" reforms. While many of these same ideas have influenced the creation of schools for boys of color, the educators who founded and lead these schools have framed their work around a profound moral imperative: creating schools that can save Black and Latino boys from prisons, gangs, and early deaths. While the emphasis on resilience may sound familiar, the urgency these educators exhibit is drawn from an awareness of the dire threats confronting those they serve. As we will show, given that the challenges confronting their students extend well beyond the boundaries of the schools, their clarity of mission sets them apart in numerous and important ways.

The Schools

Each of the schools in this study was established with the clear and explicit mission of doing something to improve opportunities and life chances for Black and Latino boys. For example, at Salem Academy on Culture and Justice, a ninth- through twelfth-grade high school in a

Northeastern city, the founder had a vision that placed history and citizenship at the center of the school's values and culture. The goal was to create a school that would provide students with a moral center that would make it possible for Black and Latino boys to overcome the obstacles they are likely to face in this country. He explained: "By grounding them in their history and culture we hope to help them to understand their extraordinary potential for greatness and leadership." Each of the other schools was created with a similar mission, and although there were important differences in how they were organized and structured, the schools shared several features that are attributable to this mission. We provide richer descriptions of each school in appendix 1, but here, in table 1.1, we offer a broad demographic description of the seven schools in the study.

Overall, the schools have similar demographic characteristics, the primary one being that they serve Black and Latino male students from low socioeconomic status families (as indicated by their eligibility for free or reduced lunch). There were far more Black students than Latino students in these single-sex schools. In fact, two of the schools, Thomas Jefferson and Bethune, served almost exclusively Black student populations, while two others, Westward and Kennedy, had Black enrollments of 90 percent or above. In the other three schools, Black students made up slightly more than half the student population, with the remainder made up of Latino and, in a few cases, South Asian students. It is important to note that among the Black students, there are also a number of students of African and Caribbean heritage. Moreover, some of the Black students also identify as Latino; however, identifying these students was in many cases more difficult because the schools did not collect data on ethnicity, only race.

All of the schools are located in major America cities and in inner-city neighborhoods where poverty is concentrated. At the time of the study, Thomas Jefferson had the largest number of students per grade, with one hundred fifty students in a single ninth-grade class. In contrast, Washington Academy is a small school that averaged fewer than twenty-five students per grade. Similarly, the schools vary with respect to teacher-student ratios—ranging from 1:10 at Washington to 1:21 at North Star—and in terms of type, with Westward, Salem, Bethune, and North Star being noncharter public schools, Washington a private school, and Kennedy and Thomas Jefferson charter schools. Washington is the only school in the study with selective admissions criteria. The other schools employ nonselective methods with limited screening mechanisms (e.g., interviewing students and/or parents).

The core of these schools—instruction, curriculum, socioemotional development activities, out-of-school-time activities—all appeared to share similar features. For example, all of the schools maintained an afterschool program designed to support students who were behind academically. In some of the schools attendance in these programs was mandatory, because the activities were incorporated as part of a longer school day. At other schools only students who needed additional academic support were required to attend. There were also many similarities in the approach that the schools took toward curriculum and instruction. Each school made attempts to ensure that the curriculum and teaching were "culturally relevant" with respect to the racial, ethnic, and gender identities of the boys they served. In chapter 3 we provide greater detail on how they defined and implemented strategies to ensure cultural relevance. Most importantly, each school was created with a mission or vision that served as the anchor for its culture and character-building practices. The mission was reflected in the schools' newsletters, Web sites, and social media, and also served as the rationale behind certain practices such as the mandatory school uniform, a practice that was common to all seven schools. As we will show, the boys at these schools were never at a loss for knowing the mission of the school; in each case it served as the glue that provided students with a sense of community and collective responsibility.

We should point out that despite the energy that went into the development of these schools, not all of them were successful. In fact, two of the schools, Salem and Westward, were ultimately closed by the school district due to a track record of poor performance. All of these schools were under enormous pressure to demonstrate that they could meet

TABLE 1.1

School characteristics

	Thomas Jefferson Academy for Young Men	Westward Leadership Academy	Salem Academy on Culture and Justice	North Star Academy for Young Men	Washington Academy for Boys	Kennedy College Preparatory Academy	Bethune Academy
Year opened	2006–2007	2005–2006	2004–2005	2004–2005	2003–2004	2007–2008	2007–2008
Grades served	9–12	6–12	9–12	9–12	4–8	5–8	6–8
Selective or non-selective (public, private, or charter)	Nonselective (charter)	Nonselective (public)	Nonselective (public)	Screened/ nonselective (public)	Selective (private)	Nonselective (charter)	Nonselective (public)
Enrollment[1]	565	116	253	449	116	252	283
Percent by race (%)							
American Indian	0	0	Less than 1	0	0	0	0
Asian/Pacific Islander	0	1	0	0	16	0	Less than 1
Black/African American	99.8	96	54	57	51	90	99.8
Latino	0	3	42	30	33	10	0
White	Less than 1	0	2	1	0	0	0

	Thomas Jefferson Academy for Young Men	Westward Leadership Academy	Salem Academy on Culture and Justice	North Star Academy for Young Men	Washington Academy for Boys	Kennedy College Preparatory Academy	Bethune Academy
Not reported	0	0	0	10	0	0	0
Percent special ed (%)	15.2	26	26.4	21.7	0	7	18
Percent ELL (%)	0.2	1.7	8	11	0	0	0
Percent qualified for free and reduced lunch (%)	84.1	59	79.2	71.1	95	89	96
Percent proficient on state ELA exam (%)[2]	24.6	19.6	NA	NA	NA	82[3]	73.3
Percent proficient on state math exam (%)		11	24.5	51.5	71.2	65[4]	67.6

[1]Based on 2009–10 enrollment figures.

[2]Based on 8th-grade proficiency rates.

[3]Based on 2010–2011 state exam scores.

[4]Based on 2010–11 state exam scores.

the academic needs of their students, and the four noncharter public schools were subject to the accountability requirements of their districts while charter schools were subject to the accountability requirements of their state charter.

In this book we offer a critical analysis of these seven schools and their efforts to meet the academic and social needs of the boys they served, not to hold them up as models of success, but to learn from the strategies and methods they employed. In our final chapter we discuss the implications of creating schools that are protective for boys of color and discuss the constraints of doing this during a time when rigid methods of holding schools accountable have been adopted by states all across the country.

Understanding the Risk: The Research on Boys of Color

Before presenting our analysis of the seven schools and delving into the findings from our study, it is important to situate this study within existing knowledge in the social sciences pertaining to the plight and status of Black and Latino males. From our vantage point, there are two competing discourses regarding the factors that contribute to the hardships experienced by Black and Latino males, both of which have influenced the development of single-sex schools for this population. We refer to these simply as structural versus cultural explanations. In the social sciences, explanations of human behavior—especially behavior associated with poor people—have been the subject of considerable scrutiny and debate. Over the past several decades epidemiologists, sociologists, anthropologists, and psychologists have waged an ongoing debate over the causes of poverty. On the structural side of this debate are social scientists such as William Julius Wilson, Sheldon Danzinger, Douglass Massey, and others who have argued that lack of access to jobs, health care, nutrition, and decent housing contributes to patterns of delinquency among inner-city youth in racially isolated neighborhoods where poverty is concentrated. When young people are raised in impoverished single-parent households, have a parent in prison, or are exposed to substance abuse at a young age, the likelihood that they will drop out of school, experience violence (as either a victim or perpetrator), or end up incarcerated, increases substantially.[19] Such conditions have been identified as risk factors within social environments that, when combined, are thought to have a multiplier effect increasing the likelihood of negative outcomes in the lives of children, and especially Black and Latino males.

Structuralists generally focus on the ways in which social institutions and the political economy (e.g., the availability of jobs and economic opportunities, class structure, and social geography) affect status and social mobility.[20] From this perspective, individual behavior is viewed as a product of access to opportunity (or lack thereof) and the socialization that occurs within the social environment. Similarly, structuralists maintain that changes in individual behavior, such as reduced violence or substance abuse, finding and retaining a job, or improved academic achievement, are more likely to occur as a result of changes in the structure of opportunity. For this reason, structuralists generally take the position that holding an individual responsible for his or her behavior makes little sense, since behavior is seen as being shaped by forces beyond the control of any particular person. Drug abuse, criminal activity, and dropping out of school are largely seen as the social consequences of inequality and institutional failure. According to this view, the most effective way to reduce socially objectionable behavior is to reduce the degree and extent of poverty and inequality in society.[21]

In contrast, those who might be grouped under the category of culturalists tend to downplay the significance of environmental factors and treat human behavior as a product of beliefs, values, norms, and family socialization. Scholars such as John Ogbu, John McWhorter, and Shelby Steele have focused on cultural explanations of behavior which they believe are tied to the moral codes that operate within particular families, communities, or groups. A central argument made by culturalist scholars is the idea that poor people are trapped within a "culture of poverty," which has the effect of legitimizing and perpetuating criminal and immoral behavior (e.g., having children out of wedlock, substance abuse, etc.). The culture-of-poverty argument and similar variants have dominated the analyses put forward by culturalists over the last fifty years of social scientific research.[22]

In contrast to the structuralists, the culturalists argue that changes in behavior can only be brought about through the adoption of new moral codes that lead to cultural change. For this reason, culturalists are less likely to call for providing more money to inner-city schools or increasing services to inner-city children and their families. Such actions, it is argued, will do little to improve behavior or academic performance because attitudes toward school, like attitudes toward work, sex, or crime, are perceived as being shaped by the cultures of their homes and neighborhoods. According to this view, culture provides the rationale and motivation for behavior, and cultural change cannot be brought about through social programs, changes in governmental policy, or increases in funding for schools.

Culturalists have documented ways in which certain values and norms can lower the aspirations of Black and Latino males and contribute to the adoption of self-destructive and oppositional behavior, particularly within school. For example, the anthropologist John Ogbu[23] has argued that community-based "folk theories" related to the perceived lack of social mobility have the effect of lowering the aspirations of Black youth. He suggests that, because of the history of discrimination against Black people in the United States, there is a pervasive belief in many low-income Black communities that even those who work hard will never reap rewards equivalent to those available to Whites. This in turn has an impact on the attitudes and performance of Black students within school because of the belief that expending effort to succeed in education will not result in access to good jobs and upward mobility later in life. In a similar vein, the anthropologist Oscar Lewis[24] has argued that intergenerational poverty contributes to lowered aspirations and patterns of behavior that perpetuate poverty among Latino families. These researchers and others in the culturalist camp have argued that values, beliefs, and norms contribute to the adoption of self-defeating behaviors that reproduce poverty across generations.[25]

In recent years, the structural-versus-cultural debate has influenced discourse among scholars, journalists, and others over the plight of Black and Latino males. Some, like the comedian Bill Cosby and psychiatrist Alvin Poussaint, have argued that many Black and Latino males view sports and music as more promising routes to upward mobility than academic pursuits.[26] For this reason they are less likely to invest time and energy in their education. Similarly, anthropologists such as Diego Vigil have argued that Latino males in inner-city communities are more likely to engage in violence and criminal behavior because they perceive gangs as support groups that can provide security and access to economic mobility.[27] Finally, some researchers have argued that, for some Black students, doing well in school is perceived as a sign that one has "sold out" or opted to "act White" for the sake of individual gain.[28] According to this perspective, the goals of school are rejected out of fear that a successful student will be ostracized by members of the peer group with whom he identifies.

Not surprisingly, the debates among the structuralists and the culturalists have influenced the thinking of the educators who created the seven single-sex schools in our study. How they understood the nature of the risks facing the boys they serve—whether emanating from the values, norms, and culture the boys identify with, or from the structural conditions and lack of opportunities in their communities—had great bearing on the approach they took in organizing their schools. As will be apparent, most of these educators cannot be easily placed on one side or the other of this debate. Instead, their perception of the risks confronting their students is rooted in an understanding of the potential harm created by adverse conditions that might be attributed to both cultural *and* structural conditions. For this reason, the protective environments the educators sought to create at each of the schools in this study cannot be regarded as rooted in an adherence to either a cultural or a structural perspective, though both perspectives clearly had an influence over how the boys and the risks they faced were perceived.

During our research we learned that despite their importance and relevance to academic performance, risk variables and cultural pressures were not used by the educators to explain individual behavior. As we will demonstrate, these educators sought to help the Black and Latino boys they served to navigate societal pressures and avoid negative outcomes. Confronted with a variety of obstacles and challenges, their hope was that the young men in their schools could become resilient by attending their schools, and even excel. This study aims to critically examine the strategies they utilized to assist their students in overcoming obstacles related to poverty and racial segregation so that they could succeed academically and live healthy and productive lives.

Protective Environments for Boys of Color

Like the educators described in this study, a growing number of researchers are trying to find ways to work in the middle ground of the debate between the structuralists and culturalists. Dissatisfied with the determinism of structuralists, which reduces individuals to passive objects of larger forces, and with the "blame the victim" perspective that is often associated with the culturalists because of the tendency to view individuals as hopelessly trapped in a particular social/cultural milieu, these researchers have synthesized elements from both the structural and cultural perspectives to incorporate a greater focus on the importance of individual choice and agency.[29] By "agency" we are referring not merely to the ability of individual students to overcome obstacles but also to collective agency, manifested in the work of educators, parents, and community groups that refuse to passively accept the failure and ongoing demise of Black and Latino boys. As we aim to show, both forms of agency are being actively cultivated in the schools we studied.

A dual framework, drawing upon the strengths of structural and cultural analyses while avoiding the pitfalls, makes it possible to focus on the vulnerability of Black and Latino boys while at the same time recognizing their potential for agency. For those who believe that education can play a role in breaking the cycle of poverty, such a focus is more likely to yield greater possibilities for devising coping strategies and school-based interventions. This framework acknowledges the risks students are exposed to within and outside of their school contexts, and takes these into consideration as schools develop protective measures to counter them. Such a framework also recognizes that individuals have the capacity to make choices and take actions that will impact their future outcomes (e.g., the grades they earn, whether or not they graduate from high school and go to college, etc.) as well as the capacity to adopt coping strategies that lead them to avoid some of the same risks to which their peers may be more likely to succumb.[30] Theoretically, the application of this dual framework should make it possible for schools to take deliberate measures to counter cultural and structural constraints within the local environment by building the capacity of their schools to mitigate the hardships and risks. As we will show, the schools in our study sought to develop such protective interventions with varying degrees of success.

Social and cultural reproduction theories have provided robust explanations for how schools are organized to reproduce social and economic stratification in society.[31] The goal of reproduction theory has been to explain how schools reproduce the dominant ideology and class structure through the distribution of skills that reinforce the social division of labor.[32] Reproduction theory recognizes the relationship between schools, the state, and the economy as being central to how schools function and the outcomes they produce.

For the purpose of this study we used reproduction theory to analyze the ways the seven schools explicitly or implicitly addressed three important questions:

1. To what degree were these schools aware that they might be providing their students with knowledge and skills that would be likely to reproduce their respective places in a labor force stratified by class, race, and gender?
2. To what degree did these schools deliberately seek to provide students with forms of knowledge that might make it possible for them to critique and resist the dominant culture so that they might be able to subvert the tendency to reproduce their place within the class structure?

3. Given that schools are part of the apparatus of the state, to what degree were these educators willing to take risks to challenge state policies that might be perceived as contributing to the reproductive tendencies within schools?

We posed these questions because, as we will show in chapter 2, the school founders and their staff told us repeatedly about the need for these schools to disrupt the negative cycles and stratification patterns for boys of color. As we examined these schools we sought to understand the strategies they utilized to promote agency among the boys and the practices they deployed to disrupt the tendency for schools to reproduce existing patterns of stratification.

In keeping with our desire to combine a structural and cultural analysis into our examination of these seven schools we also focused on understanding the approaches the schools took to shape the attitudes and behaviors of the Black and Latino boys they served. Psychologist Margaret Beal Spencer has developed a theoretical approach that can be used to understand how the behaviors of boys of color are influenced by their perceptions of society and how they believe they in turn are perceived. Spencer's PVEST (Phenomenological Variant Ecological Systems) model argues that perceptions of context (e.g., schools, society) influence the types of coping strategies and behaviors an individual may decide to use. For example, if boys of color perceive the police as a potential threat, it will in turn influence the stance they adopt when they are in the presence of police officers and may result in the adoption of behaviors that are perceived as suspicious or threatening. The intensity and prevalence of stress-inducing factors have been shown to shape the ways in which individuals act and behave.[33] In our research we sought to understand the strategies these schools utilized to shape the identities (e.g., attitudes, values, character) of their students, specifically in response to the stresses and threats in their environment.

In the schools in our study, Black and Latino male identity construction was at the center of the educational mission. Since it is on the basis of their identities that Black and Latino males are presumed to be at risk, marginalized, and endangered, both in school and throughout American society, the schools sought to find ways to help their students create identities that would protect them. As we studied these schools we paid close attention to the ways in which students might be labeled and sorted, recognizing that such processes often form part of the hidden curriculum and play a central role in the way students are socialized. We also sought to understand the factors that enabled some students to resist pressures to conform to the identity constructions that occurred within school, particularly as it related to masculinity.

Again, the goal of this study has been to understand how the educators who founded, led, and taught at these schools attempted to create a protective environment that could mitigate the structural and cultural conditions that might otherwise put Black and Latino boys at risk of failure. We use our research to show how the schools sought to promote resilience among their students and develop learning environments that were successful at meeting the needs of their students. We also analyze the obstacles and limitations encountered in carrying out this important yet complex work.

For readers who may be wondering whether schools can succeed at successfully educating Black and Latino boys, this book offers a mixed message. As you will see in the pages ahead there are some schools and some measures that appear to be relatively successful in meeting their students' academic and social needs. These schools, and the responses of the young men to them, remind us that *the problem is not who we serve but how they are served.* This point must be impressed upon educators who have lapsed into blaming the students they serve for their own failures or, by extension, blaming the parents. At the same time, readers will also recognize the limitations and flaws in the approaches taken in some of the schools to address the challenges confronting Black and Latino males. We hope that these too will prove valuable to others who seek to serve this population and avoid their mistakes.

Poverty, crime, gangs, drug abuse, and other social problems that are endemic to some neighborhoods pose formidable challenges. The pull of the streets and all of the dangers associated with it are drawing many young males of color onto the path of delinquency at an early age. It would be naïve to suggest that schools alone can counter the effects of these deeply entrenched problems. However, to the degree that some of the efforts undertaken in these seven schools have been successful in protecting young men of color from the dangers in their environment, we hope readers will see that these obstacles can be countered and even overcome when educators work closely with parents and community to design positive learning environments that meet the needs of the children they serve.

What is not determined through this research is whether separating boys of color into all-male educational environments is necessary or even a good idea. To answer this question we would have needed to incorporate more schools, including some coeducational schools, into the study. However, we do believe that this book will provide insights into the practices and strategies being utilized in single-sex schools regarding how to meet the needs of young men of color. To the extent that some of what we describe is seen as constructive and promising, we would encourage readers to make further inquiries to find ways to adapt these strategies to their schools and programs. Our hope is that this book will prove helpful to those who want to ensure that more and more young men of color can be spared from the harm that is presently destroying so many lives and depriving so many communities and families of young men who might otherwise be a source of strength and hope.

2

Assumptions and Strategies

A Model for "Saving" Boys of Color

Every single child in here is going, "Oh, I'm going to go to college." You know, we have, every once in a while these really, really close conversations, where we can get intimate and a kid will say, "So, I'm really kind of worried. Like, I'm kind of mixed into this whole college thing, but I'm not real smart and I don't know." When I was in high school, I thought college was not for me. I was not going to college. That was something that really smart people did . . . that was just never even a consideration. There was nobody in my family who went, none of us were smart. When I got into high school one of my teachers kind of set me straight, "What do you mean, you're an idiot, you're going to college. Shut up." And it was like, *Oh, OK*. That's why for these kids it's got to happen early. We've already dropped that idea "you're going to college," but now we have to counter the expectations they've been exposed to that's got them thinking to themselves, "I'm-not-that-smart."

—*School Administrator, Thomas Jefferson Academy*

Shaping the educational trajectories of Black and Latino boys is the mission that drives the seven single-sex schools studied for this book. As the administrator from Thomas Jefferson reflects in the quote above, ensuring that the Black and Latino boys he serves go to college is an ongoing struggle, but also a nonnegotiable outcome. Similar sentiments with equivalent passion were expressed by the educators we met at all seven schools. Over the course of the three years that we carried out our research we were struck by the passion, zeal, and dedication with which these educators pursued their goals. As we listened to their stories and heard them reflect on their obstacles and challenges, we were impressed by the way these practitioners framed their goals for the young men they serve. Naturally, we became curious about how they intended to achieve these goals.

Early on, we learned that the ways these schools went about shaping the long-term educational trajectories of their students were rooted in a variety of assumptions and largely untested theories. Some of these assumptions were explicit—such as the repeated refrain that "we are in a struggle with the streets"—while others were more subtle, reflecting an implicit understanding about their students' needs and the nature of the obstacles they face. While many educators in inner-city schools approach their work with missionary-like zeal, the educators we encountered in these seven schools often framed their work in life-or-death terms. On numerous occasions, teachers and administrators told us that they were "saving" their students from the streets, prison, violence, or an early death. One of our goals in this chapter is to explore the assumptions that guided these educators' work and that underlay the strategies they developed at the different schools to shape the educational trajectories of their students. We analyze what the strategies tell us about how these educators envisioned "saving" Black and Latino boys, and we document their efforts to develop academic resilience.

As we pointed out in chapter 1, although single-sex schools have been in existence for many years, there is relatively little research on the educational experiences of boys that the administrators of this new wave of single-sex schools could turn to for guidance. In recent years, several studies on the educational, psychological, and emotional challenges facing boys of color have been released.[1] However, few of these studies specifically consider how the social construction of race, ethnicity, class, gender, and related stereotypes impact the identities and social experience of these students. Hence, when the educators who founded and designed these schools began thinking about what they would need to do to create a curriculum, train teachers, and implement support systems to positively influence the outcomes of the young men who would attend their schools, they found little research to support them.

The absence of such research is due in part to the limited focus of existing scholarship on the status of boys of color. Existing studies on Black and Latino boys have focused largely on an explication and analysis of the broad array of problems confronting them.[2] In recent years, there have also been a number of relatively controversial books published that have argued that boys' brains operate differently than girls', and for that reason they need to be taught differently and separately.[3] Despite its growing influence, this line of research remains controversial because most claims about inherent differences in boys have not been supported by geneticists, neuroscientists, or brain researchers.[4] Moreover, most of the existing studies have largely ignored the way in which masculinity interacts with race, ethnicity, class, and context (e.g., neighborhood, school, family, etc.) to influence behavioral outcomes and the social construction of identity.

As we conducted our research at these seven schools we began to understand that how the educators conceived of the problems and challenges confronting Black and Latino boys had profound bearing on the types of programs and strategies they implemented. For example, if they located the problems facing their boys within the *culture* of their communities and families, they were more likely to adopt strategies that would counter these influences in an attempt to inoculate them from what they perceived as threats. Conversely, if the educators perceived the primary threats to their boys as being located in the *structure* of opportunities (e.g., lack of decent jobs, schools, etc.) at the local and societal level, they were more likely to adopt strategies to broaden and expand their access to opportunities. Rather than being at odds, there was evidence that both approaches were in place at all seven schools, along with an accompanying rationale to justify their existence.

Our second goal in this chapter is to describe the educational practices adopted by these schools and to examine what they reveal about the assumptions held toward Black and Latino boys. Additionally, we discuss how these assumptions influenced the implementation of strategies designed to counter the negative pressures and obstacles that contribute to the vulnerability of Black and Latino males, both within and outside of school. Our hope is that by exposing the implicit theories that guided the development of these schools we will be in a better position to understand why certain approaches were taken to make a difference for the students they served.

While there is no question that the overwhelming majority of individuals spearheading efforts to create single-sex schools have been well-intentioned, motivated by a genuine desire to "save" boys by ameliorating the problems they encounter and reducing their vulnerability, we learned that good intentions may not be enough to ensure good outcomes. Given the complex and pernicious nature of the problems they face, creating schools that can be successful in educating Black and Latino boys is a task that requires considerably more. In the following pages, we explore how these educators went about translating "good intentions" into effective school-based interventions for Black and Latino boys.

Designing School Environments to "Save" Boys of Color

Throughout our research we employed a theory of change (TOC) as a research strategy to make explicit the multiple, interwoven assumptions and theories that served as the rationale for the creation of single-sex schools for Black and Latino boys. Though the educators who designed these schools did not confer with one another when planning curriculum or training teachers, we were struck by the similarities in their thinking and in the design of the programs and interventions they created. Given these similarities, we think it is important to make the theories that guided their work explicit so that the logic behind their ideas can be assessed.

To accomplish this task we opted to utilize the implicit TOC that guided the creation of these schools. We understood that the assumptions about the challenges faced by this student population, the assumed role that single-sex education could play in addressing these challenges, and the expectation that these factors could in turn influence the academic and social outcomes expected of their students, could be treated as a theory of change. As is true in other research that utilizes TOC, this approach serves as an effective means for explicating the assumptions that make a particular strategy seem logical and warranted, and serves as a tool for evaluating its implementation.[5]

Figures 2.1 and 2.2 illustrate the overarching theoretical framework that emerged from our interviews with various members of the schools' staff. The theory of change that we heard articulated over and over included a framework for defining the problem, illustrated in figure 2.1, and a framework for the solution, shown in figure 2.2. The definition of the problem reflects an explicit awareness of the external pressures and threats present within the community context (e.g., gangs, negative

FIGURE 2.1

Theory of change for single-sex schools

Framework of the problem

School- and community-based problems	Social and emotional struggles
• Lack of curricular relevancy	• Lack of self-esteem
• Lack of challenging curricula	• Race and gender identity crises
• Inconsistent school quality	• Lack of parental involvement and/or connectedness
• High rates of teacher turnover	• Absentee fathers
• Presence of gang activity	• Valorizing of money and "bling"
• Absence of employment opportunities	

FIGURE 2.2

Theory of change for single-sex schools

Framework of the solution

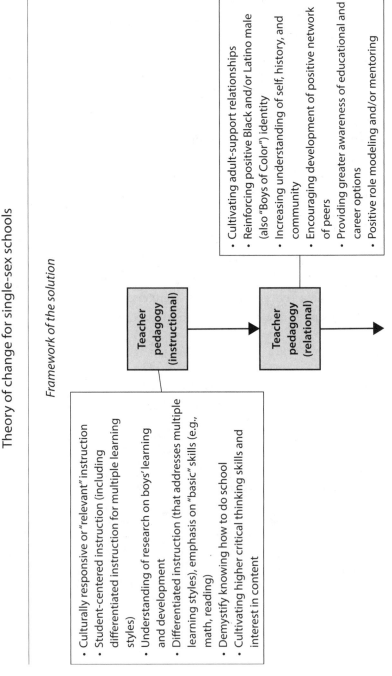

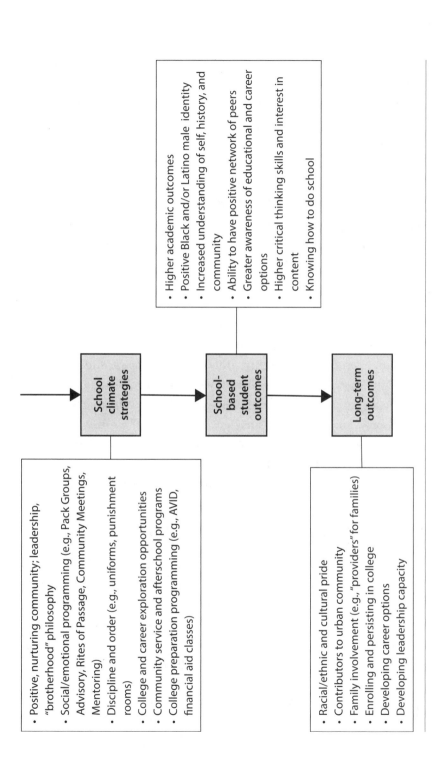

- Positive, nurturing community; leadership, "brotherhood" philosophy
- Social/emotional programming (e.g., Pack Groups, Advisory, Rites of Passage, Community Meetings, Mentoring)
- Discipline and order (e.g., uniforms, punishment rooms)
- College and career exploration opportunities
- Community service and afterschool programs
- College preparation programming (e.g., AVID, financial aid classes)

School climate strategies

- Higher academic outcomes
- Positive Black and/or Latino male identity
- Increased understanding of self, history, and community
- Ability to have positive network of peers
- Greater awareness of educational and career options
- Higher critical thinking skills and interest in content
- Knowing how to do school

School-based student outcomes

Long-term outcomes

- Racial/ethnic and cultural pride
- Contributors to urban community
- Family involvement (e.g., "providers" for families)
- Enrolling and persisting in college
- Developing career options
- Developing leadership capacity

peer pressure, pop culture, etc.) that draw young men away from school and undermine academic success; it also implies a critique of practices utilized in traditional schools, describing the ways in which they fail to address the socioemotional and academic needs of Black and Latino males and contribute to pervasive patterns of failure. The framework for the solution comprises the design features these schools identified as important, including a pedagogy for culturally relevant, rigorous instruction; a relational pedagogy that focuses on factors like behavioral engagement and race/ethnic and "male" identity development; and schoolwide strategies for creating a supportive and achievement-oriented school climate. The framework also defines the long-term outcomes that can be expected from successful implementation of this approach.

Taking the perceived needs and challenges of boys of color into account, the educators developed programs and strategies related to curriculum, instruction, counseling, out-of-school support, and a variety of other support systems, as interventions they hoped would buffer their students from perceived vulnerabilities. Their hope was that the single-sex school would operate in such a way as to help these boys surmount the obstacles they often faced at traditional schools and to withstand and counter the effects of the hazards awaiting them outside of school as well. In traditional schools, the obstacles include punitive discipline practices that result in boys of color being more likely to be suspended, low teacher expectations that result in disproportionate numbers of boys of color being referred for remedial academic services or labeled as a student with a disability (particularly an intellectual or behavioral disability), and sorting practices that make it less likely for boys of color to be referred for advanced academic courses (e.g., advanced placement, honors, and college preparation courses). The staff at the schools we studied were clear that they did not want to reproduce such practices in the schools they created. They were equally concerned about creating protective mechanisms within these schools that could make it possible for their boys to avoid the out-of-school hazards—gangs, drugs, violence, etc.—that ensnare so many young men of color in urban areas.

Meeting the Socioemotional and Educational Needs of Black and Latino Boys

A vast body of research has documented the importance of a school environment that provides students with feelings of trust,[6] and an understanding that the adults who serve them care about them.[7] There is also abundant research showing that strong relationships between students and teachers lead to improved academic outcomes and higher levels of academic engagement.[8] Each of the single-sex schools in this study sought to create a nurturing learning environment for the young men they served, as a way both to instill safety and order and to develop character through the cultivation of values and norms that reinforced the importance of learning.

When asked about the purpose of and need for single-sex schools focused on Black and Latino boys, the administrators we interviewed spoke unequivocally about the need to address various social and emotional challenges confronting Black and Latino boys; they also stressed the particular academic challenges these boys faced. In varying ways, each of the schools emphasized the need to "undo" or "counter" negative cultural influences and stereotypes that were perceived as harming boys of color and contributing to academic alienation and the pervasive achievement gap. These influences included the impact of gangs and the culture of violence on city streets; "gangsta" rap music that glorified violence, degraded the image of women, and valorized the importance of money and "bling"; and broken or dysfunctional homes, absentee fathers, and a host of other familial disorders that were seen as contributing to delinquency and "at-risk" behavior. In many respects, the concerns we heard expressed by educators at these schools about family and community disorder is not unlike the culture-of-poverty arguments made popular by scholars like Oscar Lewis,[9] or more recently by the comedian Bill Cosby and his coauthor psychiatrist Alvin Poussaint.

However, in addition to these conservative critiques of urban poverty, we also heard many administrators who keenly understood the economic and political obstacles facing Black and Latino boys. Pervasive unemployment, racial discrimination, and police abuse and misconduct were all mentioned with great frequency by educators who seemed to understand that many of the students they served had little chance of being successful because of a broad array of obstacles created by an unjust and even racist society. Some used terms like "conspiracy" to describe the threats against boys of color (without ever identifying who the conspirators were), while others made oblique reference to the "system" keeping young men of color down.

The complexity of their perspective was conveyed in the way each of the principals framed their school's mission. In each case, they described the need to mold the identities of their students to protect them from the adversity that might otherwise undermine and destroy them. For example, Darrell Trust, the principal at North Star Academy for Young Men, a 9th–12th-grade high school, stated that his school's goal was to "make our students proud and dignified young men who are college and not prison bound." Similarly, Clem Carver, the principal at Westward Leadership Academy, a school serving 6th–12th-grade students, said his school's goal was to "protect these young men from the dangers of the streets by empowering them as learners and leaders."

Redefining Masculinity

Many of the school staff we interviewed stated that it was necessary to develop a new masculine identity among their male students because the "street" images they were exposed to contributed to the negative behaviors that many of their students displayed. Masculine traits such as toughness and cool were seen as threatening to the goals of the schools because they were viewed as contributing to the occurrence of interpersonal conflicts among their students along with a de-emphasis on the importance of learning. Additionally, although all of the schools had athletic teams, many of the educators we interviewed were also worried about overemphasizing the importance of sports. As one teacher explained, "If my students put as much time into their homework as they do into playing basketball they would have straight A's."

At Westward, several teachers spoke about the need to counter the presence of negative male role models in the community who lack a strong work ethic, engage in criminal activity such as drug dealing, and do not hold respectable jobs. One administrator at the school stated that what their male students need is exposure to men with a strong work ethic:

> [In] many cases our students have things going against them as far as, you know, economic background and things of that nature. So they need to understand that as men, in order to succeed you need to work hard. It's really as simple as that, but many of them just haven't had the exposure. They don't know men who get up every morning, put on a jacket and tie, and go to work. That's not their reality. So we have to change what they expect of themselves.

Westward's mission is to develop boys of color, grades six through twelve, into strong, positive men who will be leaders in their community. They aim to do this by preparing their students for success in college and nurturing the aspirations of their students so that they will seek to pursue a professional career. "Strong, Capable, and Conscious" are the words featured in school brochures to describe the kind of leaders Westward seeks to cultivate. As future male leaders, students are encouraged to be morally strong with banners adorning the walls of the school reading "Do what is right no matter how hard it might be." One teacher explained, "Our students must be capable of discerning right from wrong. We want them to do what is required, both with respect to their academic performance but also regarding their ability to exercise good judgment outside of school."

The educators at North Star Academy were so concerned about the lack of adult male role models that they made it a priority to find adult mentors who could serve as role models for young men for each of their students. Professional adult males, many of whom belonged to a civic association of African American men, were recruited to serve as mentors for the young men at North Star. The goal of the mentoring initiative was to use the mentors as role models who could alleviate some of the anger and confusion associated with not having access to a father figure. The organization that partnered with the school played a major role in shaping the school's focus on character development. It also provided ongoing support to the school in the form of volunteers who staff events and fundraisers. According to the staff, many of their students expressed a considerable degree of anger over the absence of their fathers that manifested itself in conflicts with authority figures. One teacher at North Star explained that his students are "not equipped to know how to deal with this anger. It is deeply rooted within the boys who know that their daddy abandoned them and left them and their moms to fend for themselves. Unless they learn to channel this anger or to overcome it, their anger will get them into serious trouble."

Acknowledgement that many young men had trouble coping with anger, short-temperedness, and other difficult emotions was a challenge cited by staff at many of the schools as an aspect of masculinity that they had trouble dealing with. Some confided that they didn't understand where the anger came from, either because they were from different backgrounds with respect to race, class, or gender, or simply because their students were incapable of explaining their feelings. One White female teacher told us, "I've never been in a fight in my life so I really don't get it when I see my students go off on each other. It just doesn't make any sense to me that they carry so much rage inside of them." Others claimed to understand the anger that was occasionally expressed by their students as a response to poverty or absence of positive family ties. As one older guidance counselor explained, "I had a brother who used to fight all of the time. Today he's in prison because he never learned to control his temper. I understand that the world treats Black boys differently, but that's not an excuse to use violence."

Addressing violence and anger was seen by many of the educators as an aspect of masculinity that these schools would have to learn to deal with. However, many of those we met readily admitted that they were struggling to find ways to help their students cope with difficult emotions. For example, at Thomas Jefferson, the administrator spoke openly about the challenges his school faced in addressing the social and emotional issues his students brought with them to school:

> We spend a lot of time thinking about what does it mean for our boys to be successful. If it was just getting up and going to school every day, that wouldn't be hard to do. Right? We understand that there are some environmental factors that play a big role in how our students come to school—their state of mind, their mood, etc. We also know that when they leave school each day their feelings will affect whether or not they have the ability to complete homework. That in turn will affect how they experience the next day of school. If a student is unprepared, he'll be put on the spot, and he's probably going to have a bad day if he gets punished for not completing his work.
>
> So when you look at cumulative effects of these responsibilities and then how they are influenced by your emotions as a young adult in your formative years, it's quite complicated. These guys are still trying to figure out what their identity is, trying to figure out who they are, and all these things are happening simultaneously while they're trying to be successful in school. You don't get to be a scholar here and then be a Black male over there who is trying to figure out how to fit into the neighborhood. It's all happening inside of this young, confused person at the same time. So, it ain't easy. That's why we try to use an integrated framework that considers how the social, emotional, physical, and intellectual parts of a person are influencing their development.

With this complicated understanding of the boys they served, these administrators also admitted that they were figuring it out along the way. In some cases this meant relying on their own experience to make sense of what to do next and how to understand their boys, as the administrator at Thomas Jefferson highlighted in an interview:

> We're still trying to figure all of this out. I rely in part on my own lived experiences and having gone through a lot of this myself. I'm from a big family and I had younger brothers and a bunch of cousins. I know what it's like to have conflict at home and then try to come to school

and be focused. So we're trying to figure out how best to help them to deal with these types of situations. It's very hard because even though they're all Black males, they're also all different. What works for one of them in a particular situation might not help the next person, because they might not have the same root cause.

Staff at the other schools raised similar concerns about the challenges of providing support to young men who are beginning to understand their masculinity and struggling with how to be successful in school at the same time. As this administrator made clear, helping young men learn how to manage their emotions is a central part of this work. One teacher at Washington told us, "Many of these boys have no idea of what a man really is. They haven't seen one, at least not one they could respect or learn from. So their image of manhood is distorted." An elderly African American woman at Kennedy College Preparatory Academy said, "You can't blame them for being angry. They don't know no better. All they see is men who have experienced failure. They need men they can look up to so they have a concept for how they want to be as men."

At Salem Academy on Culture and Justice, the administrators described their work as a "struggle between the school and the streets." They identified individual and societal issues that they see as operating in an interactive fashion to present particular challenges for their students. At the individual level, the administrators described students who were experiencing an "identity crisis" as a result of the tension between the school's expectations and the pressures they experience at home and in their neighborhoods. If these pressures cannot be addressed, particularly as the students enter adolescence, they believe that they will lose many of their students to the negative influences present in the broader community.

Another administrator at Westward noted that poverty and home/family life posed significant challenges for their young men because academic pursuits were not reinforced or rewarded: "The life outside this [school] building is a challenge the young men must contend with.

Outside they value being a ball player, a rapper, being popular with the ladies. Those are the things that give a young man a sense of value and respect. We're trying to change all of that by developing a sense of pride in learning. It's a huge challenge that is heightened in the absence of a secure sense of self."

One counselor at Salem said she conceptualized this challenge as multifaceted and multidimensional. She explained, "When a student is feeling the pull of negative influences, it affects their academic identities within school. If they have an older brother or someone they look up to who is in a gang or who is experiencing some hardship, they often feel as though they have to choose between being loyal to their family or friends or staying true to the values of the school. For most of these kids, that's a very tough choice."

Another administrator described how "students are bombarded with negative imagery" and told us, "They feel the need to be hard and that's sometimes at odds with being smart." He went further in saying that "the street culture is how they define what qualifies one as a man."

For these reasons, each of the schools was concerned about developing an alternative masculine identity, one that placed great value on academic success and the elements of character they saw as related to positive social development, such as integrity, honesty, and empathy. The schools conceive of themselves as institutions that will deliberately mold boys of color into positive adult males, but they are keenly aware of how difficult it is to accomplish this task. The schools understand that they must counter stereotypical "street" images that they regard as a threat to positive development and academic success, and they seek to do this by promoting values and norms that they hope will lead to the emergence of positive male identities. In other words, the boys are being taught *not* to be the kind of man stereotypically associated with the communities that the students come from. However, this work involves more than merely critiquing and deconstructing negative male images. It also involves propagating masculine images that they believe will contribute to success at school and society.

At Thomas Jefferson, staff members who participated in a focus group described the debilitating effect of not having positive images, specifically for Black boys, in American society:

> **Teacher 1:** We're trying to build character so that our young men will be successful in school and on the outside, but it's hard because where they live they don't see positive images of a strong man.
>
> **Teacher 2:** That's right. This society has painted a negative picture of what it means to be a strong Black man. Our youth—Black youth—look at a strong man as someone who is being successful in sellin' drugs, drivin' a car with rims, 20-inch rims, and the attire they have is so flamboyant.
>
> **Teacher 3:** They may look at that type of man as someone they want to be like when they grow up. It is a strong influence. We're trying to counter that influence by instilling in them a positive sense of what a young Black man can be. But they see us as caseworkers, social workers, an office person, and a professional educator. That's a person who is not connected to their everyday life.
>
> **Teacher 2:** We want to show them that they can be someone who becomes vice president or even president at a company . . . And that's where the modeling comes in . . . We are instilling in them that we believe they can defy the statistics of failure. They can be a success by goin' to college and raising a family.
>
> **Teacher 1:** Convincing them that's possible really isn't so easy.

The teachers at Thomas Jefferson, like the other educators we interviewed at the schools in our study, were profoundly concerned about cultivating a new sense of masculinity among their students. They understood that this work is integral to their efforts to support academic success and must be handled with utmost care and sensitivity. A counselor at Westward described the importance of this desire as follows:

> I think that this notion of manhood that a lot of your urban boys are exposed to is pretty one-sided. It pretty much looks at the importance of strength and power and equates that solely with sexual prowess, the ability to earn money, and the ability to defend oneself. It's one-sided because the pursuit of knowledge and the ability to navigate

conflicts and obstacles without resorting to violence is not really considered. So when you look at the realities they face, when you consider the realities and the images that they see for themselves, once again it's kinda one-sided. I mean, you see these same images of men that are constantly projected upon them, rappers, gangsters, etc., and it's easy to see why they don't necessarily seek out responsibility . . . That's why when we first encounter many of our kids, reading is looked at as something that is not for them. They see it as feminine. Automatically in their head, they put reading in the context—reading books leisurely or what have you—as something that is for girls, not something that guys do. Guys play video games or maybe they play sports, but they don't read. So we've got a lot of work to do. We're trying to eradicate those ideas because we want them to know that in order to be powerful, strong, and a mover-and-shaker among men they will have to be scholars who read and use their minds.

Many of the educators described their work as "inoculating" students from negative male influences. This was a common theme raised at several of the schools. Many of the school staff described their efforts as a battle between students' home lives and their school lives. The School-Community Liaison of Westward, for example, explained the conflict this way:

[It] gets very frustrating for students who have to be fighting at home, fighting from the time they hit the streets when they leave this school. I mean, we have some parents that are really supportive, but we have many others that are not. These kids have to walk through neighborhoods where they see all kinds of negative things. They can't be seen as wimps or punks or they will be victimized. That's real. There are very few positive male role models in this neighborhood so we have to do everything we can to counter those images.

After listening to the School-Community Liaison describe the challenges in the local community—challenges that were reinforced by the school counselor at Westward—we were not surprised to hear them frame their work as a struggle to save the lives of their male students. They see this as a battle between good and evil, and the effort to redefine masculinity is at the heart of that struggle. The school counselor was particularly troubled by what he perceived as the mixed messages about masculinity that the boys were getting at home versus what they see and hear at school:

> A lot of times, students get mixed messages as to what is masculine and what is an acceptable form of communication between a man and a woman. If there is some argument going on at home between the mom and her man, or if there are some tough times related to the lack of money at home, students will be exposed to a lot of negative commentary about what men do. This can be very emotionally disturbing because they may hear their mothers describe a man, perhaps even their father, as someone who ain't shit. Sometimes there's physical abuse too. How do you think that affects their image of men? A lot of times our students are uncomfortable with expressing affection towards their teachers or appreciation towards their peers because they may not be seeing that at home. They harden themselves as a way to cope with the abuse they have been exposed to and that hardening can make it harder to reach them.

He adds that "sometimes there is a dysfunctional relationship between the parent and the child and you can see some of that in school. Some children are given way too much responsibility at a young age. They are expected to grow up too fast. Some of them are not given enough responsibility at their age. They don't get chores or any clear expectations about contributing to the household. All of this will create problems for them at school. We are aware of it and we realize that we've got to help them grow up in a responsible way."

At Washington, the only private independent school in the study, the masculine identity the school would like to develop was described as one in which boys embrace qualities that others may perceive as feminine. Kindness, honesty, integrity, and empathy are character traits that we were told the school actively tries to nurture. The staff wanted to shift their boys' focus away from a masculine identity centered on sexual prowess and violence, and replace it with one rooted in respect, sensitivity, and understanding. They were well aware that this would be a challenge, but their hope was that since their students were in the early stages of adolescence, and their ideas about masculinity still emerging, it would be possible to foster a different masculine image. At this school, alternative images of masculinity were promoted through the adoption of books that encourage students to reflect on their attitudes, ethics, emotions, and behavior. For example, while reading *The Bluest Eye* by Toni Morrison, students were asked to reflect on the motivations of the central male character, and to write about the decisions he made. Additionally, the school has adopted a rigidly enforced discipline code that negatively sanctions rude and aggressive behavior, or any conduct deemed to be inconsistent with the character traits Washington is trying to encourage. Finally, as discussed in the following section, students at Washington are exposed to adults regarded as positive male role models who also serve as mentors.

Exposing Young Men to Positive Male Role Models

At several of the schools, one of the primary methods for countering hardships and ensuring the success of their students has been to increase their exposure to individuals they regarded as positive male role models. Although all of the schools employed women as teachers, counselors, and administrators, and all hired non-Black staff in a variety of professional roles, we repeatedly heard about the importance of exposing the students to positive, adult males of color who exhibit the character traits they seek to instill in students. The goal of such exposure is to make it possible for the boys in these schools to attach a different vision of masculinity to an actual person. According to a counselor at Bethune Academy, the school had to do everything it could to "offset the negative effects of absent fathers and single mothers." She elaborated: "Many of these boys are coming from broken homes and they haven't been exposed to positive male role models. We are trying to create an environment that counters the negativity in the community by building a peer culture that supports the development of low-income boys of color. We do this by exposing them to positive adult males who can set a different example."

The use of role models was a prominent strategy of reconstructing the masculinity narrative. According to key administrators at North Star, the goal of the school is to "help" young Black and Latino men "realize that what they see out there in the streets" (drugs, gangs, violence, etc.) is not the only option for them. As a way of countering these negative external influences, the administrators described trying to expose the boys to Black and Latino men who would encourage them to develop their intellectual abilities so that they would move forward educationally. According to the principal, "We are trying to do all we can to create a school where it's cool to be smart."

Several of the educators we met explained that positive role models would change their students' ideas about the meaning of masculinity by providing them with examples of men who excelled academically and professionally and who possessed leadership traits worthy of emulation. It is noteworthy that all but one of the principals at these schools was a Black male, and all of the schools made it clear that they went out of their way to recruit Black and Latino males as teachers and counselors. Equally important, each of the schools found ways to invite professional Black and Latino men to their schools as guest speakers to introduce their students to role models they believed would exert a positive influence on their students.

Becoming an Academically Oriented Black or Latino Boy

Reconstructing masculinity by countering the influence of the streets and exposing their students to positive male role models is only part of the strategy employed by these schools to ensure the success of their students. We met staff at each of the schools who stressed the need for boys of color to adopt academic identities that make it possible to contend constructively with obstacles that arise outside of school. One of the obstacles mentioned frequently was racism, which was described as both an institutional and interpersonal barrier. The college guidance counselor at Westward described the presence of this structural force in the challenges faced by boys of color:

> I really think that the greatest challenge our boys face is institutionalized racism. I know that's a broad term but what I mean by the institutionalized racism is the idea that there's a whole system designed to keep our boys back. It's reflected in school funding, in the segregated system that we have . . . it's even the cause of much of the violence in minority communities. These communities are economically bankrupt and educationally bankrupt, and people are trapped with no opportunities, so it's not surprising that many folks turn to drug dealing and crime. Those things don't just happen by themselves. So I think that overall, if we are going to speak broadly about the obstacles our students face, we have to talk about institutionalized racism. It is a big problem and it plays out in a lot of different ways.

Although not typically as clear as this individual, administrators and staff at many of these schools cited the presence of institutional racism as an obstacle that constrains the opportunities available to boys of color. Many pointed out to us that in comparison to middle-class White boys who have access to a wide array of supports and second chances if they make mistakes, their students are "set up to fail" early in life. For example, at Thomas Jefferson, one school staff member mentioned what she described as "missed developmental opportunities":

> Our boys just don't get the same opportunities to receive help with their academic growth. Many of our boys have to get their other siblings to school in the morning so they consistently arrive late. They have to go to work to support themselves and their families so they can't do things like sports and theater. Some of them haven't been allowed to be kids at all. You look at White kids, they're allowed to do activities, and they're allowed to do a lot of things. If there's a younger sibling, they're not responsible for them, there's a babysitter or their parents handle it. For Latino and African American homes, that's not the case. It's almost expected, "Hey, you're the big brother, take care of your little brother or sister until I get home." That's how it's done

because the families don't have other options. So I think that if we're going to help these boys we've got to understand what they face. We want to allow them to do the things that are necessary for their development—arts, music, sports, etc.—the things that middle-class White kids get to do, but we're going to have to make adjustments for them and give them some time to grow. Being able to be boys who get to have some fun as part of their education is a new experience for many of them.

In addition to institutionalized racism and what we described in chapter 1 as structural obstacles (e.g., inequity in school funding, racial segregation, etc.), the staff in all of the schools were particularly aware of the cultural obstacles that negatively impacted the success of their students as well. Rap music, peer pressure, gangs, and advertising that emphasized athletics were also cited as forces that had a negative impact on the development of the students' academic identities. Unlike the structural obstacles, which were described as concrete and measurable, the cultural obstacles were typically seen as pervasive and simply part of the environment, making them particularly difficult to address. Principal Brown of Bethune discussed how negative cultural influences in society impacted his students' definition of masculinity. He explained, "We live in a nation where an identity as a learner isn't something Black men come to value as [much as] an identity to be tough or sexy to women. This is what our boys think it means to be a man." Like the tension between the school and the streets, the cultural influences that shaped the social construction of Black and Latino masculinity was seen as creating a disconnect between "what it means to be a man" and what it means to be a learner. This dichotomy posed a real challenge for the schools' efforts to socialize young men to see themselves as scholars.

The Obstacles Posed by Past School Experiences

In addition to the structural and cultural obstacles, the educators were aware that the students' previous school experiences created tensions related to attitudes and behavior that had to be addressed. All of the schools in the study were serving students whose parents had chosen their schools to escape the negative experiences they'd had at previous schools. Low teacher expectations were cited more frequently than any other issue as an aspect of traditional public schools that these single-sex schools would have to address. According to a teacher at Washington, "In the public school system our students never really saw themselves as learners. They weren't pushed to excel and no one really cared if they developed core academic competencies. They were just passed through. That's why so many of them come to us barely able to read. It's a damn shame."

Countering the effects of previous school experiences was seen as essential if the schools were going to succeed in cultivating academic identities among their boys. According to Principal Trust, "We have to give them a space where they can learn and make mistakes. It's important that they do not have to compete with girls for academic success, or feel the need to show off as young men who are 'too cool for school.' We finally have them in a space where we can deal with their academic needs, but getting there requires us to reorient them to what school should really be about."

The assistant principal at North Star stated his belief that the work of his school was so difficult because the desire to learn "hasn't been instilled in these young men." In describing the key challenges of boys of color, he explained:

> I would say that getting them to identify with being a learner is one of the most important things we try to do. In the public school system, they never really saw themselves as active participants in their own education. They just showed up as if that was good enough because no one challenged them to do more. How can you embrace the identity of being a learner if no one treats you that way? This is why our students have a fear of breaking the stereotypes associated with Black masculinity. They've embraced an identity that allows them to be comfortable in their ignorance. Really getting at the academic orientation so that they're comfortable seeing themselves as learners and scholars is the key to what we're trying to do here. It's very different from anything they have ever experienced before.

45

One aspect of their past school experience that was frequently cited as a primary obstacle to academic success was the perception that many of these students have formed oppositional identities toward school because they associate learning with White norms. Several of the educators we interviewed stated that the boys in these schools face "the acting White stigma." Scholars such as John Ogbu and Signithia Fordham[10] have described how Black students sometimes fear that if they adopt certain manners and attitudes toward school their peers will accuse them of acting White. According to one science teacher at Kennedy, "If [they're] trying to achieve too much or if [they] talk a certain way they'll hear it—'you're acting like a White boy.' I mean I understand where they're coming from. A lot of them have not seen Black scholars before and they have gone to all-Black schools where being academically oriented isn't valued. That's what we're up against here." Several of the teachers we interviewed told us that whereas Blackness is associated with being cool and tough, Whiteness is associated with being well-behaved and smart. For this reason, changing how students connected their racial identities to their academic identities was seen to be as important as altering their notion of masculinity.

Each of the schools sought in a variety of ways to provide students with a secure sense of self, one that would reconcile the idea of being academically successful with becoming a well-rounded Black or Latino male. Repeatedly, we heard that this type of socialization and identity construction was an essential component of single-sex education as well as a key component to the mission of the schools. Given the psychological issues plaguing boys of color, acquiring a positive academic orientation and identity was perceived as essential to student success.

At Washington Academy, the principal reported that he believed the greatest challenges his students face are psychological. He explained this view to us during a formal interview:

> You know, as much as we're caring and nurturing, these youngsters bring their stories and experiences with them and, you know, there's only so much one can do at school. There are so many hours in the

school day and once they leave here they are still being bombarded by the negative images. I mean one of the reasons I wasn't able to meet with you earlier is that I was dealing with a young man who is constantly being subjected to verbal and physical abuse by his father. His notion of living the "Christian way" is all about not sparing the rod. The boy gets beat regularly for the littlest things and it takes a toll on him. We are trying hard to build up his self-esteem and disabuse him of the notion that he is worthless, but it's so hard to counter what he's going through at home on a regular basis. I had another two kids who were acting up on the bus and getting into mischievous little games. Now they shouldn't have behaved that way but the bus driver responded to the kids in a totally inappropriate fashion. This kind of abuse takes a huge psychological toll on our kids and it holds many of them back inside.

The principal mentioned his concerns about how young children are susceptible to the influences surrounding them, describing his male students as "psychic pincushions" because they absorb so much of what goes on around them. He also pointed out that many parents, especially single-parent mothers, often try to counter the psychological assault on their sons by overcompensating with support that can lead to them becoming dependent and less capable of doing things for themselves. As the principal pointed out, "The mothers try to make up for the threats they know their sons are under by monopolizing their time. Some of them treat their kids like princes and they're not used to doing anything for themselves. Their mothers carry their stuff around for them and don't make them do chores at home. In the long run, that really doesn't help them or prepare them for life in the world." He sees this type of parenting as contributing to a sense of helplessness among the boys and filling them with unrealistic expectations about how they will be treated by the rest of the world.

Overall, one of the complex endeavors of these educators is acknowledging that the various obstacles in the lives of boys of color can potentially interfere with their school-based efforts to build a new set of social identities. Although there is no body of research or theory that these

47

educators mentioned as guiding them in their efforts, there was a surprising degree of consistency in how they framed the problems they were trying to address and the approaches they were taking to intervene. According to the school leaders, much of their knowledge about what needed to be done came from having a deep understanding of the communities where they worked and the challenges facing their young men. The following quote from an administrator at Thomas Jefferson clearly illustrates how many of these educators conceived of their work at these schools in preparing the academic futures of their students:

> So, we understand that there are some environmental factors that play a big role in how our kids come to school and in what they face when they leave school. Whether or not they have a stable place to live or their parents have steady jobs will play a role in their ability to complete homework or how well they perform on a test. If their parents have a fight or if they have some problems with kids on the street on their way home from school, it's going to affect how they experience the next day. . . Our work is to shape their identities during their formative years so that as they figure out who they are as adults we can have a major impact. All these things are happening simultaneously to you and many of these kids don't know how to process it. That's why we want our boys to feel safe here, to know that they can be Black and male here and not have to stress over how people will judge them.

Creating a Positive Peer Culture

To counter the effects of external pressures, negative prior school experiences, distorted societal images, and parenting that fosters dependency, and to develop social identities among their students that would value academic success, each of the schools in our study worked to create a peer culture among their Black and Latino male students that would reinforce their goals. In their own way, each school sought to establish a sense of "brotherhood" among their students to develop and sustain their emerging academic identities. Many of the schools drew their models from the Black fraternities that the administrators, teachers, and staff belonged to when they were college students. In that model, peer groups would support and encourage each other and serve as each brother's "keeper" so that they could achieve success together.

In several of the interviews we conducted, and in many of our observations, we heard staff refer to students as "brothers" and to the school as a larger "family." Repeatedly, we heard that the purpose behind creating this sort of collective consciousness rooted in familial ties was to establish a safe space where students could support each other and create a space where the boys could "be themselves." Recognizing that many students were developing identities that might not be accepted outside the school doors, the educators hoped to create a climate that would provide social and emotional support and cultivate a sense of resilience among their students that reinforced academic success.

All of the schools spoke of the importance of building positive peer networks as a way to protect their students and help them in persisting toward their goals. When we spoke with the educators about the concept of brotherhood that they were fostering at their school, we learned that there was a hope and expectation that such an environment would not only insulate the boys from the effects of institutional racism that they were likely to encounter, but also counter their own community's low expectations of them. Both of these external threats were seen as contributing significantly to their vulnerability, and the peer group was seen as a primary strategy for reducing the risks the boys would experience.

Developing Future Leaders

Each of the schools also understood that helping the boys develop coping mechanisms in dealing with the myriad of psychological and social challenges they face is not enough to ensure their success. While teaching their students to avoid negative peer pressures and buffering them from the harmful effects of stereotypes that undermined their academic orientation was important, the schools also sought to cultivate identities among their Black and Latino boys that would make it possible for them to become "leaders."

Leadership was envisioned as more than merely acquiring a position or title that connotes authority. For the educators we interviewed, the leadership qualities they hoped to instill in their students were envisioned as an affirmative expression of the values and character that each of the schools regarded as important. The idea of leadership was rooted in a belief that if the young men actively embraced the ethos of their schools, its effects upon their development would be manifest long after they graduated. Leadership was also described as a way to influence the kinds of choices students made about their education and their lives. The goal we heard expressed was to make students less susceptible to the negative influences around them by equipping them with critical thinking skills and a moral foundation that would help them to make good decisions.

Clem Carver, the principal of Westward, explained the need to develop what he termed "urban leaders" in a manner that was typical of what we heard from other educators:

> Sure we want our kids to get good grades and to get admitted to good colleges, but we're actually trying to accomplish more than that. Our hope is that some of these kids, after they've gone to college and graduated, will want to come back to this community. Or at least, you know, go to another urban community and try to have an impact there. We are hoping that they will become men who will become leaders in their communities as fathers, teachers, businessmen, and even politicians, who will work to improve urban life somehow.

In each of these schools, the educators we met sought to transmit the message that their Black and Latino male students should become positive examples and find ways to "give back" to their communities. The schools sought to accomplish this by creating experiences they hoped would develop the leadership qualities of their students, such as community service projects, schoolwide assemblies, and a variety of learning activities.

Each school had an explicit set of strategies aimed at cultivating qualities of leadership in its young men. Aware of the ways in which their students were likely to be influenced by the negativity of street culture, the schools encouraged their students to take control of their lives and to take what they learn back to "the community." Several of the schools created community service projects that provided students with the opportunity to tutor younger children, assist the elderly, or clean up their neighborhoods. These activities were all intended to encourage leadership through service and to give the students a chance to show gratitude for the opportunities they had been given. Repeatedly, the educators we interviewed told us that their young men are expected to go out into "the world" and help others. Education within these single-sex schools is designed to develop a new sense of Black or Latino masculinity that is characterized by the ability to effect positive change for greater societal good.

By developing young men who would become leaders, the educators within these schools are in effect preparing these young men to become agents of change in the world. Their hope is that these young men will become adults who can transform conditions around them rather than merely adapting to them. The promotion of this affirmative and active form of male identity is seen as an essential component to "saving" Black and Latino boys from themselves and their surrounding environments. The words of Westward Principal Clem Carver conveyed this part of the mission of single-sex education most effectively: "If we want to save these boys, then we have got to take action. At this school, we are taking action via education to make it possible for them to rise beyond low expectations, and beyond being victims of the streets. We want them to view their futures optimistically and to understand what is necessary for them to do to become successful men. If we succeed, they will pass their success forward to their future families and communities."

Saving Boys of Color Through a Resilience-Building Program

What is clear about what we came to describe as the implicit theory of change that is driving these single-sex schools is that they see their primary mission to be one of building resilience among their Black and Latino male students in the face of the structural and cultural obstacles that confront them. The administrators and teachers we interviewed understood the role so often played by environmental challenges (e.g., family disengagement and disorganization, absence of father figures, absence of community youth development outlets, pervasive crime and unemployment, etc.) in setting these boys up for academic failure. As such, they see their work as designed to provide students with the social and academic skills that will enable them to successfully navigate these obstacles and avoid the pitfalls that have taken down so many others.

In some ways, the efforts undertaken by these educators are similar to the approach taken to assist girls in science and math during the 1980s and 1990s. Many of the interventions that were implemented during that time placed less emphasis on academic support and far greater emphasis on redefining or expanding notions of femininity.[11] Advocates for girls believed that by empowering young women socially, a greater number would obtain the confidence and resilience to succeed in traditionally male-dominated fields. Similarly, these single-sex schools for boys are operating on the premise that if they can redesign and reorient their students' notions of masculinity, they will be able to save them from academic and social failure.

Given this goal it is hardly surprising that the administrators and founders designed their schools and framed their mission around meeting both the socioemotional and the academic needs of their students. As we have seen, a critical part of that work is redefining masculinity so that academic excellence is perceived as compatible with what it means to be a man. While the school leaders understand that they will ultimately be judged based on the academic performance of the students they serve, they also realize that the socioemotional needs of their boys cannot be ignored. Addressing these needs is a complex and difficult process because the social milieu and the cultural influences within their communities and the larger society contribute to distorted male images, a lack of self-esteem, and for many, an inability to manage negative external pressures (e.g., community, familial, peer, or pop-cultural). The hope of these educators is that these pressures can be countered by exposure to positive male role models and by an educational environment that has been deliberately designed to instill character and educational ambition.

In the following chapters, we explore in greater detail how these schools have gone about implementing their theory of change to develop resilience and promote academic success at the school and classroom level.

3

Curriculum and Instruction

Striving for Rigor and Relevance

Right now I am really struggling with the freshmen to get them collaborating effectively and productively in small groups, discussing a book. The sophomores, because we've done that, and we've really worked that skill, they can jump in and do that, and we can go on to higher-order discussion skills.

—*Teacher, Thomas Jefferson Academy*

What I'm trying to create is, I guess, a sense of family—there's a basic need for acceptance in my room, then we can move on to learning. I think we're getting there—but to get that foundation going and then move on to the actual work, they need a lot more guidance . . . Eventually I'd like for them to be able to do a lot of group work, a lot of cooperative learning, but first we have to learn to accept each other and respect each other. It's coming along.

—*Teacher, Bethune Academy*

Creating positive educational environments where high-quality teaching is the standard and students are fully engaged in learning was a primary goal for each of the seven schools in our study. However, the creation of such environments proved to be a complicated task. As the two teachers above describe, there is a need to establish a classroom environment where respect and collegial cooperation can engender trust and a sense of safety in the learning process. Simultaneously, these teachers are also struggling to meet the learning needs of their students and to push them to develop their higher-order thinking skills. The teacher at Bethune was in a unique situation. Her school was the only one in the study that was attempting to utilize what it described as "gender-based instruction" based on training the staff had received from the Gurian Institute. Bethune is located in a Southeastern city and serves students in grades six through eight. The school opened in 2007–2008 beginning with a sixth-grade cohort of nearly 150 students. The professional development and instructional conversations that we observed focused continuously on using "gender-based" strategies. Although we found considerable confusion among the staff about what this actually meant in terms of classroom practice, the instructional challenges they faced were not unlike those confronting educators at the other six schools.

During interviews with teachers from the various schools, we heard several of them grappling with the question of how to address the skills deficits of their male students and promote higher-order thinking and social and emotional development. They understood that the time and energy spent trying to build relationships often comes at the expense of the time needed to develop skills and encourage students to challenge themselves intellectually and analytically. Yet, as discussed in the previous chapter, each of these schools was engaged in a deliberate effort to create an environment that would provide protection and achievement for their boys. Given the goals and obstacles they faced, the quality and form of instruction provided at each of these schools typically entailed far more than merely developing academic skills. It also involved a conscious effort to help students develop a degree of resilience that the educators hoped would reduce the vulnerability they experienced in their lives.

In this chapter we focus on the approach to instruction that we observed in these seven schools and the specific strategies utilized to promote engagement and learning. As we observed classrooms and interviewed teachers and students about what was occurring, we sought to understand how instructional strategies were developed and deployed to provide a protective shield for boys of color. Specifically, our focus was on understanding the choices made by the educators in these schools regarding the type of instruction students received. We also sought to understand the choices that were made about the curriculum, and how the students in turn responded to these choices. In our examination of the instructional environment we closely monitored classroom practice, the stated purpose behind particular strategies, and the materials that were used. We also looked closely at how the educators addressed what they described as the need for cultural relevance in curriculum and instruction as well as for skill development and academic challenge.

Working with the Constraints: Meeting the Academic Needs of Black and Latino Boys

As educational institutions that are judged primarily by the academic performance of their students, the seven single-sex schools were all preoccupied with developing academic strategies and interventions that would produce high levels of achievement. Each of the school principals was well aware that one of the chief reasons why these schools were created was to address the academic needs of Black and Latino boys whose school outcomes are typically distinguished by failure. For example, James Jackson, the principal at Thomas Jefferson, explained that his school was specifically created to address the dismal college graduation rates for Black males:

> Out of all Black male students who enter the public school system, only 2.5 percent will earn a college degree by the time they are twenty-five years old. This means that 97 percent of young African American males . . . are left to pursue avenues to make a living that do not

require a college degree . . . Everyone knows that while it's not abso-
lutely necessary to have a college degree to succeed, all of the indicators are that if you graduate from college you have a greater likelihood
of success in life than if you don't. And if all the research shows that
going to college and finishing will result in a better standard of living
and greater success, then how can you look at a segment of your population and accept the fact that only one of forty of you get to do that?

Similar concerns were expressed even in the elementary and middle
schools in this study. In such schools the goal of sending young men to
college was embraced as the ultimate goal of single-sex education. Well
aware of the dismal track record for Black and Latino male students in
traditional public schools, the educators at these schools sought to provide boys of color with an educational foundation that they hoped would
make it possible for them to succeed in high school and college.

To accomplish their academic goals, the schools focused on four areas critical to meeting the academic needs of their students: addressing
gaps in skills, preparing for college, raising expectations for a future,
and establishing a culturally relevant curriculum and instruction. In
the following sections we describe each of these approaches and analyze how they sought to accomplish the ambitious goals that were set.

Addressing Gaps in Skills

Across the seven single-sex schools, the educators we interviewed expressed an awareness that many of the students they served, even those
they considered capable of high performance, came to them with major
gaps in their content knowledge and basic skills due to the poor education they had received in their local schools. Repeatedly, we were told
that before students could excel they had to make up for missing skills,
especially in areas such as literacy, math, and critical thinking. To address these needs, the educators generally expressed support for traditional approaches to remediation as the best way to fill these gaps. This
typically included double period math and literacy courses and a relentless focus on completing homework. Although we were repeatedly told
that they hoped to provide their boys with a "rigorous" and "challeng-

ing" education that would ultimately help them to succeed, the narrative we heard expressed over and over by the educators suggested that the schools prioritized the need to teach the basic skills that their students were lacking.

Some of the educators we interviewed expressed the belief that the learning deficits of male students could be explained by the fact that in traditional public schools the boys were being taught in ways that were more appropriate for girls. For example, a number of educators we interviewed told us that boys have lower attention spans than girls, and that they benefit from more physical activity. Several teachers told us that boys need "more hands-on kinds of programs and projects" to suit their learning needs. In addition to "hands-on" work, several educators stressed the need to address "multiple learning styles" or to provide "differentiated instruction" to meet the learning needs of each of their students.

According to a math teacher at Bethune, learning conditions in traditional public schools were "inadequate, unchallenging, non-rigorous, and promoted mediocre learning." In contrast, the teacher asserted that single-sex schools like Bethune aimed to provide an equitable alternative for Black and Latino boys. The principal of Thomas Jefferson made a similar point: "Well, it's quite evident that the school system is underserving or not serving urban young Black and Latino men. We've tried to create an environment that gives our guys some options. Our school has to have the leeway to do some things a little differently. Quite frankly, it seems to me that the traditional ways of education for young Black men aren't working."

Interestingly, although several of the educators we met spoke about the need for instruction that met the unique learning styles of boys and for single-sex schools that could offer an "innovative approach" to learning, most of the instruction that we observed seemed very similar to what one might see in any typical public school. This was particularly the case in the remedial classes that were designed to improve basic skills in math and literacy. Later in this chapter we take up an analysis of the instruction observed in the seven schools in greater detail, but for now it is sufficient to point out that there was not much evidence that the schools devised creative interventions in response to the skills gap of their students, or that they had discovered any unique instructional strategies that were well suited for Black and Latino boys.

Preparing for College

In order for Black and Latino male students to be prepared and on an equal footing when they got to college, each of these schools reported that they were intentionally building and implementing a college preparatory curriculum. Despite these assertions, we saw very little evidence that the curriculum developed by these schools was designed to ensure college readiness. Very few of the schools offered honors and advance placement courses, and a close examination of the curriculum revealed that most of the courses offered at these schools were typical of what is available in most urban schools.

Instead of a college preparatory curriculum, at several of the schools we were told that they were attempting to adapt certain elements from the college experience to the culture and structure of the school. For example, the principal of Westward Academy described developing a college preparatory curriculum that was similar to his own college experience at a prestigious private university:

> They need to get as much college stuff before they get to college. My experience going to a prestigious private university is that the kids who did well in the freshman year were kids who knew a lot of that stuff before they got there. Being exposed to college-level courses while you were in high school just put them on a much more solid footing. That's why for these kids coming from this neighborhood . . . it's their only real way of getting a shot . . . Even if they have some of the other skills: good note taking, paying attention, showing up every day, being prepared, it's not going to be enough. I mean if the kid next to you took calculus the year before, and you didn't, you know, you're not going to do as well. So they need as much of the college prep courses as possible to succeed. At a minimum, they need some exposure to it or some level of proficiency or mastery.

Although all of the high school principals in the study expressed great concern about preparing their students for college, the primary strategy for achieving this goal consisted of visits to colleges and universities. Several of the schools invited college students to speak to their boys about college life in order to demystify the experience; they also took their students to college fairs, where they would be exposed to several colleges at once. Principal Clem Carver at Westward confided that despite his desire to prepare his students for college, he was not in a position to offer the kinds of courses that he felt would meet their needs. Other principals expressed similar concerns. Despite the stated goal of preparing all of these students for college, we were told that that the reason why more challenging courses were not offered was that the students lacked the academic preparation to succeed in them. Although research by the College Board and other organizations has shown that such courses can be highly effective in boosting college enrollment among students who have historically been underrepresented,[1] the schools in our study had not yet found ways to make these courses as widely available as they would like.

Instead of offering rigorous college preparatory courses, the schools offered classes that could provide students with organizational and study skills that they hoped would give them a chance to be successful in college. Privately, Principal Carver described such courses as less important, but he also told us that he was at a loss for coming up with a more effective approach. The guidance counselor at Salem Academy explained the rationale for such an approach to us in this way:

> It would be great if they could actually get some credits before they start college, but most of them are too far behind when they get to us so we're playing catch-up. We do offer the AVID[2] program and it's great because it teaches them how to take notes, how to get as much as you can from a lecture, how to look at a text and pull out the important information. You know, all those kinds of things. Like I said, it would be great if we could offer AP Bio and Calculus, but we're not there yet. We're still trying to convince these kids that they are smart and bright, that they have the aptitude . . . It just doesn't come naturally for

them. They were never taught that, so by learning these skills we hope there's a chance that when they get to college they'll be ready.

Raising Expectations

The educators at these single-sex schools were driven by a clear sense that raising achievement among their boys was only possible if they raised their expectations and held them to higher academic standards. However, at most of the schools we noticed a gap between what they said about high expectations and what was actually happening in the classrooms. While most of the educators we spoke to acknowledged the need for higher expectations, in practice this primarily meant insisting that students show up to school and to class on time, come prepared for class, participate as expected by the teacher, and turn in homework. These expectations represented what might be described as activities intended to ensure behavioral engagement. Achieving higher levels of cognitive engagement was described as a goal they were still aspiring to achieve.

The academic and social needs of the students, combined with the environmental impediments they face growing up in racially isolated communities with concentrated poverty, were cited as barriers that constrain the ability of the schools to raise the achievement of their students. While the educators we met and interviewed expressed optimism about their ability to help their students succeed, they also expressed a sense of realism about what might not be possible during the limited period of time they had responsibility for their students. For example, during a tour of Bethune, Principal Clayton Brown explained that most of his students entering sixth grade were classified as Level II, meaning they were below proficient in reading, writing, and math. Although Level II is not at the lowest level (Level I) of achievement, for many students it meant that basic skills were lacking. With a profound sense of resignation, Principal Brown pointed out that most of his students could barely read. "They've gotten good enough at taking the tests so they can find enough right answers to score at Level II, but if you ask them to read something you'll see that most of them are reading at a second- or third-grade level. We want to push them to achieve at a higher level than that, but for the next two years we'll be playing catch-up, making sure that they get skills they should have gotten back in elementary schools." He pointed out a reality that exists in many persistently low performing urban school systems in which test preparation has taken the place of instruction designed to meet the learning needs of students. Brown and others told us that the emphasis placed on test preparation is creating generations of Black and Latino children who lack the ability to succeed in school or college.

An administrator at Thomas Jefferson suggested that his school was trying to counter the effects of "deep structural racism" in a system that prevents Black students, in particular males, from making educational gains:

> When you see kids arriving in high school who can still barely read and write, I call that structural racism. I mean how do you let a kid get that far and not stop at some point and say "this kid has got to learn something"? I would say that being a young Black male you're constantly dealing with racism. It's the racism of people who have low expectations of you, who have no expectations of you. We're trying to create an environment that's different, but to raise the achievement we have to reverse years of miseducation.

While this administrator's comment is linked to the "social issues" facing Black males, one of the most common structural issues their students would have to contend with are the low expectations that others hold toward them. Each of the schools mentioned low expectations as being a significant factor contributing to the achievement gap.

The effort to elevate expectations was apparent in nearly every classroom, hallway, and cafeteria that we visited. Over and over we were told that creating a culture of high achievement was an unrelenting effort that was working against a tide of low expectations. An administrator we spoke to at Thomas Jefferson explained how the effort to raise expectations affected the school's ability to seek funds from a private foundation:

I remember one time when I was doing some fundraising for the school and I went down to talk to a donor from a fairly large foundation that had recently made a fairly large contribution to a predominantly White, affluent school. So I was down there talking to them, you know, trying to get them to see why they should give us some money. You know what this guy said to me—point-blank—and he is the head of the foundation, he said, "Well, what we don't really understand is why it's so important for these guys to go to college. I mean, maybe you should do some type of technical/vocational focus because it's important that we have people who deliver the mail and drive the buses . . ." And he was very nice about it, and just kept going through this long list of blue-collar jobs. And, you know, I said to him, "Did you ask Somers [pseudonym for the private school they donated to] to implement a vocational program like that before you gave them that million dollars?" He immediately became uncomfortable and said, "Oh, well, Somers is different." I explained to him that I know it is, it's very different; I went to Somers. Then I said that I think that these guys should have the same type of experience that those guys get. I mean, I don't think that anyone of us would say that every person in the world needs to go to college. But I think all of us would agree that enough Black men aren't going to college. And so there's no harm in us saying all of our graduates are going to college. Because there are plenty other places out there that aren't sending any . . . Well I guess you wouldn't be surprised to hear that we didn't get the money. [He laughed loudly.]

Making Curriculum and Instruction Culturally Relevant

Existing research suggests that not only do students need teachers who are highly skilled, they also benefit from teachers who are culturally sensitive and have the ability to make the curriculum culturally relevant and responsive to their learning needs.[3] Throughout our study we placed considerable emphasis on what teachers did in the classroom to ensure that the material was culturally relevant and challenging. We adopted such a focus because we were repeatedly told by teachers that this was one of their primary goals. As we mentioned in the previous chapter, a critical part of the implicit theory of change guiding these schools was the assumption that a culturally enriched, academically rigorous curriculum would succeed in countering the effects of weak academic preparation and the numerous distractions in the communities where the boys reside. In order to meet the academic and social needs of their students, the teachers we interviewed told us that cultural relevance and academic rigor were required to produce cognitive engagement for boys of color. Many of the educators suggested that in order to address the educational needs of boys of color, teachers must employ a set of "hooks" in their pedagogical routines. Several described these "hooks" as strategies that would allow the young men to "see themselves" in the curriculum. Others described the importance of instructional strategies that have "real-world application."

It is important to note that several education scholars[4] have made similar points about the importance of curricular relevance and identity affirmation to cognitive engagement in relation to adolescents generally and students of color in particular. However, what we found to be unique to these schools is how they framed the choices they made with respect to curriculum and instruction. Much of what we observed is very much aligned with the broader view that we described in chapter 1, regarding what these educators believe it takes to "save the boys." Through hundreds of hours of classroom observations we documented and then analyzed how these schools attempted to realize that goal. We also examined how the educators imparted what scholars like Lisa Delpit describe as "the culture of power"[5] and Theresa Perry describes as "counternarratives of excellence."[6]

At each of the schools, the administrators reported that the curriculum needed to extend beyond the walls of the classroom in order to prepare the boys for academic success not only in school, but throughout the rest of their academic careers. Most of them maintained that the curriculum needed to connect to the lives of their students in positive and constructive ways. However, while some had clear plans related to what they thought of as a culturally relevant curriculum in their schools, others described their efforts in fairly vague terms. Still others described this as something that *should* be done, but did not have a clear plan as to how it would be put into practice.

In the research literature, culturally relevant instruction is defined as the use of learning materials and instructional strategies that are directly connected to the heritage and lived experience of students.[7] In other words, cultural relevance is being conceptualized as a remedy or intervention that can be used to address the educational needs of students of color.[8] Several of the administrators we interviewed stated that they believed academic disengagement was caused in large part by the boys' disinterest in what they were learning and by their inability to "see themselves" in the curriculum of traditional public schools. As one administrator at Washington commented:

> I think the students learn best when they can learn about or experience something that is meaningful to them. Students are not very good long-term thinkers. They tend to be short-term—me, right here, right now. This is my world. And so when you can kind of show a student how what they're learning is applicable to their world, I think they can make that connection and begin to learn . . . If the material connects with them, specifically as African American males, then the capacity for learning is greater.

According to Washington's vice principal, the education the boys receive should "connect" to each "student's life, their world, their existence." When this happens, we were told, the material would be more meaningful and solicit a greater degree of cognitive and behavioral engagement. According to several administrators, the students in single-sex schools need to know that what they are learning connects directly to "their world." When asked to speak more specifically about what this connection entailed, the administrator at Washington said that it could be "along any lines pertaining to their identity, socioeconomically, racially, gender, or just within their particular interests."

Many of these educators assumed that if students could see the applicability of the material they were learning—its connection to their current experiences or their "interests"—they would be more likely to be invested in learning. Inherent in this belief is an assumption that this particular population of students—African American and Latino males—has a limited ability to feel "connected" to the subject matter in more traditional educational settings. The educators hoped that cultural relevance could be the antidote to alienation, boredom, and disengagement—attitudes and behaviors that are common among boys of color in many traditional urban schools. In many of the schools we were also told that the material found in traditional settings is biased (racially or by gender) or not conducive to the boys' learning processes.

Implementing Culturally Relevant Instruction

All of the principals recognized that while cultural relevance was important in the curriculum, it was even more important that teachers understand how to make the curriculum relevant to their students. In each of the schools the principals emphasized the importance of hiring a diverse and knowledgeable staff, but many administrators also acknowledged that there was a gap in the depth of knowledge about the experience of Black and Latino boys among their staff. At Salem, the principal spoke adamantly about the need for what he described as cultural competence among his staff:

> I would say that many of the staff lack some cultural competence. They are well-meaning and really do care about our students, but I would say they really don't have an appreciation and understanding for the culture and history of the students that they serve. This is especially true with the theme of history. We would like for all of our teachers to be able to integrate that within their discipline at some point because that is a central theme of this school . . . However, it's just as important that they have some knowledge about how to work with boys. They really must understand this stage of development: where they are, what they're going to bring. . . . There's no school, or very few schools of education in American institutions, that focus on the psychosocial development of young men of color.

It's very important for us [to] have professional development that focuses around the socialization of young people of color, particularly
young men.

In addition to concerns about cultural competence and how the lack
of it might affect the effectiveness of teachers, several administrators
also expressed concern about the strategies teachers relied on to engage
their students. Principal Trust of North Star emphasized the importance of instructional methods that he described as "student-centered."
He expressed his concerns in the following way: "Right now our lessons
are still very teacher-dominated and we would like to move more away
from that. Our boys get bored and fidgety when the teachers talk for too
long. They need hands-on activities." To address this problem Principal
Trust confided that his teachers "need more classroom management
skills and extra professional development on group activities. This is
especially true for some of the inexperienced teachers. Whenever our
teachers have trouble relating to our students it usually shows up as a
classroom management problem. I try to get at the underlying causes
of the problems that may be related to their lack of experience in working with or even being around Black people. But that takes time. In the
meantime, we have to help them maintain some kind of order so that
learning can take place."

Although it was not always framed in terms of cultural competence,
the ability to connect instruction to the students' lives was a theme that
we heard mentioned frequently in our interviews. Several administrators expressed concern that class differences between teachers and students were as significant as racial differences in separating teachers
from students. Most of the teachers in these schools were from middle-class backgrounds and came from neighborhoods that are very different than the ones where their students live. As a result of these ex-
periential differences there was a concern that they would not be able
to relate to the challenges their students confront on a daily basis. The
program director at Salem let us know that this was a major concern for
him: "In order to be successful every teacher in this environment has to

be prepared to have some conversations around the issues these boys face—gangs, youth culture, drugs, thug life . . . If they can't integrate this stuff into their instruction the boys are going to tune out. They're going to say 'this ain't for me because it's not about my reality.' We can't afford to allow that to happen." Despite his concern, when pressed about what should be done to address this lack of understanding, he admitted that he was at a loss over what to do.

Several of the principals said that because there is a shortage of teachers who can be effective at single-sex schools, there is an ongoing need for professional development to increase the effectiveness of teachers with the Black and Latino male students they serve. Many of them told us that the teachers needed to have a clear understanding of the research on the educational strategies that were most effective with Black and Latino boys. When we pressed them for concrete examples of the research-based strategies they felt would be most effective, we were generally given broad statements about cultural relevance and the need for more hands-on activities.

As we observed classrooms we learned that one way teachers attempt to engage students is by incorporating material that they believe the boys can relate to and identify with in the curriculum from a racial/ethnic and gender standpoint. In many of the lessons we observed there were explicit references to figures such as Malcolm X, Harriett Tubman, Emmett Till, and other prominent figures from African American history. Other teachers sought to use contemporary figures from popular culture such as Kanye West, Jay Z, Drake, and Fifty Cent. The heavy reliance on Black icons served as a pointed reminder that although Latino boys were present in some schools, there was not an equitable representation of Latino figures in class materials. This may have been because there were also relatively few Latino educators at these schools. Interestingly, even when the goals and focus of a lesson varied—from test preparation, reading comprehension, question-and-answer sessions related to math or science, or even a film screening—the underlying commonality in many of the classes was the deliberate attempt to tap into the students' presumed interest in historical/cultural figures and contexts as a way of engaging them in the lesson. Even though it was not clear that such an approach consistently elicited the desired effect, teachers at each of the schools described the importance of students "seeing themselves."

For example, after observing a Spanish teacher discuss the history of slavery in Cuba and the Dominican Republic, we were given this explanation as to why she felt it was important to put what she described as "cultural components" up front:

> I do this because I think it's part of what it takes to really connect with my students. Given the group that we're teaching, we're working with African American males many of whom have been turned off to school, so just even doing things like readings must include their culture. To me, incorporating the cultural component of Afro-Latinos and Cuba and the Dominican Republic makes it so that they are more conscious of what's going on in the world around them. I had an interest in Latin American literature and politics while I was in college. I feel that I have brought a lot more of that into my classroom. This might not be what is typically covered in the Spanish 1 classroom, but I make sure it's covered in mine.

Another teacher at Kennedy Academy explained that his primary concern when choosing what literature to use in reading was whether he thought the material would connect with his fifth graders: "I actually review the lists and stuff that we're using in reading, I then realize that I have to skip a lot of the stories because I ask myself: Would a fifth-grade African American or Latino boy like this story? I have to be mindful of the literature and the activities I'm using. I feel it's important for them to relate to what's going on the classroom."

Interestingly, when we pointed out that several of their students told us that they enjoyed reading Harry Potter, a book series that few educators would describe as culturally relevant in a narrow sense, the teachers seemed undeterred about their choices. Several of the teachers we met made it clear that they thought of cultural relevance in fairly narrow terms, and for this reason they focused on materials that were specifically about Black or Latino people, history, and culture. Some teachers acknowledged to us privately that they felt such efforts were a bit of a stretch, and that they were not convinced that it always worked. One White, relatively young female teacher at Westward described how she found the expectation that she be able to speak to the cultural experiences of her students to be a little difficult:

> I don't try to get into the standpoint that because of who you are you will learn this way or that way, or because of where you come from. I can't speak to their personal experiences and I don't know that much about the communities where they live. I do try to connect with them through their gender. For example, I pick literature based on what I think boys would enjoy reading. Like right now we're talking about the election and I'm trying to draw on their interest in the campaign. They're very much convinced that Obama is going to win, so we have a lot of discussion about how—which states is he likely to win and why will he get certain states but not others. You know, there's difference in attitudes toward Obama in the country, and I try to help them understand why that is. But I don't pick things simply because I think that because they're Black or Hispanic they will find it interesting. I don't change the way that I talk to them based on my perspective of where they're at. In order for me to do that I would have to know more about them and I'm really not that informed about their culture.

As the teacher in this example shows, though cultural relevance was valued as the pedagogical approach that should be utilized at several of the schools, the ability of teachers to utilize it effectively varied considerably.

At all of the schools the notion of cultural relevance also included a concerted effort to make instruction relevant to the lives of students. Several of the teachers used examples in their classrooms which seemed to be drawn from experiences that they believed their students could identify with. Additionally, in several of the schools, courses were created to recapture or "hook" the students' interest by focusing on their racial/ethnic and gender identities. The following are some of the course names:

- M.A.L.E. (Make All Learning Exciting) middle school math class
- M.D.R. (Men Do Read) high school English language arts class
- History of African- and Latin-Based Music
- Indigenous Latino History
- The African and Latino Experience in the 20th and 21st Centuries

These classes were created to develop a learning experience that the educators hoped would be seen as relevant to the boys. However, based on our observations of hundreds of classrooms, we would have to conclude that such efforts were not always successful. Even in classrooms where the course material or the course name indicated that it was specifically geared toward males of color, we found students who were distracted, disengaged, and at times disruptive. This suggests that there is much more that educators need to consider when striving to solicit sustained intellectual effort and engagement. As several of the administrators noted in chapter 1, there was a perceived need for the boys to have classes that reflected their experience. This was based on their theory that the boys were suffering from a racial identity crisis that could best be countered by a heavy dose of cultural relevance. As we learned from our observations, however, to produce sustained intellectual engagement the educators would have to do much more than merely incorporate some materials that they regarded as culturally relevant.

In several of the schools the educators sought to engage their students by framing specific academic activities, particularly reading, as culturally oriented activities that they hoped would be more attractive and compelling to their students. During several focus groups we were told that some boys previously thought of reading as something that only girls do. Cultural relevance was seen as the tool that would counter this sort of alienation. But our observations revealed mixed results from such efforts. For many of the educators, cultural relevance was merely a matter of infusing the curriculum with information from African or

Latin American history. In many classrooms this did not appear to result in high levels of behavioral or cognitive engagement. Rather, such efforts appeared contrived and did not lead to the creation of a learning environment where male students willingly embraced learning.

There was a surprising degree of similarity in the effort to create a culturally relevant curriculum among the teachers and administrators at the seven schools in our study. Most often these efforts consisted of making explicit race and gender connections to the course material and the learning process. Even when the materials used did not result in higher levels of engagement, the educators seemed convinced that eventually the approach would work. An administrator from Thomas Jefferson told us that he supported the idea of using material that he deemed culturally relevant, and he described it as central to his philosophy of learning: "You've got to try your best to connect the subject to that student's life, their world, their existence." This need was echoed in several of the other schools, as both teachers and administrators described the importance of meeting students where they are culturally. Although one could argue that this was based on a more inclusive notion of culture that went far beyond race and gender, it also appeared that the approach was based on broad generalizations about who their students were and what would interest them.

In some respects, the use of cultural relevance at these schools followed patterns that are consistent with findings from the research on multicultural education, but in other important respects the approach taken also diverged significantly. Among leading scholars in the field it is commonly asserted that "culturally relevant" curricula and instruction will effectively engage students—especially those from marginalized groups—by providing them with subject matter and learning activities that they can "relate to" or "identify" with.[9] The assumption is that by including content knowledge from their ancestral heritage or from popular culture, students will be more willing to embrace the knowledge and information presented in class. Scholars such as James Banks, Christine E. Sleeter, Gloria Ladson-Billings, and Geneva Gay[10] (to name a few) have suggested that educational inequities may be partially remedied through more "inclusive" learning practices. Others, such as Jackie Jordan Irvine, have argued that by adopting a pedagogical lens that takes into account the diversity of students' racial, ethnic, and/or socioeconomic identities, students will respond with higher levels of academic engagement. However, our observations of classrooms in all seven schools revealed that cultural relevance in curriculum and instruction was no guarantee of higher engagement.

Interestingly, while many interviewees made explicit reference to the need for "culturally relevant" instruction, the term was rarely defined or articulated in a way that made specific reference to *how* this would appear in instructional practice. During one administrator's discussion of the type of professional development teachers at his school needed in order to reach their population of boys, he stated, "We are really trying to build the capacity of the entire staff, Black and White alike, on cultural relevancy within the curriculum—*what that looks like*, why it's important" [emphasis added]. Statements such as these—focusing on the need to educate teachers about culturally relevant practices, including the types of activities that are essential to these practices—led us to believe that the way they have conceptualized cultural relevance is very much a work-in-progress. Based on their experience these practitioners have come to recognize that there is no guarantee that students will respond positively to their instruction simply because of cultural inclusion. Their experience in working with their male students led them to understand that engaging students intellectually and addressing their academic skills was a complex task that would not lend itself to simple solutions.

Student Responses to Instruction

Not surprisingly, we observed a wide range of responses to the material by students when we sat in classrooms. While some were clearly motivated and engaged by the material utilized and the learning strategies employed, others were not. Variations in the responses of students reinforced the importance of connecting efforts aimed at promoting cultural inclusion to professional development designed to improve teacher effectiveness in clear and practical ways.

The need to get students actively engaged in learning was combined with a concern among educators about the importance of developing their capacity to think critically. Cultivating critical thinking and other higher-order skills was a continuous focus in many of the teachers' discussions. Several teachers reported that one of the ways they promoted critical thinking was by developing a classroom discourse that encouraged collective inquiry. An English teacher at Kennedy explained her approach in this way:

> We do the critical thinking in our classroom meetings. I always try to push them by always asking why. So if they got the right answer I follow up by asking why? Why did you choose that answer? Why did you solve the problem in that way? I do this to push them, to push them to think critically about everything that they're doing . . . That's why we always ask why. I want them to know that getting the right answer is only important if you can explain why it's right because in the real world you have to know why you're doing what you do.

The need to go beyond basic skills to address the gaps in student's analytical thinking did not emerge initially. Many of the schools were focused on creating positive, disciplined learning environments, but they didn't have a clear sense of what the learning needs of their students might be. Several teachers talked about it taking a while for them to fully grasp the extent of the academic needs of their students. For example, a math teacher we interviewed at Westward described how she learned about her students' needs:

> I've figured out that you have to meet the students where they're at. When I first met them I was so focused on my expectations, which were very high. It took me until like last Tuesday to actually figure out where they were in terms of their prior math knowledge and their fears about math. I'm beginning to know how to assess them and their learning needs; now that I know that, I know how to revamp my instruction to meet them at their level. If I want them to rise on up

then I've got to start where they are. And that's something that took me a while to figure out. I mean, I've taught before but it's always a new deck of cards that you get every day.

Despite the fact that we noticed inconsistency in the level of challenge and degree of rigor in classrooms during our observations, many of the boys reported that their teachers and administrators expected a lot from them. Table 3.1 illustrates student survey responses on indicators of teacher quality and expectations in English language arts (ELA) classes for the middle and high schools in our study. A large majority of middle and high school students agree that their ELA teachers expect them to do their best all the time and to work hard. It is also striking that most of the students believe their teachers think they can do well in school. While a slightly smaller majority of students noted that their teachers help them catch up if they are behind or notice if they have trouble learning something, about one in every eight middle and high school students "disagree" or "strongly disagree" with this statement.

As we became aware of these patterns in the way students were responding to the instructional strategies of their teachers, we were com-

TABLE 3.1
Indicators of ELA teacher quality

The teacher of my English/ELA class . . .	Disagree		Agree	
	MS	HS	MS	HS
Expects me to do my best all the time	6.8%	7.1%	93.2%	92.9%
Expects everyone to work hard	7.2%	8.1%	92.8%	91.9%
Believes I can do well in school	7.2%	7.4%	92.8%	92.6%
Helps me catch up if I am behind	13.9%	14.3%	86.1%	85.7%
Notices if I have trouble learning something	14.4%	17.6%	85.6%	82.4%

Note: Disagree combines the responses "strongly disagree" and "disagree"; Agree combines "agree" and "strongly agree."

pelled to raise additional questions about how teachers decided what might be possible for their students. An administrator at North Star elaborated on the limitations of the teaching staff during one of our interviews: "We get our instructional staff from the same pool regular schools get their staff. Not all of them understand how to work with struggling students or how to strike the right balance between challenging them and helping them." His point compelled us to consider how inconsistency in the instructional strengths of teachers was being addressed in these schools. While using cultural relevance as a way to "hook" students and get them engaged seemed to work with some students, it was not necessarily a sufficient strategy for addressing deficiencies in knowledge and skills. In the following section, we use data obtained from student surveys and focus groups to analyze how effective these strategies have been.

Giving Students What They Need

Some teachers reported that the most important skills students needed to acquire involved knowing how to function in school, or as some put it, "to do school." Several of the administrators and teachers we interviewed spoke about the importance of helping students to develop organizational skills like note taking and using a schedule to keep track of assignments. Others focused on issues of comportment, attitude, and presentation. Many of the teachers complained that their students did not display behaviors that they felt were conducive to learning. For example, a math teacher at Kennedy described student behaviors that interfere with the learning environment and the importance of teaching a student to look like "a good student":

> I tell them they must sit up straight, listen, ask a lot of questions, not to interrupt the speaker, and track who's talking. I want them to understand that we must respect and learn from each other. This is basic stuff, but a lot of these boys never got this before. I have to let them know that there is a reason they have to conduct themselves in this way. When you're an adult and you're in a meeting talking to other adults you need to show that you're listening. A lot of kids don't come

in knowing that. . . I want them to have the social skills that are necessary for success. That's something that we're really working on with them every day in every single setting, so that once they leave eighth grade, these behaviors will be natural.

Similar comments related to the importance of getting their boys to "act" like serious students were made by teachers and administrators at all of the schools. One administrator at Washington explained that the goal was not merely to teach their students to be good at school, but to be leaders who would know how to carry themselves in their communities. A deliberate focus on behavioral socialization within the context of the classroom was mentioned by several teachers, including one who talked about using literature to develop leadership skills: "We have four books, three of them that focus on leadership and individuals who overcame obstacles. One of the books is *The Autobiography of Malcolm X*, the others are *Lord of the Flies* and *To Kill a Mockingbird*. We use every opportunity we can find to develop character even as we are simultaneously developing their academic skills."

Instructional Strategies

When we examined the types of instructional strategies that were utilized in the schools it was clear that open-class discussions served as the primary and most common instructional tool. In looking at a representative sample of classroom observations (social studies, English, and math), there was a consistent pattern of teacher-centered instruction (see table 3.2). In most cases, the teacher led the discussion for the entire class period and took full responsibility for how the content would be applied. In our data analysis process we utilized thirty-five codes to examine the classroom observations (see appendix 2). These codes allowed us to examine various dynamics of classroom environment, such as the direction of conversations in the classroom (e.g., one-way, two-way, or additive conversations), the types of questions posed (e.g., comprehension, analysis, synthesis), the types of tools used during instruction (e.g., worksheets, manipulatives, textbooks, novels, etc.), the ways content was delivered (e.g., lecture, small group, cooperative groups), and the amount of time spent on various activities (observations were of the entire class period). Interestingly, there was very little variation between the schools with respect to the type of instructional strategies that were utilized. For this reason, we present the patterns we observed by school levels (middle and high school) rather than for each school individually.

Overall, there were six types of instructional strategies that were consistently utilized in all seven of the schools. These included: whole group discussions, question-and-answer forms of direct instruction, reading (aloud and independently), writing activities (with and without prompts), worksheets, and a variety of hands-on activities. Table 3.2 provides an overview of the frequency that each action occurred. At both the middle and high schools, discussions occurred in almost all of the observations. This was the case even in math classes, and the discussions typically involved teachers engaging in a give-and-take with

TABLE 3.2

Frequency of instructional actions

Instructional actions	Middle schools	High schools
Discussions	35 discussions in 47 observations	45 discussions in 48 observations
Question-and-answer	Average 4.5 questions per class	Average 3.25 questions per class
Reading (includes aloud and independent)	18 out of 47 observations	23 reading activities in 48 observations
Writing activities (prompted and unprompted)	33 writing activities out of 47 observations	36 writing activities in 48 observations
Worksheets	41 worksheet assignments in 47 observations	23 worksheet assignments in 48 observations
Hands-on	5 hands-on activities in 47 observations	6 hands-on activities in 48 observations

students over the nature of their responses rather than simply accepting one-word answers to questions. We found that the average rate at which questions were posed at the middle schools was slightly higher than in the high schools. In many cases the questions posed were robust and challenging, evoking a rich discussion over the subjects being raised. However, relatively few of the classrooms we observed utilized reading to drive learning activities. In contrast, we observed several classrooms where teachers used worksheets as instructional tools. When we asked one social studies teacher why she relied so heavily on worksheets, she explained, "I believe in doing a lot of reading. I believe in writing. I believe in having discussions and in talking about different issues and hearing different points of view. But these kids get distracted very easily. If I don't keep them busy they become disruptive. I would like to have debate and even some drama so that students could be more actively involved, but I haven't been able to do any of that this year because of the discipline needs."

Additionally, looking more closely at the classroom observation codes, we found that out of the 41 observations conducted in the middle school classrooms where we found worksheets being utilized, the majority (24 out of 41) were in math classes. Interestingly, at the high schools, the worksheets as an instructional tool were mostly present in social studies classes (12 out of 23).

In general, while the mode of instruction by itself may not be an indicator of intellectual rigor, when combined with the detailed notes that were taken they reveal a consistent pattern of teacher-centered instruction. While there was some degree of variation with respect to the types of strategies teachers relied on in their classrooms, more often than not students were engaged in fairly passive forms of learning: listening to a teacher explain a concept or lesson, answering a question, or carrying out an in-class assignment. Project-based learning, group activities, and other learning modalities that could be described as active or student-centered, were quite rare.

The patterns we observed were corroborated in the student surveys. We asked students a variety of questions regarding the frequency in which specific instructional activities occurred in their classroom. We opted to focus on English language arts as a central course, since students appeared to be taking at least one and sometimes two different types of ELA courses. Table 3.3 illustrates student responses to questions about literacy activities and whether or not these were perceived as being related to college preparation. Given that all of the schools had a major emphasis on college preparation, we decided to collect data on the types of instructional activities being employed in classrooms in Years 2 and 3 of the study. The majority of middle and high school students identified the following activities as occurring at least once a week: explaining what you've read in a class discussion; discussing how something you read connected to real life; studying something that is about an issue you care about; and explaining something in writing about how you solved a math problem. In contrast, writing an essay or a research paper, working in groups to solve a problem, and speaking or presenting in class occurred less than once per week.

Though relatively few of the learning activities we observed in the literacy classes appeared aligned with what are typically regarded as college readiness activities, the majority of students surveyed stated that they considered their teachers, and at times the material, to be challenging. Table 3.4 shows responses to indicators on ELA course challenge, that is, to what extent middle and high school students perceived their ELA courses as challenging. A little over a quarter of middle and high school students reported that they never found the work in their ELA classes difficult. The remainder of students reported that they found the work to be difficult at least once a month. An overwhelming majority of middle and high school students reported that they have to work hard at least once a month to do well.

The student survey responses suggest that most of the students report that they have to work hard to do well and that they feel challenged. However, our observations revealed that relatively few of the classrooms deployed learning activities that would be regarded as meeting the standard of college preparation. Undoubtedly, because most of these young men came from schools where relatively little was expected of them,

TABLE 3.3

Literacy activities related to college preparation

How frequently did the following occur in your classes?	Never		Less than once a week		Once a week or more	
	MS	HS	MS	HS	MS	HS
Explaining what you think about something you've read in a class discussion	11.2%	6.9%	11.6%	17.6%	77.3%	75.5%
Writing an essay or paper that is more than three pages for your English/ELA Class[1]	12.0%	15.5%	47.4%	50.2%	40.6%	34.3%
Discussing how something you read connected to real life situations or real people	14.3%	7.4%	30.3%	28.8%	55.4%	63.8%
Studying or reading something in class that is about an issue you care about	19.1%	13.6%	27.1%	33.6%	53.8%	52.9%
Working with 2 or 3 other students on a big class project	8.8%	10.5%	49.0%	48.6%	42.2%	41.0%
Speaking or doing a presentation by yourself in front of the class	12.4%	10.2%	48.6%	59.3%	39.1%	30.5%
Explaining in writing how you solved a math problem for your Math class	14.7%	10.0%	21.5%	30.7%	63.8%	59.3%

Note: Less than once a week combines the responses "less than once per month" and "less than once per week"; Once a week or more combines "once or twice a week" and "every day or almost every day."

[1] In the middle school student survey, the item referenced a two-page written essay and a high school student survey referenced a three-page written essay.

TABLE 3.4

Indicators of ELA course challenge

In this English/ELA class, how often ...	Never		Less than once a week		Once a week or more	
	MS	HS	MS	HS	MS	HS
Do you find the work difficult?	29.5%	25.2%	36.3%	38.8%	34.3%	36.0%
Are you challenged?	14.7%	13.8%	16.3%	23.1%	68.9%	63.1%
Does the teacher ask difficult questions on tests?	12.0%	16.0%	23.9%	33.8%	64.1%	50.2%
Does the teacher ask difficult questions in class?	14.3%	15.7%	21.5%	29.0%	64.1%	55.2%
Do you have to work hard to do well?	6.8%	10.5%	13.9%	13.6%	79.3%	76.0%

Note: *Less than once a week* combines the responses "less than once per month" and "less than once per week"; *Once a week or more* combines "once or twice a week" and "every day or almost every day."

just being required to work on a regular basis represents a significant increase in the degree of challenge and rigor. However, whether or not the schools are actually succeeding in preparing them for the ambitious goals they have set is a question that nagged at us throughout our study.

The Limits of Cultural Relevance

We observed several cases where despite the effort of the teacher to utilize material that might be regarded as culturally relevant, a significant number of students were not responding. For example, during one classroom observation at North Star, we witnessed a young first-year Black male teacher struggle when trying to teach a lesson focused on the murder of Emmett Till. The teacher explained to the researcher that he had deliberately chosen the material because he hoped it would capture his students' interests. In addition, he had incorporated hip-hop lyrics into his lesson, hoping that this would help his students to see the relevance of this important incident in the history of the Civil Rights movement. Despite these efforts, we observed the class become disruptive and watched with great discomfort as the teacher struggled to gain some semblance of order and control.

Interestingly, even though his students already knew the lines to several of the songs he introduced by heart, they resisted his attempts to get them to analyze them and think about their significance. After playing a portion of Kanye West's "Through the Wire" twice (despite one student's plea to play the entire song), Mr. K. asked the boys to write an answer to the question: "Who was Emmett Till?" Relatively few students complied with this request. He then told them to consider West's reference to a woman who, after the artist's car accident, fears his face will look like Emmett Till's. He tried to get the class to discuss Till's murder and link it to Kanye West's relative disfigurement upon having his jaw wired shut after an accident. Growing increasingly frustrated with their disengagement, the teacher asked his students, "Is there a direct tie between the way Emmett Till acted and the way you act?" In response to this provocative question, several students referred to the way they act around their peers, the ways in which they try to impress girls or brag about sexual acts they claim to have partaken in. For a moment the teacher thought he had regained control through the use of his "hook," but as the exchange below reveals that moment of engagement quickly transformed into something else:

> **Mr. K.:** Now let's look at their time and space . . . A young gentleman from the North comes down to the South and has the nerve to whistle at a White woman . . . How do you think this would have been interpreted within this social order?
>
> **Student A:** They probably didn't like that he had so much pride.
>
> **Mr. K.:** What about the disrespect shown toward the woman? Maybe the real problem might have been his masculinity. Think about how many men see women as sexual objects . . .
> Look at the time in which they lived.

Student B: The White man could've taught Till a "verbal lesson," rather than doing what they did. They didn't have to kill him.

[Some students agree, with one yelling out (**C**)]: Hollering at a woman ain't no crime. If it was most of us would be dead or in jail.

[Others laugh and disagree, with one student (**D**) saying]: The White man's reaction should have been expected during that time period. What was he thinking? Till should have known better than to speak to a White woman in the first place.

Student A: The only reason Till's face was unrecognizable was because of how much time he spent under the water.

[Students at tables 5 and 1 begin to discuss the fact that Till had been under the water—a fact they seem to be learning for the first time. Students at table 3 are not discussing the lesson at all. They appear to be talking about something that happened during lunch.]

Student B: They wouldn't have done all the things they did to him if he hadn't spoken to the White woman. They were trying to kill him.

Student E: At the homecoming dance at another school there was a fight between two boys over a girl.

[The students at table 3 begin laughing. Apparently this information is related to what they had been discussing in their group.]

Student B: Back in that time the Whites wanted to teach Till a lesson, to keep him in his place. They had no remorse about killing a Black boy.

It is not clear from watching this discussion what Mr. K.'s goals were. At one point he tells the boys that "time and space" are important for understanding the Till murder. However, he doesn't say much about time or space, apparently assuming that the students can make these connections themselves. He also attempts to connect the killing of Till to the current situation of Black males, pointing out that some students "are letting a ghetto mentality and ghetto culture get into our school."

It is not clear from this statement if he is implying that the killing of Till was justified because, like the boys in the school, Till had a bad attitude. Even if this is not what he was trying to suggest, it was clear that the larger purpose of the discussion got lost somewhere along the way.

It is worth noting that Mr. K. went to great lengths to utilize the story of Emmett Till and the lyrics from the Kanye West song because he believed this material would help him to engage his students. However, it was not clear what particular skill he was hoping his students would learn through this activity. During our follow-up interview with the teacher we discovered that the point of the activity was to have the students learn how what we think of as acceptable behaviors are related to a particular time and place. When we asked him if he thought that idea came through, he admitted that he didn't think so. Even though several of the students in the classroom were actively involved in the discussion, the learning objective of the lesson had not been met.

We present this example because it is illustrative of one of the problems we observed with efforts to make the curriculum and instruction culturally relevant. In many of the classrooms where we observed teachers utilizing culturally relevant material we saw students who demonstrated behavioral and emotional engagement. However, it was not always clear that the intellectual engagement solicited from these activities was furthering the school's larger objective of preparing students for the rigors of college. Several teachers acknowledged that even when their students were able to "see themselves" in the material, it was not always enough to get them involved in the learning process.

For example, Ms. S., a young White female teacher at one of the middle schools, was observed conducting an ELA lesson in which students in the eighth grade were required to fill out a type of graphic organizer known as a KWL (What you Know, what you Want to know, what you Learned) chart pertaining to Harriett Tubman. The teacher was about to begin a series of readings on the Underground Railroad in order to prepare her class for the impending standardized ELA examinations. She gave her students instructions to record all of the things they knew about Harriett Tubman. The following dialogue (using pseudonyms) was captured during this observation:

Ms. S.: You have about one to two more minutes with this.

Ms. S. *(to Devon)*: Do you understand what you need to do?

Devon: I don't have anything to write with.

Ms. S.: So you're just going to sit there? . . . Maybe you should ask. That would've been a smart thing to do about twenty-five minutes ago.

Wilson: Harriett Tubman shot slaves who would tell about the Underground Railroad.

Ms. S.: That's interesting. I hadn't heard that before.

Devon: See Ms. S., there's a lot you don't know about Black history.

Ms. S.: Devon, you just get to work. You haven't done anything all period.

Christopher: All I know is Harriett Tubman was Black and she was old . . . How old was she when she died?

While many of the students in Ms. S.'s class were on task, completing the assignment as she had instructed, Devon was not. Moreover, as most teachers know, when one student is off task it often has an effect upon other students in the room. It was only after his teacher's prompting that he used the excuse of not having a writing utensil to record what he knew about Harriett Tubman. Although the material being covered by Ms. S. could be viewed as culturally relevant in that it focused on an important element of Black History, it did not seem to be enough to engage this particular student. Whether it was the subject matter itself, the task, or something that was not easily observable, it is clear that even if Devon did "see himself" in the material, his level of engagement appeared just as low as administrators suggested their students' interest levels might be in more "traditional" classrooms. A number of other factors, such as teacher style, classroom dynamics, and the use of other learning materials, are undoubtedly equally relevant to the relationship between teaching and learning.

Examples such as these do not prove that the inclusion of culturally relevant material is not helpful in motivating students. However, during our many classroom observations we observed several such attempts that struck us as not just unhelpful but misguided as well. In one focus group, a student cited an instance in which a teacher referenced a "kilo" of drugs as a way of teaching about the metric system. The mention of illicit drugs certainly seemed to pique student interest. Nevertheless, while using examples of this kind may induce a higher degree of engagement, it clearly runs counter to the desire expressed by all of the administrators to combat negative stereotypes and harmful community influences. Though such examples of cultural relevance were not common, the fact that they were used in some classrooms suggests that teachers may need greater guidance in how to incorporate appropriate material into their lessons.

Relevancy and Real-World Applicability

In addition to providing instruction that made it possible for the students to "see themselves" through various forms of cultural relevance, educators in the seven schools were also preoccupied with finding ways for students to connect to learning by finding some real-world application to the content. This goal was pursued in many different ways. For some, it was through the examples used in the curriculum; for others, it was through cultural activities that could "bring learning to life." This might include trips to local colleges, or meetings with the authors of books that students were reading in their English class. Finding ways to help students apply what they were learning in the classroom to "real-world" situations emerged as an important engagement strategy in all of the schools. As teachers at Thomas Jefferson explained in a focus group, "Everything has to go back to real life. Our students want to know: How is it that this thing here is going to apply to my real life? Sometimes it's a real challenge for us to make these connections to something in real life. I have to figure out what I have to do as far as skills are concerned, to make sure that this means something to them."

In most of the classrooms we observed, teachers were making a concerted effort to develop activities that demonstrated the real-world application and the utility of the knowledge or skill being introduced.

Sometimes this involved making it clear to students how skills such as critical thinking or public speaking might relate to concerns about social justice or conditions in their home or community. By scaffolding core concepts in this way, the educators hoped that students would more readily embrace the material and retain the knowledge and skills they were attempting to impart. In many cases, it seemed to work. For example, a North Star student described his experience with learning public speaking:

> It gives me a chance to articulate my thoughts and grow my vocabulary. I'm also learning how to speak with others. I always thought that being loud was the best way to get my point across, but when I started taking public speaking class I started to realize that I don't have to be obnoxious to get my point across. I have to listen to what a person has to say so that I can respond intelligently. Public speaking has taught me to calm down and keep my composure.

In another example, a Westward student spoke with us enthusiastically about a class writing project: "We had this 'change the world' project. I made a flyer on gang violence and why it was so bad." He then shared how he would like to use this information to educate people outside of school throughout his community. The student's apparent excitement over the possibility that what he had learned in school might prove to be helpful in solving a major community problem suggests that the goal of connecting what they learned in the classroom to a variety of real-world applications worked well for many students.

In another example, a teacher at Salem described using a letter-writing campaign and petition drive as a way to provide "real, meaningful, relevant education" at his school. In this case, the letter campaign focused on the controversy involving radio talk show host Don Imus, who made racist comments about the Rutgers University Women's Basketball team in 2008:

> I truly believe in the adage that "all kids can learn." I believe in getting kids to be as engaged in the learning process as possible. For me, this involves being as hands-on as possible. I don't find that direct

instruction and lecture-type of teaching works very well for my kids. Actually, I don't think it works for boys or girls. I think there is a time for direct instruction but at some point you have to turn it over to the kids and let them learn by doing. They need to be engaged in real relevant kinds of things. For example, I'm teaching a class this fall called "Principles in Leadership" to the ninth-grade students and right now we're looking to do some things around the issue of the recent Don Imus controversy. I've given them a chance to listen to his comments, to study who he is and understand why he's been so influential as a radio personality. After our investigation some of the students suggested that we launch a letter-writing campaign to voice their opposition to having him on the radio. Another student suggested that they begin by sending in petitions. This all came from them, so to me, that's quite profound. They can see that what we're learning is real, meaningful, and relevant.

We observed numerous lessons that created meaningful educational moments for students. At times, this involved teachers posing dilemmas to the boys that they knew were "real" for them. For example, a Thomas Jefferson teacher talked about using relevant examples, some of which involved challenges that he knew his students were confronting on a daily basis, to support the curriculum. He explained: "We were talking about the global struggle for resources . . . To get the point across one of the examples I used in class one day was a guy who has an iPod, and another guy who is hungry. What are the ethical issues involved when this guy is sitting here with his $500 iPod but you haven't had anything to eat for a few days?" The teacher explained that several of his students had been robbed on the subway and while walking to school. Most often, the thieves took their iPods or cell phones. In some cases, force was used and his students felt violated. In this class focused on global economics he attempted to connect the struggle for resources to something they had faced personally. His hope was that such an application would not only help the boys understand the content, but also make it possible for them to see how what they were learning applied to the real world.

In some of the classrooms we observed, teachers utilized emotionally powerful subjects as a way to demonstrate the real-world application of what they were teaching. Topics that they knew might elicit a charged emotional response were sometimes used as a bridge into content that these boys might otherwise see as disconnected to their realities. An example from a high school American government class at Thomas Jefferson illustrates how this was often done:

> My approach with American government in all of my classes is from the bottom up. In every case, I try to show my students how this relates to *you* specifically. Once I make these connections, then I put it in context of American government. For example, right now we're learning about feminism, women's issues, and the women's rights movement. I know that for many of my students the one person that all of them have strong feelings about is their mother. As soon as I bring mothers into the conversation it brings up all of these emotions. Recently, a very emotional, very sensitive young man began to cry when he talked about the struggles his mother faced. No one in the class laughed or reacted in a way that would make him feel uncomfortable. You might not think that would happen in a class full of boys, but I would say that in many ways males are more sensitive than females. We looked at bell hooks' article "Mom and Love." And then from there, I started to explain to them what feminism is, how it relates to women's issues, and various aspects of public policy. I get the students to think about why the Constitution leaves them out, not just as African American men but women who represent more than half of the population. Once they can see the tie this has into their personal life it's easier for them to relate to it.

This teacher began by hooking students with an issue that was close to their hearts and homes and gradually led them to a new interpretation of the American Constitution. Interestingly, he was not afraid of touching on a subject that he knew would be emotional for many of his students. It was clear to us from observing his class and the way he interacted with his students that this approach was highly effective. Not only were his students engaged, but in interviews we learned that many students left the lesson understanding and caring about what the Constitution meant to them, as opposed to memorizing facts that may be recalled on an exam and then forgotten later.

There was considerable diversity in the types of social experiences that teachers used to bring real-world applicability to instruction. For example, in a social studies classroom at Salem students were asked the following questions: "Do you think a decrease in parental involvement contributes to the crisis with Black boys?" and "Do you think that (peer pressure) is one of the factors that contributes to the decline of African American males?" These questions allowed students to share their thoughts on the issue, and compelled them to have a deep and critical conversation about a set of issues that are directly relevant to them. In another social studies class at Bethune, students were asked: "How do people show pride in their culture?" and "What do people need to come together to create a nation?" These questions were designed to get students to apply what they had learned about patriotism and nationalism to their own personal knowledge of the world outside the classroom. It also led to a meaningful and lively discussion. In a Westward class students were prompted to think critically about their world by using examples from current events for the class discussion. One student shared, "Well, I don't usually read the newspaper but because we are learning more things that are going on in the world and all around the country, I tend to read the paper more. I feel like this class is helping you to think critically about what's going on, and that's why I try to stay up on the current events."

Other examples of real-world application came from teachers who found ways to get students to analyze topics through multiple perspectives. In order to get their students to see how an individual's social position might influence the perspective they take on an issue, a Salem teacher had her students write a play involving a conversation between Thomas Jefferson and Black abolitionists. In addition to immersing students into the topic, students were also engaged by the creativity the activity allowed. Another teacher at Westward immersed his students in a unit on Darfur, in the following way:

We were doing a unit on Darfur and I knew that my students might have trouble relating to the issues because the material is so removed from their realities. I decided to use one of the books we're reading— We Beat the Street by the Three Doctors—and connect it to another book we're reading about the Lost Boys of Sudan. Although the unit we're looking at is focused on the war in Darfur, I used the struggles described in The Street, which is all about kids growing up in Newark, to get my students to see how young people are affected by violence. For the class assignment, the kids had to develop a hospital and a pharmaceutical company to address the needs of the boys in Sudan and students in Darfur. By reading about the Three Doctors in Newark they were able to see how health became a part of the response to the violence.

In addition to the simulation activity, students read fiction and nonfiction accounts of the events in Darfur. After the readings they were well prepared to think about how they might address the situation in Darfur through the creation of a hospital and pharmaceutical company. It's fair to say they were immersed deeply into the topic. In addition to learning about current events in the world, students were also reading, writing the types of nonfiction expository essays they will be expected to write on state exams, and thinking critically. Moreover, students were analyzing a difficult world situation and creating scenarios that assisted children in Sudan.

A teacher at Washington took a similar approach with a different historical topic that he felt his students might have trouble relating to:

At first I wasn't sure how I could get my students to connect to the Iroquois people, their system of government, and the civilization they created. However, as I spent time thinking about the kinds of resources we had access to I realized a lot of it could be done utilizing supplemental material that is available on the Internet. This made it possible for them to see some of the artifacts from Iroquois villages, and pictures of what their civilization actually looked like. We even made a lot of Iroquois stuff, like wampum, wampum belts and headdresses. By coming up with these hands-on activities the students were able to enter the content with an attitude of exploration and openness. I could see from what they wrote in their journals that they appreciated what they had learned and could relate to the material.

Overall, the strategies we observed for organizing instruction and using real-world applications to address missing gaps and skills demonstrate how many of the schools were attempting to respond to the socioemotional and academic needs of their students. As it turned out, the greatest challenge for many of the teachers was using their knowledge of social identities to implement instruction with sufficient academic challenge. Not surprisingly, among the seven schools in our study we found a great deal of variability with respect to the instructional rigor in the classrooms. There was a great reliance on open-classroom discussion which helps to build students' oral and cognitive capacities; however, the absence of robust reading strategies, given the students' prior academic achievement, raised questions as to whether the staff had sufficient expertise. Though we witnessed a number of highly engaging classrooms, the low levels of proficiency among students in these schools (discussed in chapter 1) made us wonder whether the culturally relevant practices were sufficiently balanced with high-impact strategies for students who were significantly behind. Despite the inconsistency of high-impact instructional strategies for this population, the students described feeling challenged by their work at least once a month. Many of the boys stated in their interviews and focus groups that this was a new experience for them. The instruction we found at these schools sought to develop the students' socioemotional identity through culturally relevant application, including reflection of cultural assets in the curriculum (e.g., Black and Latino history) and youth cultural assets (e.g., hip-hop); however, it is not clear that the students in these classrooms were actually academically pushed. Even so, the absence of consistent high-impact instructional strategies (e.g., college-ready literacy and math activities) raises questions as to whether achievement outcomes, specifically state test scores, can be improved with this one-sided instructional program.

4

Building Community

A Climate That Supports Resilience

I like the fact that I don't have to hide my personality. I can state my opinions without being called any names or anything like that. This is an environment where people want to learn.

—Student at Thomas Jefferson Academy

This simple, straightforward comment made by the student above may not seem striking, but the fact that it was made repeatedly by several of the young men we met at the seven schools in our study suggests that for many of the boys, "an environment where people want to learn" was a noteworthy circumstance given that it may have been lacking in the schools they previously attended. In interviews with dozens of boys at these schools, what was most salient was the importance the students placed on being in a place where they believed learning was possible. The schools made a deliberate effort to create climates that they hoped would be supportive and conducive to learning. As we show in this chapter, they went about this based on their understanding of how to protect their students from the factors that contribute to the vulnerability of Black and Latino males in American society.

To a visitor, the most obvious sign that these schools are working to create climates that are conducive to this goal can be seen in the types of images portrayed on school walls. Kennedy Academy, founded in the second year of our study, is a college preparatory charter middle school (grades 5 to 8) located in a large Southwestern city. The Academy is located on a strip mall that the charter management organization and foundation purchased in order to create a K–12 school campus. In order to accommodate new students as it expanded, the school facility has been renovated, making it possible to add a new grade level each year. The space is organized into a U shape with large classrooms, a cafeteria, a greeting area for the receptionist, and a playground area in the back of the strip mall that was still under construction at the time we carried out our research. The walls of the school are lined with posters of prominent African American figures as well as the colleges the teachers and administrators attended. The highlight of the space is an expansive mural in the entryway of the school with a portrait of Frederick Douglass painted by a local artist, along with a quote: "It is easier to build strong children than to repair broken men." We soon learned that attending to the vulnerability of these children involved careful attention to the physical space and the social interactions that occur within the school.

In chapters 2 and 3 we described the strategies and instructional practices implemented by the educators at these seven schools to create a climate that would support the achievement and development of boys of color. In this chapter we explore how the schools worked to encourage social interaction that would lead to higher expectations and a sense of community within the school. As we will show, the actions taken by these educators have strong similarities, even though they never consulted with each other about what they were doing. Repeatedly, and often with very similar words, the educators we met told us that developing resilience among the young men they served was the key to enabling them to cope with the adversity they encounter in society and in their neighborhoods.

The concept of resilience as understood by these educators is closely aligned with research on behavioral and mental dispositions associated with the development of academic resilience. Key among these dispositions are: persistence,[1] personal optimism about one's future possibilities,[2] and motivation,[3] as well as confidence in one's abilities, the mastery of social skills and social intelligence, and resourcefulness.[4] With respect to these single-sex schools, the hope shared by the educators was that they could instill resilience in their students by pursuing five core goals: 1) getting students to believe in education and to see it as a college pathway; 2) encouraging strong, positive, and caring relationships between educators and students; 3) responding to the challenges and risks that arise from neighborhood experiences; 4) raising self-esteem; and 5) developing supportive peer relationships, or what some referred to as a "resilient brotherhood," among the students.

Believing in Education: "We're Going to College"

I came from Madison [pseudonym]. And [when] I was in Madison, I had the mindset that after high school I was going to the military. College was never in my mind. I had the grades and everything, but in Madison they don't encourage that idea. You know, they just let you do what you want . . . you can basically go with the flow. But then I transferred and when I came to this school, I had a college advisory class. Next thing you know I was thinking about going to college. This year I was admitted to four colleges.

—Student at North Star Academy

Several national studies have found that Black and Latino students disproportionately attend schools where expectations are low and a college-going culture is not present.[5] In these seven schools, there was a pervasive belief in the importance of college, and it was promoted as the critical lever for insuring that students would succeed in the future. As we describe in appendix 1, the schools offered a wide variety of activities designed to help the boys embrace the belief that a positive future was attainable through college. This included visits to colleges throughout the country as well as listening to popular artists and authors (e.g., Spike Lee, Henry Louis Gates Jr., Common, Jawanza Kunjufu) speak

97

about their personal journeys to college. Hearing stories from their teachers about the colleges they attended and what they gained from those experiences was also a consistent part of the effort. At North Star there was a particularly strong relationship between the school and several Historically Black Colleges and Universities. Other schools had partnerships with local colleges that provided various forms of support. The goal of these activities was to build an expectation among the boys that college would be part of their future and provide them with tools to ensure that this would happen.

Surveys and interviews with boys at each of the schools revealed that overwhelmingly the schools' strategy of instilling a desire to go to college has worked. Nearly all of the young men at all seven schools reported that they not only wanted to attend college, but had concrete plans for how to get there. Despite the significance of this self-reporting data, we were aware of previous research by sociologist Roslyn Mickelson that showed a discrepancy between what she called abstract versus concrete aspirations toward college.[6] In her research, Mickelson found that while many African American students reported an *abstract* belief in the importance of going to college, when prodded further she discovered that many had no *concrete* plans of college attendance. To determine whether or not a similar discrepancy might be present among the boys in our seven schools, we utilized Mickelson's Academic Educational Beliefs[7] scale to measure the strength of their beliefs about college attendance.

As table 4.1 shows, the boys consistently identified a good education as important to future success. However, this belief—when phrased in different terms—was also tempered by doubt. At least one quarter of the students disagreed that "if everyone in America gets a good education we can end poverty"; one-fifth disagreed that education was "the way for poor people to become middle class"; and over half felt that success in school "is not necessarily a clear path to a better life." The variation in responses suggests that some of the boys were aware that there were other factors that may influence whether or not a person achieves social mobility and earns a higher income, even if they obtain

TABLE 4.1

Beliefs about the efficacy of education

	Disagree	Agree
Education is the key to success in the future.	8.2%	91.8%
If everyone in America gets a good education, we can end poverty.	25.1%	74.9%
Achievement and effort in school lead to job success later on.	12.0%	88.0%
The way for poor people to become middle class is for them to get a good education.	20.1%	79.9%
School success is not necessarily a clear path to a better life.	45.4%	54.6%
Getting a good education is a practical road to success for a person like me.	13.2%	86.8%
Young people like me have a chance of making it if we do well in school.	10.6%	89.4%
Education really pays off in the future for a young person like me.	9.9%	90.1%

Note: *Disagree* combines the responses "strongly disagree" and "disagree"; *Agree* combines "agree" and "strongly agree."

a college degree. Skepticism among students that education is always a guarantee that one will experience upward mobility is reinforced by other research.[8]

Despite the divergence of responses, the survey showed that overwhelmingly students appreciated the importance of college and held a general belief in that value of education. For example, an eleventh grader at Thomas Jefferson told us that he saw no other way for himself to succeed except by pursuing his education:

> I know it is very important . . . I'm nothing without my education, you know what I'm saying. I can't do anything, you can't go anywhere without a degree. You used to be able to get a good job with just a high school diploma, but it's not like that anymore . . . you need your college diploma. That's why I want to get a degree, and I know I can.

Throughout the interviews it was clear that the importance many students placed on going to college influenced their attitudes and behaviors in school. They often talked about how important they thought studying, earning good grades, and gaining knowledge were for success in life. A seventh grader at Washington explained that education was helping him achieve his goals:

> I think it's gonna help me understand what people say to me, especially if they use complicated words. In the past, if I didn't understand something, I might just sit there and not do anything. Now, I ask questions so that I make sure I understand. That's why education is important to me. I know it's helping me to be able to achieve my dreams and to feel better about myself.

The students also made clear to us that their belief in education was centered on college as the pathway for success. Most of the boys understood that going to college and graduating was the key pathway. Many described themselves as college bound and unwilling to settle for just a high school diploma. A ninth grader at North Star described it well:

> Everyone is here to help you succeed. Because from here then you go to college and if you do well in college, you can get a good job . . . Here [at North Star] our teachers want us to know the stuff we'll need for college . . . it makes you more confident in yourself because you know you are being well prepared. My parents always talk to me about doing the right thing too. They really want to see me go to college because they know that if you're not going to college life is going to be a lot harder. That's a given. That's why I really appreciate what they do for me at this school. They are committed to seeing me go to college so that I can do good for myself, my family, and my community.

The ways the schools went about creating a college-going climate can be seen in the kinds of activities that were built into the school day. For example, this description of a community meeting at Thomas Jefferson, transcribed from our field notes, shows how the theme of going to college was reinforced:

Community Time is a daily community meeting that is held in a section of the gymnasium. School leaders stand on the bleachers to address their students. The young men are lined up in their "Packs" [advisory-like groups that are led by a teacher who stays with the group for all four years]. Mr. Langston addresses the student body: "Good Morning." The students respond, "Good Morning!" Langston continues, "You look intelligent, how are you feeling this morning?" "Good!" the students respond. At this time, the entire student body recites the "To Be on Time" daily mantra: "To be on time is to be early, to be early is to be on time . . ." When they finish, everyone claps. Mr. Langston continues, "Even though it's a short week, we have a lot going on this week. Today the sophomores are taking a big step; they're taking the practice ACT! [Entire room claps and cheers.] Most schools wait until the last minute to get their students prepared. The ACT is a predictor of how well one does in college; we have a practice one today. Let's concentrate. Your teachers gave you work to do in your Packs. Use your laptops to research our guest speaker tomorrow." The students are whispering to each other about the speaker and the news cameras that will be present. Mr. Langston continues, "Now gentlemen, yesterday I began creating a list of those gentlemen who participate in an afterschool program. After progress reports [we have students] that need extra time to get their homework done who are not being successful. As we said before, you may be mastering the skills but some of you are still getting Cs or Fs, why? It's because you are not doing homework. You have to be diligent about getting your assignments done. Homework is like practice; the basketball team had practice this morning. If you don't practice how can you be successful on the court? It's very important. Homework is practice.

Some version of community time was held at each of the schools. Sessions like these instilled the possibility of a college-bound future. In activities such as these the schools promoted what Theresa Perry describes as a "counternarratives"[9] based on a new definition of Blackness, Latino-ness, and maleness—one centered on a future orientation that cultivates personal responsibility, character, and social mobility. Such rituals reinforce the hope and promise that the educators repeatedly told us is so essential to student success. Through assemblies and town hall meetings, core values are lauded and a sense of community among students and staff is cultivated. They serve as moments when the boys and the staff can reflect on the larger purpose of education and be reminded that the goal of preparing them for college is the reason why they are at this school.

Believing in the Importance of College

When we asked students why they wanted to attend college, the boys overwhelmingly told us that college was essential to success in life; most described it as a critical step on their journey toward a middle-class future. In the second and third years of our study we began cataloguing how many students believed they would go to college and eventually graduate. As shown in table 4.2, over 80 percent of the students in the seven schools reported that they believed they would graduate from college. This pattern exceeds findings from recent National Center on Education Statistics reports that show 67 percent of Blacks and 56 percent of Latinos expect to graduate from college.[10]

Compared to many schools serving middle class children, where most students hold aspirations and plans for attending college, such numbers may not seem particularly noteworthy. However, it is impor-

TABLE 4.2
Expectations for educational attainment

As things stand now, how far in school do you think you will get?	Year 2	Year 3
Leave high school before graduation	1%	1%
Graduate from high school	6%	7%
Attend college, but not complete a degree	1%	2%
Graduate from college	40%	43%
Obtain an advanced graduate degree (e.g., PhD, MD, MBA, JD)	43%	40%
Don't know	9%	7%

tant to keep in mind that most of the students attending the schools in our study transferred from schools where dropout rates were high and college enrollment was low. As we learned, changing their goals and aspirations was a process that required time and a relentless focus on cultivating their aspiration and developing their academic skills.

Despite the efforts by the educators in these schools, the obstacles perceived by the boys that might prevent them from getting to college cannot simply be wished away by bold exhortations. Concerns about the cost of a college education were the ones we most frequently heard. However, we also heard students express fears about being far from home and family. Despite these doubts, all of the schools worked assiduously to cultivate a belief in education and to get their students to see going to college as a worthwhile goal. For the students who embraced this aspiration early, the desire to attend college appeared to be based on their experience at their single-sex school. For example, in a focus group with tenth graders at Thomas Jefferson, the participants spoke at length about why going to college was an important step for dispelling myths about Black boys. Several also told us that they were also seeking to mirror their teachers' experiences:

> **Student 1:** For me, I'd say this school sets an environment where we can never fail because they are committed to us. They let us retake tests to make sure that we really understand the material. They make us redo homework assignments so that we have [the] opportunity to learn everything that was covered. At my old school they really didn't care if we did our work or if we failed. At this school it's really important.
>
> **Interviewer:** Why do you think this school cares so much?
>
> **Student 2:** Well I think, for me, it's kinda more like a family. They really know me and let me and the other students know they care about us. It's an Afrocentric school so they are trying to provide us with a sense of direction related to our identities as Black young men.
>
> **Students 3 and 4:** That's right. It's more like a family.

Student 5: So they kind of take more interest in what they are do-ing for us. I guess what they feel is we are the next generation. We are the future. They want to make sure that we are really pre-pared when we leave this school.

Student 1: I mean there's not so many African American men that go to college. A lot leave even before they graduate from high school.

Interviewer: Okay. What do you think about the school's mission of getting you to go to college?

Student 2: I know that many young African American men are drop-ping out. I don't fully understand why that is but I know from my own experience that I didn't even want to be at my last school. It was hostile and I don't think they even wanted most of the stu-dents who were there to graduate. This school really wants to see all of the students graduate and they support us to make it pos-sible. They know that we have to get our graduation rate up be-cause despite all the hard work they put in, we're pretty much at a really low percentage. We have to try harder or else our school could be in trouble.

Student 3: I think that like the teachers here really like and care about all of the students here. And not all of our teachers are males. Like our science teacher is a young White female, but she really cares about us. She pushes us and makes sure we get our work done. She also makes sure that we really understand the material. I never had a teacher like that before. It's our teachers who are really setting an example for us. We can look at our gym teacher and see that he cares too. He wants us to go to college and he tells us so. I can look to any teacher at this school for guid-ance. That's why we wanna be like them so that we can improve our lives by going to college.

Student 1: They really set a good example for us. You look up to them.

As the dialogue captured from this focus group reveals, the students' belief in education and a desire for college is cultivated through the strong relationships they develop with their teachers. As the boys make clear, getting to college was also predicated on having the information they needed. Access to information about college—how to apply for financial aid, the importance of taking an SAT prep course, and the importance of developing the appropriate academic and social skills—is critical for these students. The educators we met understood that the requirements must be made explicit, since the vast majority of these students would be the first in their families to enroll in college. In developing their college pathway policies and practices, the administrators and other adults were well aware of the importance for students to acquire what they described as "basic academic literacy." The staff we spoke to seemed to clearly understand that their students will need to know how to navigate the university system. They must come with basic information about how to register for classes and how to choose an appropriate major. They must also have the patience to persist when they encounter administrative hurdles and to navigate the financial aid system. Students who lack an understanding of what will be required to succeed in the college environment, and who enter college without the essential psychological and emotional resources needed to function independently in a strange environment (especially one that is far from home), will have a more difficult transition to college.[11]

Our research showed that the high school students knew quite a lot about the college admissions process. Tables 4.3 and 4.4 show that they

TABLE 4.3
College pathway knowledge

Do you have opportunities in school to . . .	Yes	No
Find out about college?	88.5%	11.5%
Explore careers?	77.6%	22.4%
Learn about what you need to do to apply to college?	86.0%	14.0%
Learn about ways to pay for college (e.g. loans, scholarships)	81.3%	18.7%

TABLE 4.4

Feeling prepared for college

	Strongly disagree	Disagree	Agree	Strongly agree
My meetings with counselors or teachers to discuss my future have been helpful.	13.7%	18.2%	47.1%	21.0%
I know where to get applications for college.	10.1%	18.4%	47.0%	24.5%
I know how much college costs.	7.6%	18.2%	51.6%	22.5%
I think I will do really well in college.	5.1%	9.9%	55.1%	22.1%
Overall, I feel well prepared to apply to college.	7.3%	23.0%	43 .9%	25.8%

were receiving appropriate information and felt prepared to apply for college. The overwhelming majority of the high school boys stated that they had plenty of opportunities to gain college pathway knowledge (table 4.3). And the majority, in turn, felt prepared as result of this intentional pathway knowledge (table 4.4).

At several of the schools we visited there was evidence that parents as well as students were supported in the application process. This included offering workshops specifically aimed at informing parents about the college process. For schools with graduation cohorts, staff worked with students to complete their applications during advisory periods or during workshops held after school or on a Saturday. Some students worked one-on-one with counselors or teachers as well in developing their essays and getting all of their application materials together. At Thomas Jefferson, North Star, and Salem, the college counselors not only worked with seniors on the college applications, but they also developed a process to have ninth to eleventh graders apply for summer internships. During one of several interviews the college counselor at

Thomas Jefferson talked about how he gets the boys involved early in "college-like experiences" in order to get them in the mindset of college.

One of the strategies used by several of the schools to develop a pathway to college was to arrange for their students to visit nearby colleges. For example, at North Star the college counselor explained, "We're trying to have day trips for all of our ninth-grade students just so they can actually see what a college campus looks like. We want them to start to envision themselves on those campuses." They followed up in tenth and eleventh grade with overnight trips. College admission representatives also visited several of the schools to give presentations and answer questions from students. At Thomas Jefferson students visited local community colleges as well as more elite colleges and universities.

In addition to exposing students to college, staff members often shared their own experiences from college. Students reported appreciating what teachers shared with them about what they went through in college—being away from home for the first time, making new friends, finding a mentor on campus, and so forth. Students told us that hearing about their teachers' experiences gave them a clearer sense of what to expect and reduced some of the anxiety they had about the process.

In addition to these strategies, the schools also employed a variety of other explicit and implicit measures to impart the expectation that all students should go to college. Buddy systems were established at several of the schools for the explicit purpose of helping students prepare for college. The buddy systems were used to reinforce the importance of dressing appropriately so as to develop the image of a college student, and to promote necessary social skills such as punctuality, organization, and follow-through. The guidance counselor at North Star created a structured buddy system modeled after the successful college readiness approach developed by the nationally acclaimed Posse Foundation.[12] In assisting students with deciding which colleges to apply to, he attempted to get small groups of students (3–4) to apply to the same schools so that each student would have support from their peers while away at college:

My whole thing is making sure that there is a support network once they get there. Are they going to be comfortable with this campus? Are there other brown faces among the students and the staff so they can feel comfortable? Who are they going there with? I was trying to develop my buddy system or posse-style program so that my students would not be alone when they go to college. It can make a real difference when you get to college, particularly if it's a long way from home, if you have someone around who you know has your back.

In several of the schools students also noted that they felt like they were gaining important college-ready skills like time management, note taking, and overall organization skills. Students told us repeatedly that they recognized that the schools they attended were preparing them in ways other schools had not. One student who was part of his school's AVID program—a program that has developed a successful supplemental curriculum designed for students from populations underrepresented in college—noted: "One thing that this school does is give us different classes that will help us improve our organizational skills. AVID has been really good at helping me with time management. This will help me in college when no one is telling me to get to class or to go and study. They are also helping us to get scholarships . . . they give us the tools and information we need that we wouldn't get at other schools."

Although not all students were enthusiastic about school uniforms, several students described them as part of their college readiness training. Each school used uniforms as a symbol for creating a studious atmosphere. The uniforms typically involved a mandatory tie, button-down shirt, khaki pants, and at some schools a jacket. By requiring their students to dress in ties and blazers, the schools hoped their students would develop a sense of pride. Through the focus groups we learned that in many cases the boys also interpreted the uniforms as part of the process for getting ready for college. In a focus group with seventh graders at Bethune, one of the boys talked about uniforms as part of their college preparation:

One thing that helps us in getting ready to go to college is making us dress in uniforms. I think this is helping us go to college because now we understand how to dress for success. Mr. Brown is in ties all the time. He tells us that if you want people to take you seriously, you have to put on a tie and jacket when you're taking care of serious business. I'm glad that we have teachers who break things down for us like that. If I go to college, I would be the first one in my family to graduate. So I don't have anyone at home telling me how to do all of this. I'm lucky to have a principal like Mr. Brown who really explains how to be successful.

Eleventh graders at Thomas Jefferson also considered uniforms as part of the symbolic curriculum that was essential for entering the pathway to college. When asked about the things they were doing to get ready for college and beyond, students in the focus group responded that wearing uniforms was a part of that preparation because it was changing the images they held of themselves:

I think like all the focus on getting ready for college really started with the uniforms. I didn't really like it at first but now I realize that when you look good you feel good. Like when I'm wearing a jacket and tie and I walk downtown, I notice that I see other people in ties and these are people that got a lot of money and stuff. So I think that them having us in ties and jackets is about us getting used to dressing like people who are successful. Some of the kids still don't like it. They don't want to wear the ties because some people make fun of them out on the streets. But if you wear it every day then you will probably keep wearing them when you're old. That's going to start getting you ready for like a good life. It's changing the image you have of yourself.

Concerns About College Readiness

While students and teachers alike were optimistic about their college pathway programs, teachers at one of the schools worried that their graduating seniors were not really ready for college. They were concerned that they hadn't developed the academic resilience among their students that would be necessary to ensure that they could be successful at a four-year university. Specifically, teachers worried about their students' study habits and feared that they wouldn't be ready for the behavioral expectations of a college classroom. This fear grew out of their concern that they might be helping their students too much, and in so doing, they were not fostering an orientation of independence that would be critical to success in college. For example, by providing students with numerous opportunities to receive help with their work, by giving them the opportunity to retake exams they had missed, or not insisting that they be prepared and maintain classroom etiquette by raising hands, several teachers told us their students might not really be ready to meet the challenges of college. In a conversation with a teacher at Thomas Jefferson we were told that "a lot of students try to just do the minimum, and they can get away with it here. That's not going to cut it when they get to college and I'm worried about that."

At Salem, some of the graduating seniors in the final year of our study also worried about being ready for college. Their teachers had told them to expect the work to be harder, and one student worried about his writing skills. Reflecting on his experience, one student told us, "I just wish I would've taken advantage more of English. I like to write but I haven't had too many opportunities to write research papers. All the teachers tell us about the length of the papers that we will be required to write in college and that using proper grammar, bibliographies, and all this stuff will be necessary. I don't feel my writing is up to par and I'm concerned about that."

Using Out of School Time to Build School Climate

Another important component of school climate we examined was Out of School Time (OST) activity. Supplemental programming plays a central role across the school sites; therefore it is important to try to capture the extent to which participation in such programs contribute to academic achievement (see appendix 1 for descriptions of school programming). To account for the wide variation of programs covered, we divided them into the following seven categories: academic enrichment; leadership; creative arts; tutoring or home/schoolwork help; sports; technology; and programs/clubs related to students' racial, ethnic, cultural, or religious background. As we analyzed the data we collected about the effects of OST activities we found a pronounced difference between middle and high school grades, so we present the patterns of participation in separate tables by school level.

A total of 676 middle and high school students completed all the questions on the student questionnaire related to OST activity in the middle year of our study. The overwhelming majority reported participating in some sort of OST program either at school, out of school, or in both settings. Among the middle school students, the most popular activities were sports and athletic activities, followed by community service and tutoring, homework, or schoolwork help. Participation was generally higher in school-based activities as compared to out-of-school activities. Middle school OST activity is presented in table 4.5 in the chapter appendix.

The OST activity of high school students in our sample is presented in table 4.6 (also in the chapter appendix). Participation was generally slightly higher in school-based activities than in non-school-based activities, but the difference is not as pronounced as it was in the middle school sample. Similar to their middle school peers, the participation was highest in sports-related activities, which as we describe later is an important and unique predictor of relational engagement. Leadership-related programs such as community service or student government maintained relatively high participation rates. This is notable because participation in leadership programs was the only supplemental program category that was found to be uniquely predictive of cumulative GPA in the resilience-achievement model we describe later. About one-half of the students reported involvement in arts-related programs, the tutoring or homework/schoolwork help programs, and the academic enrichment programs.

The majority of high school students also reported having some kind of outside responsibilities during their time out of school. Over one-half of students reported that they took care of younger siblings or relatives, and nearly three in ten reported being employed. In our achievement model (see chapter 6), we discuss why there was a negative association between GPA and those who reported that they were responsible for taking care of relatives.

Independent sample t-tests were performed to determine if there were individual relationships between involvement in each OST activity (including supplemental programs and outside responsibilities) and cumulative GPA of students. Some activities were more highly predictive than others when placed within the context of all the variables tested (see the chapter appendix for a fuller discussion of t-test results). The tests revealed that there were some statistically significant differences in the grades for those students who participated in supplemental programs and those who didn't, as well as between students who spent their time involved in outside responsibilities and those who didn't have those commitments.

Sometimes statistically nonsignificant findings are as important as, if not more important than, statistically significant ones. One example is academic remediation. Students who are receiving extra help with their schoolwork have generally been assigned such help because of their poor academic skills. Indeed, our initial examination of the kinds of afterschool programs provided at the seven schools suggested that remediation was targeted at low-skill students or students who were behind in turning in their work, with the expectation that participation in these programs would place them on a par with their higher skilled peers. Our t-test analysis revealed that this expectation was in fact being met: students who reported participation in tutoring or homework/schoolwork help programs did not do significantly worse (or better) than nonparticipants. This finding supports the notion that forms of remediation and help may in fact be serving participating students well.

Overall, our analysis of the influence of OST activity on student grades for the high school sample revealed several key findings. First, leadership programs have been shown to be uniquely correlated with cumulative GPA in our model of academic performance, and students involved in such programs, whether school-based or community-based, receive higher grades than those who are not. What we cannot discern at this time is the extent to which higher performing students are recruited to such programs at the outset, but we can safely conclude that once involved in leadership programs they are more likely to be higher performers.

And second, academic remediation and support programs appear to be working well in helping students earn better grades. In addition, our findings suggest that responsibilities outside of school, in terms of caretaking or employment, may detract from student performance. While such findings are not surprising, they do suggest that students who bear such obligations may be in need of additional support in managing their responsibilities and coursework.

Promoting Caring Relationships Between Students and Adults

> This is a very welcoming environment. I came into school I think a month late, but I didn't feel out of place. Everybody else welcomed me, trying to get me to play on the football team and stuff that made it easy for me to be here. You can really tell that the teachers care about you. They care whether you get your assignments completed or not, they care whether you're gonna make it. That's what I like about being here.
>
> —*Tenth-grader at Salem Academy*

As we have pointed out previously, the administrators at each of the seven schools in our study clearly understood that building positive, supportive relationships between adults and students was essential for academic success. In most schools, the process of relationship building began with accessibility. All of the schools stressed the importance of teachers and administrators making themselves available to students at virtually any time of day. In some cases, this involved structuring the school day to provide students and staff with the time needed for counseling, advising, and mentoring. For example, at Thomas Jefferson great lengths were taken to ensure that teachers and other staff were available to students. Teachers were all given cell phones to allow students and parents to call them outside of school. As one teacher explained, the opportunity for students to engage them outside of the traditional boundaries of the school was seen as essential to academic success:

> I would just tell them [students] to leave their cell phones on because the socioemotional piece will come at the time when you least expect it . . . I sometimes get calls 7:30 on a Sunday morning or 10:00 p.m. on a Tuesday night from students who are distressed about something. It's not easy to be so accessible because I have a personal life and a family of my own, but we understood when we came here that this job would require more from us. Being accessible is a critical part of building strong relationships.

While providing students access to adults through structured activities such as advisory sessions and extracurricular programs is important, it is equally important for adults to possess the qualities that make relationships with students possible. Many students told us that having access to an emotionally invested adult was something they valued highly. Students said that when they knew their teachers genuinely cared about their success, they tended to do better academically. They identified with those adults who related to them on a personal level, who listened without judgment, who showed them respect, and who were willing to share stories from their own lives. When such characteristics were present in an adult, students reported that they were more open to being mentored by them.

Several teachers indicated that they appreciated the importance their schools placed on developing relationships with students. A number of teachers told us that when schools are overly consumed with achievement numbers, they may forget about the relational element of schooling and that this could be counterproductive. A teacher from Bethune explained:

I've been in schools where the teachers, the faculty, and the administrators don't really care about the kids. They may say they care about kids, but when it comes down to it, they care about numbers and they care about state test results . . . They care about money and keeping their jobs, but the kids come somewhere fourth or fifth down on the line.

In surveys and interviews it was clear that the students agreed about the importance of relationships. Over and over again we heard similar responses to our question "What do you like about this school," with the most common answer being "the teachers." Of particular importance to many students was the degree of care the teachers demonstrated. Following is a very typical response from a student at Westward:

One thing I like about this school since I've been here is the teachers. Some of the teachers really care about the students. That's one good thing about Mr. D. and his staff. Even though there's just a small number of us in this school, in a few years, there's going to be a whole lot more. They are still going to have that one-on-one talk with you when you need it. You are still going to have Advisory, still going to have someone that you're going to have a conference or a talk about your schoolwork with.

Care was expressed in a number of ways. During the focus groups, the boys gave specific examples of what their teachers do to show them that they care. For some students, knowing their teachers insisted that they perform to the best of their ability was important. As one student explained:

In my old school the teachers didn't really care if you didn't turn in your assignment. They would be like, "Oh well, I get paid either way." That attitude really affects you. It makes you not care either, so I'd be like, "Oh well too." In this school, if you don't turn in your assignments, they really care. They'll ask you all these questions about why you didn't do it, and lecture you about why it's important. After a while you just get tired of them coming after you so you do the assignment on your own. They will even make you stay after school or sit with them during lunch to make sure you do your work, so you don't have any excuses.

Other students mentioned that caring was apparent to them in the amount of time their teachers spent with them during school and non-school hours. For example, students at Thomas Jefferson talked about their experiences with teachers on school trips, playing basketball with them on Saturdays, as well as going to them for help after school. One student told us, "The one thing about the teachers at this school is that you can come to them any time and they'll listen . . . Teachers will admit when they're wrong . . . We have teachers staying till like six, seven . . . Our teachers are really dedicated to help students move forward in life." Other students at Bethune emphasized the *way* that their teachers tried to relate to them:

> For me personally, if I'm just in a class and all the teacher is doing is just talking, I get bored easily. In my old school I was bored most of the time. I didn't even feel like coming to school half of the time. If you have a teacher trying to bond with you and trying to make the class interesting, you know, they don't want you to be bored, they want you to focus. Like, in my history class we were talking about the Boston Tea Party and some students in that class never even had tea before. They didn't really know what it is. So right after school, we had a tea party and she made people that never had tea some tea. She actually bonded with us. Most teachers, even though they can't play basketball, they will try. They really like to laugh with us and have a good time. If something funny happens they'll laugh with us. And that's a big part of the connection that we have here that most schools I've seen do not have. In this school, teachers have control of their students, not because we are so easy to deal with but because we like them. In most other schools, students have control over the teacher.

Students at Salem spoke with respect and appreciation about the dedication of their teachers. In their comments to the interviewers they spoke at length about how hard they work, and that they don't give up on them. This type of caring makes an impression on students and re-inforces their belief that their teachers care about their future:

> Our teachers are really trying to help you graduate, they're really trying to get you in college. Like they are here after school every day and

if you don't even want to come, they're like "come on." They push us to get the help we need even when we don't want it. If you miss some homework, they'll make you come. The goal is to make sure that everybody is graduating and going to college. I appreciate what they are doing for us because I really want to go to college. I really want to go somewhere in my life and end up like anybody else.

An administrator at Washington stated that the most optimal teacher-student relationships occurred when teachers worked beyond the basic expectations of the regular school day: "The teachers who work with students outside of class have the deepest and most meaningful relationships with them. The teachers who just leave at the end, they tend not to have such good relationships—they often have more struggles with students."

In the focus groups conducted with students in the seven schools, the students concurred with the sentiments expressed by this principal. In a variety of ways, they told us that they will listen to and follow the guidance of the teachers who they know care about them and who work hard to help them to be successful. Conversely, they are less attached to those teachers they perceive as "just being there for a job." It is important to note, moreover, that students attribute their own degree of engagement and attentiveness to the methods teachers employ in the classroom. Students see teachers relating to individual students differently depending on context and the learning needs of the student. As one student at Salem explained:

Mr. E. jokes a little bit more with him and he jokes a little bit more with Michael because he knows this stuff a bit better. But he wouldn't joke around with a kid that's not doing his work and not making any effort . . . He doesn't joke around with Sam because he doesn't know the material. So Mr. E is serious when he's dealing with Sam after school. He's all about making sure we are learning. But sometimes when I'm on a roll, he jokes with me. He loosens up and that means he knows I'm getting it.

Interactions like the one described by this student create a context for building relationships between teachers and students based on trust.

As a sense of trust and safety develops between teachers and students, possibilities for more personal interactions and life coaching open up. Trust, as one teacher suggested, is essential for building relationships with this population of boys because in the communities where they live, trust is often lacking. However, trust must be earned, and for the teachers who managed to earn the trust of their students, honesty was seen as the trait most likely to secure it. One teacher explained this dynamic to us:

> I have found that it is definitely important to be real with them. I try to be as honest as possible. As a health teacher, I have to tell them a lot about themselves that can be kind of sensitive and personal. Most teachers don't normally get into such intimate topics. But I feel that when you come to them real, when you come to them honest, then they respect you more and they're more willing to hear what you have to say, more willing to buy what you have to say.

By the third year of our study there was clear evidence that the majority of students in these schools felt cared for and supported by their teachers. Out of 1,056 students who participated in the third-year survey, approximately four out of five students agreed or strongly agreed with the following statements: "There is at least one adult in school I can always count on", "There is someone at school who makes me feel like a successful student", and "If I have a problem at school there is someone I can count on." On the other hand, very few reported that adults did not care about them, as indicated by the low agreement to such statements as "I feel that there is no one in school who can help me", "Teachers do not care about my future", and "School is a lonely place where no one cares about me."

Challenges in Building Relationships

Although all of the educators we interviewed told us that developing caring adult-student relationships with students was very important, several administrators told us privately that there were members of the staff who encountered difficulty in establishing positive relationships with their students. Several of the principals told us that many of their students came to them with a history of strained relationships with teachers. As a result of their past experience, some students had major challenges in acculturating to a school climate premised on trust and respect. Some teachers also admitted that they had difficulty in gaining the trust of their students. These challenges were frequently attributed to the cultural context in which students are embedded, including an irreverent youth culture. Some staff members specifically singled out hip-hop culture as the source of the disrespectful attitudes and oppositional behaviors exhibited by some students. Others, like the principal below, pointed to the neighborhood culture, or previous negative school experiences as the cause for strained relations with some students:

> Overall, I think that this is an environment where students learn to trust, or need to trust adults that are here. I think that as an adult, being a new teacher here, it takes time to develop that trust, to understand what this culture is all about and how to work within the culture. Rather than getting discouraged, however, we persist to gain their trust, constantly considering and reconsidering the same questions: what are the needs of the boys, what are their backgrounds? Where are they coming from, and what's the best way to reach them?

Even after years of trying to develop strong bonds between adults and students at the schools, the boys had mixed views about whether or not adults treated them fairly or with respect. Of the 1,056 boys in our third-year survey, sizeable majorities—upwards of three-quarters—agreed with the statements "In my school, everyone has the same opportunity to get good grades" and "Teachers treat students from different backgrounds in the same way"; a similar percentage disagreed that "Teachers do not treat me with respect." But somewhat smaller majorities—roughly two-thirds—agreed with the statements "Administrators treat students with respect" and "The punishment for breaking school rules is the same no matter who you are." While these are impressive numbers, indicating that most students clearly held positive feelings toward the educators at their school, the fact remains that a quarter to a third of them did not.

The need to build positive relationships with all students was identified by several administrators as an issue that required ongoing effort. For example, one principal told us that at the root of the difficulty they experienced was the lack of social skills among some of his students:

> What I see as a bigger problem among these boys is the lack of respect for adults. It's the back talk, and some of them are just disrespectful. You know, they insist on having the last word even when they know they are wrong. I mean, it's just basic rudeness. A lot of it has to do with how some of these young people are raised. A lot of it had to do with culture that they exist within that says it's all right to just say whatever you feel like saying and that there's almost no distinction between being with your friends and how you carry yourself when you are in the company of adults.

Similarly, another administrator suggested that some students lacked basic social skills and didn't know how to participate in activities such as cooperative learning, debates, and other activities that require an ability to work with others. Still others told us that their student struggled with punctuality, coming to class prepared, following procedures, and handling conflicts in a civil manner. Lack of social skills showed up in some of the classrooms we observed in the following ways: the use of foul language in the classroom, defiant and disrespectful behavior toward teachers, frequent conflicts with other students, and an inability to follow established school norms. Though we were told that such problems were an issue for only a small number of students, the presence of such attitudes and behaviors was the cause of considerable conflict between many students and teachers, and contributed to strained relationships within some classrooms. "They don't understand that they are students in a classroom and that students have a responsibility," an administrator told us. "They want to be equal to the teacher in the room, but they haven't learned how to censor or restrain themselves a bit. They constantly come back to zero instead of moving forward."

Interestingly, some teachers attributed strained relations to gender differences. Several teachers, both male and female, reported that for some students it was more difficult to build respectful relationships with female teachers. Several of the female teachers we spoke to reported that they were not consistently shown respect by their students, and that in their view this was a reflection of the values of the community. These teachers suggested that there was a high degree of disrespect shown toward women in the community and that this contributed to the low level of respect shown by some students toward female teachers.

One female teacher attributed the lack of respect she perceived to the misogynistic lyrics in popular music and the general culture. She felt that such influences had a negative impact upon her male students and the respect level they displayed toward their female teachers. "Some of the male students respond to female teachers in an unhealthy manner," she stated. "A lot of it comes from the culture, the outside culture, the media culture, the hip-hop culture, whatever it is. And so sometimes you will have to work twice as hard to get their respect as your male counterparts."

Given that many of the boys in these schools come from single-parent households where the mother is the only parent present, their reaction to female teachers requires further analysis. It may well be the case that some of these students are yearning for contact with an adult male to make up for the father they either never knew or did not have consistent contact with. It may also be the case that the resentment some show toward their mothers at home are being reenacted within school. The data we collected did not provide a compelling explanation for this phenomenon, but this is a topic that clearly warrants further investigation.

Taking on the Streets by Raising Self-Esteem

A major challenge confronting the educators who were leading these schools was to create a climate that could counter negative community influences on the boys and simultaneously counter the low self-esteem and self-destructive beliefs and behaviors that some of them exhibited. To say the least, this was not a simple task. An administrator at Salem, describing the challenges confronting the school in their efforts to counter the "pull of the streets," explained that the primary strategy utilized by the school to accomplish this goal was to focus on building the confidence of their students:

> There is a significant cadre among our scholars who express themselves very well, who have a commitment to learning and have many academic strengths. However, they don't have the attitude, the values, and the verve of someone who has the confidence to withstand the kinds of pressures they are under. There is a whole dynamic involved in embracing an identity of being smart. You have to want it, and you have to internalize the notion that you can accomplish things. Over half of our scholars would prefer to fly under the radar. They would prefer not to be known as a person who is smart because the culture they are a part of doesn't value such attributes. That's why our job is to penetrate the influences being exerted upon them in that culture . . . So, to address that, I've been thinking about finding ways to get our scholars to completely embrace the legacy of what it means to be a scholar of African and Latino ancestry. That's why we spend so much time talking about the attitudes and the values that one would have to embrace and walk with as a scholar. This is especially important for those who are about to enter into higher education.

To counter negative cultural influences of the "streets" at Salem, the program director developed a course for a select number of boys who, based on the attitude they exhibited and the number of behavioral referrals they received, appeared to be struggling the most. The course focused on identity development and self-esteem, and involved asking the boys questions such as "What's happened to you?" and "How can you change what has happened to you?" instead of "What's wrong with you?" During one interview, the Salem administrator described an exercise in which the boys held mirrors in front of themselves and described what they saw. He said some of the boys "talked about being ugly, hating their lips and noses. There is a very deep level of discomfort with who they are and how they feel about themselves. If we can't counter these self-images and replace them with a more positive sense of self, it will be very hard to move them in a different direction."

Such moments served as powerful reminders to the adults in these schools that what they were contending with in educating these boys went far beyond increasing reading fluency and comprehension. Educating these young men was also about creating a climate that could offer a different type of socialization that would lift their self-esteem.

At Thomas Jefferson, the Pack meetings, which occur at the end of the day, tended to focus on a variety of topics that were of concern to the boys and adults. In one observation, a boy described having an argument with his family before coming to school. He shared that he had been bothered by it all day and that it affected how he performed on his assignments. "I just couldn't concentrate. All I could think about was what happened before I left the house in the morning." In response to this disclosure and the obvious vulnerability experienced by the boy, the teacher had all the boys in the Pack surround the boy and chant "We are here to support you." At the end of the class, the teacher asked each boy to say the name of another student they would ask for emotional help.

Such moments, when students express their personal struggles and allow themselves to be vulnerable with their peers, can be quite powerful. They create a context for offering young men tools to cope with the negative challenges they face and an occasion for using positive peer support to reinforce the values and norms the schools are trying to instill. As a guidance counselor at Thomas Jefferson described to us, such moments offer an exceptional opportunity for developing resilience:

> Sometimes in our advisories or even in our classroom discussion we have exceptional moments when it is possible to make a real breakthrough in how our young men are thinking about themselves. I think these exceptional moments can provide them an opportunity to make a transition, from who they were to who they are trying to be.
>
> I've seen these changes occur from one year to the next. Like the freshman class to the sophomore class. When they are in their Pack time, and their Pack leader is talking to them, they kind of expand on

a lot of the things they see. There is an atmosphere of trust that has been established and that allows the young men to take some risks.

Interviewer: And have you seen it yourself?

Oh, definitely. You know what, some people shift and move earlier than others. But we've got a couple young men who are from gang-affiliated families . . . that's really all they know. But when they get their tie they dress it up, tighten it up, button it up, and show some pride in their appearance. That's because here at Thomas Jefferson they are part of a family and they feel a sense of pride in it.

They've actually shared with me that they feel safer here than they do in some of their homes. And that's powerful stuff. That's really powerful. I see the young men beginning to understand their significance and it shows in the way they carry themselves. A lot of times, I mean education wasn't important because they don't see a correlation between the hard work they put into their education and what they can accomplish later on in life. They ask themselves: "What does it got to do with me?" That's why at Thomas Jefferson we try to create a climate for learning that is positive and supportive, and we surround them with a lot of African American leaders who are not just athletes. They get more than enough of that.

Finding ways to counter the negative pressures from outside of school was seen as an ongoing battle by many of the teachers and administrators. To the degree that they fail at this effort, many felt that it could contribute to their students' being attracted to the negative influences and lost to the streets. One teacher at Bethune acknowledged that some of their students seek a sense of comfort in gangs, and she recognized that the school was in a competition to influence their students' behavior:

> I believe that the greatest challenge that faces them is their self-esteem. Because when you're surrounded by gangs and when you grow up around a lot of negativity, you really take a lot of that in. You can become negative if you don't have some other influences on you. I worry that if our boys don't find the right comfort, they will go to the wrong place for comfort. That's where the gangs come in. What they

offer is support and solace. The drugs offer them solace. Prostitution offers them solace. There are a lot of negative things out there that offer an escape from how bad they may feel about themselves, but what it's really doing is reinforcing the negative.

Repeatedly we were told that lack of self-confidence is a product of ecological factors outside of school, and the students attending these single-sex middle and high schools did not always have the positive influences to counter these forces. Unless the school can compensate by creating a positive climate that promotes resilience and social and emotional development, many educators acknowledged that their boys would become even more vulnerable to the lure of the streets.

Another teacher suggested that low self-esteem was a result of the persistent low expectations society holds for Black and Latino boys, in general, and she found it challenging to get some students to accept that she truly believed in their ability to achieve. "They've been told all of these different negative statistics," she told us:

> If I tell them, you know, "You can achieve" and "Yes, you can do this," they look at me as though I'm lying. And in fact, I'm not lying. They can achieve, they can do well and I try not to dwell on all of the negative things because then they believe the hype that "well, if ninety percent of Black men shoot each other at twenty-one, why should I think about living past twenty-one?"

To offset the years of negative acculturation and the constant exposure to discouraging messages about their potential, each of the schools sought to create a climate where relationship-building between adults and students could be combined with a culture of high expectations. The hope was that together, these strategies would result in higher self-esteem and greater academic resilience. This in turn would lead to a higher number of students graduating from high school ready for college.

In several cases we found clear evidence that the strategy was working. A number of the students we interviewed described how they had overcome insecurity, anger issues, and other behaviors associated with low self-esteem and self-destructive behavior through their positive relationships with adults in school. Some students were particularly insightful about how adults in school had helped them develop their own sense of resiliency by supporting them in finding and shaping their voice as a member of society. This included redefining the type of person they wanted to be and becoming prepared to confront life's obstacles. Several students told us that the most effective way this is accomplished was when teachers shared their own personal experiences. As one student at North Star put it, "I really do feel prepared for all the obstacles that I run into, because a lot of teachers have shared their experiences with me on things they have gone through. That gives me an idea of what I might have to do later if obstacles come up."

Some students praised their teachers and other adults in the school for helping to motivate them into thinking about the things they wanted to accomplish through sharing their own stories. The following student at Salem described the bond he forged with a favorite teacher:

> Mr. S. told me that his father left him when he was little. My father did the same thing. I appreciate that he was willing to share things like that with me. It lets me know that I can overcome this and become successful in life despite what me and my family has gone through. Sometimes I may be lost or feel like it's my fault that the situation at home is the way it is. He knows how to listen and how to take it in. He also knows what I can do to direct my feelings in a more positive way. I get frustrated and angry sometimes and it's been bottled up in me for a long time. Before it used to just come out at the wrong moments. So now I've learned to, like, calm that side of me down.

By sharing his own personal stories and hardships with the student, Mr. S. presented his vulnerability to this young man. This made it possible to establish a relationship based on trust and care between the two and propelled the student to work harder and live up to high expectations.

As another student shared, "When I came to Thomas Jefferson the people pushed me and . . . they wanted me to succeed and get better things in life. So, I stored that in my head. I thought about my career. I know I want to be a businessman so I have to think about the type of mindset I need to get to where I want to go. I want to be greater than I have been and make my grades rise."

While administrators spoke about the behavioral expectations they have of their students (e.g., adhering to the dress code, getting to school on time, holding individuals accountable for their actions), many also cited the need to provide their students with an outstretched hand. Aspiring to create a unique academic environment, administrators described offering their students a level of support most were unaccustomed to, standing by their students not just in words but also through actions. As one administrator at Salem recounted:

> You know what, being here is a privilege and not saying that we're going to throw you out but saying that you've got to meet us halfway. If we're giving you a plan and we're willing to work with you, you've got to put something into it and if you're not, then we're not going to let you slide by, we're not going to let you coast. And so when you place that aspect into it, I think it adds a level of accountability that now all the students respond to, not just the ones that were in danger at some point.

Developing Self-Esteem Through High Expectations

Teachers at all of the schools expressed the importance of developing the self-esteem of their students. Many teachers spoke about the growing competitive spirit felt throughout the student body, where their Black and Latino students were more interested in who is getting the best grade in the class than in who is wearing the best pair of shoes. They attributed this emphasis on the value of academic achievement to the supportive school environment and the recognition that administrators and teachers gave to the academic performance of their students.

Schoolwide activities such as "Student of the Week" or an academic honor roll were used to provide students with support and recognition for their academic accomplishments. Many of the educators believe that such an emphasis has been lacking in the educational experiences of many of their students. As one teacher at Salem put it,

> I'm excited because we want our young men to see themselves as scholars, and gradually, I can see them slowly starting to become scholars. They weren't scholars when they first got here. And the reason that we call them that is because, if you think it, you can achieve it. But you have to put that thought into action and let them know that they are better than they believe themselves to be. Some of them are starting to step up to the plate—smart is becoming real cool. It's hip to get the homework done; it's fly to be on time to class. And you know, it's not all the way there yet, but I feel like we're making inroads, so we'll see.

At Salem, Westward, North Star, and Thomas Jefferson there were bulletin boards hanging on walls throughout the school with the names of students with the highest attendance rates and highest grade point averages. Students acknowledge that the supportive school environment is a major contributor to the changing views they have about their academic abilities. It is instilling a sense of accountability and helping them to develop concrete plans for the future. Walking into these four schools, one is immediately surrounded by messages intended to reinforce the high expectations.

Generally, students also spoke highly about the school recognition activities and how being called out for excelling academically motivates them to continue to challenge themselves: "Like once you get up to standard you want to keep on going 'cause like they call your name, everyone starts clapping, it makes you feel really good, you know, so like you want to keep that feeling inside, keep on doing good, keep that good feeling." On the other hand, there were also bulletin boards that posted the names of students who were *not doing well*. Surprisingly, students told us that this type of attention was not seen as unfair or a type of labeling that might contribute to lowered self-esteem. Instead, several students who had been singled out in this way told us that they took this type of negative attention as a sign of encouragement. For example, one student told us that it's about being told the truth: "They [teachers] don't lie to us. They keep us straight on everything we have to do. They tell us the truth, they tell us what we need to improve on, and they help us when we need it. So I like the way teachers are with the students." Or as another student put it, "Now I know what I have to do." This finding suggests that, to a certain extent, students were buying into this strategy as something that motivated them, as opposed to disparaging their self-esteem. The students seemed to genuinely believe that their teachers were not trying to appease them or to be easy on them—the teachers "spoke the truth."

Building Resilience by Developing a Sense of Brotherhood with Peers

Research has established the importance of peer influences on student achievement and adolescent development.[13] Several studies have also shown that positive peer support can be pivotal in helping students navigate school environments and develop academic identities conducive to school success.[14] In chapter 1, we highlighted that building strong, supportive peer networks was a key component of the socioemotional strategy that the seven schools have adopted to develop academic resilience. With few exceptions, adults and students viewed strong and "growth-enhancing" positive peer relationships as important for promoting positive student outcomes.

Nonetheless, encouraging the development of supportive peer communities posed its own challenges for the adults at several of the schools. Of concern for administrators were the difficulties students sometimes had in socializing with their peers and how that impacted their ability to work with one another. One administrator suggested that some students simply lacked proper communication skills: "Every year has its own set of issues. This year it's social. Some of the boys, they just don't get along. They have difficulty working in groups. The comments that they make to one another aren't the most sensitive. No matter where or how, the littlest thing could hurt someone's feelings and trigger a confrontation."

Some students clearly responded in a positive manner to the strategies adopted by the schools to foster peer relationships. For example, students felt that strong peer bonds coupled with peer pressure fostered the creation of an environment where boys competed academically with one another. Several young men told us that friendly competition made them care more about their studies. One student talked about how his relationship with a new friend boosted his grades:

> My [grade point average] was over a 2.0 but that don't work for me. I started hanging with [a new friend] and then I had a 3.39 at the end of the semester. That was good! And then, I see that like, if it wasn't for the push that I got from him, I would have never made it. My brothers make me work harder. You know, we all love each other and I think we'll make it, if we try.

Another student shared that the creation of this mutually supportive yet competitive environment made academic engagement—rather than disengagement—normative. "If you don't want to learn, that's a downfall for you. Everybody is competitive about learning."

In the final year of our study we surveyed students about how and to what extent their peers supported their academic efforts. In both the middle schools and the high schools students generally agreed, often strongly, that they did receive peer support, but the level of agreement varied across items. Overall, students agreed that peers at both levels believed that going to school and attending classes were important. A little more than eight out of every ten students agreed or strongly agreed with the statement "My friends think that it is important to do well in school," and nearly three-quarters of them agreed with "My friends think it is important to attend every class."

Generally, they also agreed that their "friends tried hard in school." However, a key component of a successful academic help network is the provision of concrete help—such activities as tutoring or working on homework together. When students receive help and support from peers in actually completing the work assigned, they are more likely to forge supportive academic relationships. Here we see that while the majority of students agreed with statements related to tangible support, a critical minority reported that they did not find that support with their friends. For example, approximately 70 percent agreed with the statement "My friends and I help each other with homework assignments." This means that a significant number—three in ten—did not do homework with their friends. Even fewer students (though still a majority) reported agreement with the statements "My friends and I talk about what we did in class" and "My friends and I help each other prepare for tests." While the emotional support was there, the tangible help seemed to be a bit more elusive.

Students and adults acknowledged that strong peer bonds without peer pressure could have a negative impact on school engagement. One middle school administrator at Westward used a cohort in his school as an example: "Our seventh graders have very much found lifelong friends as well but there are factions and cliques that have developed in the past. We're looking at how to teach them to deal with and work with people who you don't necessarily consider your friend." Whereas academically oriented cliques could help students succeed, not being in the clique could hurt outsiders. This pattern of exclusive groupings may prevent some students from feeling connected to school, which in turn could affect their ability to "do school."

Overall, the task of creating a school climate where academic resilience could flourish posed a certain dilemma. On one side, adults had to break down students' past experiences and poor relationships with adults in the schools they previously attended—and overcome the distrust built up in those environments—in order to forge strong caring relationships that pressed students to do their best. At the same time, adults strove to create conditions where students could develop strong bonds among themselves, but only coupled with a strong academic ethic.

A Climate for Developing Resilience

Judging by these seven schools, there are several features of school climate that mattered most in improving academic outcomes and reducing the vulnerability of marginalized populations. These climate elements, along with the qualities of instruction and curriculum discussed in chapter 3, helped to create a safe environment for the cognitive, social, and emotional development of boys of color. For instance, the element of encouraging the boys to believe in the value of education and college allowed them to accept their social and emotional desire for a middle-class or "good life" as a real possibility. Meanwhile, caring and trusting relationships with adults were used as a bonding tool for sustaining that desire. These relationships also played a role in mitigating the self-esteem issues the boys struggled with, particularly around their gender, race, and ethnic identities.

Overall, our findings suggest that students responded to the environment and relationships provided to them. Although this caring environment was prominent throughout all the schools, there were challenges in developing and maintaining it. Teachers and administrators noted that some students still lacked the social skills to interact with each other in a positive manner. That said, students generally reported that they felt the school staff cared for their academic progress and future. This sense of care, according to students, was exemplified in the teachers' accessibility, honesty, and desire to connect with them.

Furthermore, research has demonstrated the importance of attending schools where both teachers and peers expect students to perform well; this appears to be especially true for students from low socioeconomic backgrounds.[15] An optimal situation would be one where key people in a student's life—teachers, other students, and parents—hold academic excellence and high academic expectations as normative, which could be collectively referred to as "relational press."

Our findings are consistent with this research, where teachers, other adults, and students all emphasized that both peer relationships and student-teacher relationships had an impact on the level of connection students felt with their school. For administrators and teachers, the outcome of these positive relationships was the creation of a strong school community where students associated adults in the school with family and vice versa. To the degree that we saw this occurring, we also saw schools becoming settings that were more conducive to learning and to higher levels of academic performance.

Chapter 4 Appendix

Tables 4.5 and 4.6 provide response patterns among students regarding the types of Out of School Time activities they participated in. T-tests were conducted to determine statistical significance between groupings of students. Students who participated in academic honors programs either in or outside of school had significantly higher cumulative GPAs than students who weren't involved in such programs [M = 75.25, SD = 12.54; t(423) = 2.82, p < .01]; however, the magnitude of the differences in the means was quite small (1.84%). This finding is to be expected, however, as it is likely that academically advanced students understand the importance of being involved in extracurricular activities to gain admission to selective colleges.

Involvement in creative activities had mixed associations with GPA. Participation in visual arts programs was negatively associated with cumulative GPA, and students who participated in art programs outside of school performed more poorly than those who didn't [M = 64.98, SD = 2.01; t(423) = −3.65, p < .01], with a moderately small effect (3.1%). Similarly, students who reported that they participated in performance-related activities tended to have higher GPA than their peers who didn't [M = 65.27, SD = 17.84; t(423) = −2.74, p < .01). However, as was the case with other supplemental activities, the magnitude of the effect was small (1.7%).

As in the overall achievement model, outside responsibilities were negatively associated with cumulative GPA. Students who held jobs were significantly less likely to do well in school compared to their non-working peers [M = 68.87, SD = 13.47; t(418) = −2.63, p < .01], and students responsible for taking care of younger siblings earned significantly lower grades than their peers who didn't have such responsibilities [$\underline{M}$ = 70.08, $\underline{SD}$ = 13.51; t(418) = −2.46, p < .05]. However, in both cases the strength of these negative effects were small, only 1.63% for employment disadvantage and 1.43% for caretaking.

TABLE 4.5

Middle school activities

	Total participation
Academic enrichment	
Academic honors-related program	15.5%
School yearbook, newspaper, or literary magazine	28.7%
Club related to an academic discipline	36.7%
Leadership	
Student govt. or other leadership program	22.3%
Community service program	48.6%
Arts	
Music program	30.3%
Performance-related program	21.5%
Art-related club	37.1%
Tutoring or home/school work help	39.8%
Sports	61.8%
Technology-related club	37.8%
Club or program related to background	
Club related to racial, ethnic, or cultural background	20.3%
Religion-related program	

TABLE 4.6

High school activities

	Total participation
Supplemental education program participation	92.9%
Academic enrichment	*48.2%*
Academic honors-related program	16.5%**
School yearbook, newspaper, or literary magazine	17.9%
Club related to an academic discipline	38.1%
Leadership	*52.9%*
Student govt. or other leadership program	23.1%
Community service program	44.9%
Arts	*52.0***
Music program	26.8%
Performance-related program	21.6%
Art-related club	34.1%
Tutoring or home/school work help	*49.9%*
Sports	*71.3%*
Technology-related club	*39.3%*
Club or program related to background	*36.9*
Club related to racial, ethnic, or cultural background	17.9%
Religion-related program	
Outside responsibilities	
Employment	
Caretaker of younger sibling/relative	

**t-test is significant < 0.01 level (2-tailed).

5

Reconstructing Social Identities

Race, Ethnicity, and Gender

There's a lot on our backs because we're young Black men . . . there's a lot of doubt and a lot of expectations on us that we have to meet. It's really heavy, so I'll applaud everyone and myself who stays long enough to graduate. Because you get so much pressure . . . all the time people are saying "You should let those (N words) from the streets stay there, because they ain't goin' to graduate, they're going to end up dead or in jail." We have to hear all these things and it wears on you but it makes me know what not to do. I focus on what I have to do so I won't hear those things no more. It's a challenge to show them that I'm not who you say I am.

—Tenth grader, North Star Academy

The students at the single-sex schools we studied, like Black and Latino boys throughout the country, are under enormous pressure to avoid succumbing to the stereotypes that characterize young men of color. Throughout our interviews we heard from young men who told us they were tired of being described as hoodlums, drug dealers, and foul-mouthed criminals who are likely to be dead before they reach their thirtieth birthday. As we described in the previous chapter, the environment these schools are working hard to develop, based on care, trust, character, and resilience, is the primary strategy the educators rely upon to counter these stereotypes and develop positive social identities.

As the young man above states, performing well in school is a challenge but also "a way to show them that I'm not who you say I am." His ability to articulate this counternarrative and to define himself in a different way provides a clear indication of how these schools are attempting to reconstruct the identities of the young men they serve. As we described in previous chapters, the hard work of implementing high-quality instruction and creating a positive school climate was undertaken with the goal of reducing the vulnerability of these students. In many respects, that vulnerability is specifically tied to their identities as young, low-income, Black and Latino males in American society. Mr. Franklin, the principal at Salem Academy, acknowledges the difficulties when asked about the greatest challenges facing Black and Latino boys and men:

> Where do I start? I think the biggest, or one of the biggest challenges they face is of the negative identity that has been foisted upon them. I believe our young men have an identity crisis . . . And I think a lot of our young men, because of the experience they've had in schools, don't really see themselves as learners. Their identities as learners haven't been nurtured. Instead, what they value is an identity as someone who is tough or cool. That's what it means to be a man, you know, they attach their identities to materialistic things, or the women you can get. So that's what I mean by identity crisis. Those who don't have a strong sense of their identity are more susceptible to the gangs. This is a huge battle we're fighting against. A lot of our guys don't have any real family structure. They are coming from single-family backgrounds, which isn't a guarantee that they're not going to do well, but when parents are working a lot of hours to provide, they're not necessarily there to provide the guidance and support and structure and the love. All of those things together I think create our challenge.

Mr. Franklin's point regarding this crisis of identity and how it contributes to the vulnerability experienced by the boys, helps to explain why the schools placed so much explicit attention on identity development work—the effort to redefine what it means to be Black and/or Latino and male, or as some schools described it, "being part of the African or Latino Diaspora."

The effort to help the boys construct new positive identities and to dispel negative ones was carried out in a variety of settings. It occurred both within regular classrooms, as teachers admonished students on how to conduct themselves, and in the hallways, advisory groups, schoolwide assemblies, and extracurricular activities. For example, if a boy was seen walking through the halls with his head covered by a baseball cap or hoodie, he would be counseled to remove it, to always wear his shirt tucked in, to wear his pants with a belt and to pull them up. Sagging—the common practice of allowing one's pants to hang below the waistline, often resulting in underpants or even part of the buttocks being shown—was not allowed at any of these schools. The educators we met described this as a constant form of socialization that is similar to what Lisa Delpit described as teaching racial/ethnic minority students the "culture of power."[1] The goal was to teach the boys to become aware of how they present themselves to others and to impart essential "code switching" skills so that they understood how to carry themselves in public settings, when and how to use standard English, and even the posture to assume when speaking to individuals in authority.[2] Several educators told us that acquiring such skills was essential for their success because it would make it possible for their students to avoid being harassed when stopped by the police, or to manage simple interactions in public settings such as a department store, a job interview, or a restaurant.

In this chapter we discuss how the racial, ethnic, and gender identities of these young men were being constructed within the schools we studied. We pay particular attention to how the educators conceived of being a Black or Latino male, and how they went about instilling those beliefs in their students. We also examine how the boys responded to the schools' efforts to reconstruct their identities, where and how conflicts developed between adults and students in this identity formation process, and how these were in turn resolved.

Racial and Ethnic Identities

Aside from gender, race is the other big issue that provides these schools with their raison d'être. The seven schools in our study, like many similar single-sex schools being established throughout the country, were not created for boys in general. Rather, they were created specifically for Black boys, though in many cases Latino boys and boys who are Black but not African American have enrolled in them as well. Because so many urban schools are racially segregated, not by law but by residence, the fact that they serve an all-Black or all-minority population is not an issue that draws much attention or public scrutiny. While the American Civil Liberties Union and others have raised various objections to using gender as the basis for school enrollment, relatively few opponents of single-sex schools have expressed concern about their de-facto racial exclusivity.

In many respects, passive acceptance of racial segregation is a remarkable political development, particularly when one considers that the U.S. Supreme Court mandated an end to segregation in 1954, with the federal government going so far as to deploy federal troops to enforce school desegregation orders (most notably, when Eisenhower dispatched the 101st Airborne Division to Little Rock, Arkansas, in 1957). Many communities throughout the United States later endured highly contentious protests over court-ordered busing and other desegregation efforts. Given this history, the fact that racial isolation in schools would now be regarded as a "nonissue" among policy makers is truly amazing.

In our seven schools, the racial composition of the schools may not be a nonissue, but it could be regarded as a contextual issue. That is, the educators who founded these schools knew they were doing so to "save Black boys" specifically, and as such, they understood that it was both the race and the gender of their students that placed them at greater risk. However, they were generally less likely to view race in itself as a cause of their vulnerability. Rather, issues related to gender and masculinity were perceived as interacting with race and class to create a broad array of hardships for young men that these schools hoped they could ameliorate.

As mentioned previously, several of the schools embraced Afrocentric themes and utilized prominent Black role models to instill pride and encourage academic engagement among their students. As we show in this chapter, the identities the boys used to describe themselves in interviews and focus groups invoked some of the complexities that lie at the intersection of racial and ethnic identification. Across the different school settings and regions of the country, they sometimes used ethnicity and race as interchangeable terms, while at other times treating race as a construct that was different than ethnicity, nationality, or culture. The students' narratives provide an insightful empirical account of how confusion related to race and ethnicity influenced the way they saw each other and themselves.

We begin our discussion of the boys' racial and ethnic identifications by describing the terms they used to identify themselves. In our student survey and interviews, we asked how the boys identified themselves racially and ethnically, and more importantly, what that meant for them. The great majority of the 1,007[3] boys in the seven schools—73 percent—identified as Black, with 12.5 percent identifying as Biracial/Mixed, 10.8 percent as Other Race, 2.1 percent as Native American, and less than 1 percent as White or Asian. This pattern was to be expected given that the Midwestern and Southeastern schools had a nearly all-Black student enrollment.

However, the fact that most of the boys identified as Black does not tell the whole story with respect to their racial identifications. In the context of the U.S. census, race is often placed alongside ethnicity as an identification option for respondents. For example, census participants may be asked "Are you of Hispanic/Latino descent?" (ethnicity) and "What is your race identification?" (race). So while the majority of boys responded to the question of "What is your race identification?" with "Black," nearly a third of the total students in the sample—29.7 percent—also identified as Latino, adding some form of ethnic identification to the racial identification to indicate they understood that race did not fully capture their subjective sense of who they were.

Among the entire population of Latino males in the sample, the majority (81%) chose to identify racially as Biracial/Mixed (35.4%), Other Race (35.4%), Black (25.7%), White (1.8%), and Native American (1.8%). What is interesting about how the Latino boys self-identified is that the majority (81%) identified themselves as belonging to a racial group—Biracial/Mixed, Other Race, or Black. Additionally, Latino boys who chose the "Other Race" category wrote in a singular national origin (e.g., Puerto Rican or Dominican), multiple national origins (e.g., Puerto Rican, Dominican, and Salvadoran), a pan-ethnic label of Hispanic/ Latino, or both a national origin and a pan-ethnic label (e.g., Hispanic Mexican and Puerto Rican). Despite the diversity among the students, in all of these schools Black or African American is explicitly established as the contextual norm. The fact that Latino students and other non–African Americans used our survey as an opportunity to articulate their difference is undoubtedly a reaction to the dominance of Black cultural identities.

Black boys who did not identify as Latino also elaborated on their ethnic identifications through their write-ins in the open-ended item, "How do you identify?" Out of 314 boys, 35.4 percent wrote in that they were also African American. Just over 15 percent of the Black boys referred to an ethnic or (hyphenated) American identification (e.g., Italian and Jamaican, West Indian, Asian-American). Lastly, about 20 percent of the boys wrote in personal characteristics with their racial identifications, most of which were overwhelmingly positive, such as "smart," "intelligent," and "good person."

The patterns of racial and ethnic identifications gleaned from the student survey illustrate some of the complex ways these boys were learning to identify as racial subjects in relation to ethnic subjectivities and other characteristics (i.e., cultural referents, skin color, hair texture). The boys also expressed these complexities in focus groups and in the interviews we conducted with nearly 120 students. Through the interviews, in addition to learning about the boys' ethnic subjectivities, we learned about the ways they identified as immigrants of a particular generation. Some boys who were first- or second-generation immigrants would use some form of hyphenated term when asked to explain their identity, while other boys would use a pan-ethnic term like Black or Latino that encompassed a lot of different groups.

For example, Pablo, an eleventh grader at North Star, used a hyphenated identification when asked to explain his racial identity. He highlighted his grandparents' identities as Cuban and Puerto Rican but also explained that his birthplace was in the United States of America. This led him to construct what he called a "Spanish-American" identification:

> All I know is I'm Spanish, that's how I define myself. I'm Spanish, I'm American. I was born in America, so Spanish-American, but not too Spanish. Like, what I mean is I won't wear a whole bunch of, like Cuban and Puerto Rican chains and stuff. You won't see me saying, "I love being Puerto Rican" or whatever. 'Cause I'm not really Puerto Rican or Cuban. My grandparents are.

For many of the Latino students, there was a tendency to use their heritage language, Spanish, as an ethnic/racial identifier, as in the statement "I am Spanish." To an outsider this might appear confusing, since none of these students were phenotypically White, and none of them claimed a connection to the nation of Spain. However, there was a tendency among many of the boys to equate language, culture, or national origin to ancestry and heritage. Some boys used their ancestry to describe a particular recognition of their heritage. For example, Cedric, a seventh grader at Westward Academy, described his identification as African American in terms of a bond with his African ancestry from past generations:

> If you're African American you might not be from Africa, but you still have like, generations and generations of people from Africa. I think that understanding where your people were from is very important.

Another student, Keith, a tenth grader at North Star, told us his identification as African American was a representation of varying ancestry in his family line:

> I see myself as Black, African American. I'm not too sure, 'cause there's a lot of different ways I could identify. Like, on my mother's

side, my grandmother, she comes from, like, Lumbee, Indian, down south in North Carolina. And on my grandfather's side, his father is from some of the Haliwa-Saponi Indians. They're both based in North Carolina. So there's a little bit of African American, a little bit of Irish, there's a little bit of Native American in me.

Overall, the racial and ethnic identifications the boys described included multiple renderings such as hyphenation, race over ethnicity, ethnicity over race, and a combination of the two. These ways of expressing their identity not only support what we already know about racial and ethnic identity development, which is that they are integrated processes,[4] but also that embedded within the boys' narratives of their racial/ethnic identifications are their connections with history and community. These connections parallel the messages of history and community espoused by many of these single-sex schools. In particular, when closely examining messages students receive pertaining to race, we found that the embedding of history and community within the boys' concepts of identity also demonstrated a pattern of identity affirmation that was intended to build resilience but also had the effect of erasing differences.

Being Black and Latino Is Being Resilient

The narratives shared by the students as they explained their racial/ethnic identity made it clear that there is a tremendous need both for them to resist stereotypes that would otherwise undermine their confidence and to demonstrate resilience in order to overcome the adversities they have and will continue to encounter. In particular, many of their narratives focused on overcoming experiences of racism and violence, some of it bound to experiences in communities where they were raised. For example, Mark, an eleventh grader at Thomas Jefferson, spoke candidly about feeling like he had "bells on my back," meaning that he felt that as a Black male he experienced a heightened sense of visibility. Rather than seeing this as a burden, however, Mark explained that he viewed his racial identity as a strength:

Honestly, being a Black male is really important to my experience. I've been exposed to a lot of things that have affected me and how I see things. I live in a neighborhood where I've been exposed to a lot of violence. This is not a good thing, but it has helped me in certain situations. I know what to do and what not to do, or how to react and how not to react when confronted with violence. I feel like if I were a Caucasian, I wouldn't have been exposed to so much. I wouldn't have these "bells on my back" that force me to be aware of what's going on around me. White kids have different problems. I feel as though what I've been through and what I've seen throughout my life, has made me stronger. It made me realize that I have to get out of here if I want to be successful. So I'm kind of thankful and blessed that I have seen those things so I won't have to live those things in the future.

There is a clear distinction that Mark is making between his experiences and that of his "imagined" White counterparts. We place the term imagined in quotes because there are no White students at Mark's school, and in all likelihood, he has never attended a school with White students before. Still, he imagines that if he were White he would not have faced so many hardships and his life would have been different. It is also noteworthy that he describes his racial identity as a burden that provides him with a source of strength and a lens through which to understand and engage the rest of the world.

Some boys also interpreted the history of their racial groups as part of their identity foundation that contributed to their sense of resilience. Peter, a tenth grader at North Star, in his description of his African American identity, explained its importance in relation to his pursuit of his education and the adversities faced by his ancestors:

In our past, many people didn't have the chance to pursue their education. They didn't have some of the opportunities that we have today. They fought for the opportunities that we have now. That's why I know that if we gain different opportunities as African Americans we've just got to grasp and take it. You have to do what you have to do because it wasn't too long ago when our people didn't get this kind of chance.

Several of the students we met during interviews, focus groups, and observations, let us know that their racial identification was not an accident. They expressed a strong sense of pride about their racial and ethnic identities, and these were strongly encouraged by the schools they attended. Throughout our field observations, teachers and administrators often rationalized the purpose of a particular activity by suggesting that it would help advance their "people," and they explained the meaning it held to their students as Black or Latino people.

For example, during a lunch period at Kennedy, Principal Howard, in typical fashion, corralled the boys into a large group conversation called "What's in the News." He asked the boys what they had seen or read in the news from the previous night. The boys shouted out various topics in response. One boy brought up the story about Senator John McCain possibly having had an extramarital affair. The conversation quickly moved from McCain to an awareness within the group that if similar accusations had been made about Barack Obama it would have turned into a larger scandal. The boys spoke with great animation about the significance of having a Black male as a presidential candidate. Principal Howard had the boys "turn and talk" to discuss the significance of Obama's historic candidacy. After a minute of conversation, they turned back to Mr. Howard, who stated, "If Barack becomes president, that's the end of excuses for us, especially if you go to a school like this one. We gotta make it happen." Such moments where appeals were made directly to the racial identities of the young male students were constants in each of the schools.

At one of Salem's annual men's conferences, lessons about history and culture were framed as an integral part of a Black and Latino identity. Mr. Lewis, the staff member who typically presided over cultural rituals at the school, made the following statement before pouring libations: "Our school is about history, activism, and social justice, developing perseverance and learning strategies, and navigating through the rites of passage to get to the core you. The best of you must come out every day of your life . . . You are part of a movement."

To the degree that messages related to race/ethnicity were made explicit, more often than not it was treated as a way to develop an identity that would contribute to their resilience. The explicit focus on history and community was so central to the educational foundation of some of the schools that it prompted some students to learn more about what it means to take on a Black, African American, Hispanic, or Latino identity. Nestor, a tenth grader at Thomas Jefferson, went so far as to study African American history in order to understand what it meant to identify as such:

> I got curious so I studied more about Black history. As the years went on, I read books on my own and studied much more Black history. I found out what the struggle was that they went through. Learned about the arduous times we experienced during slavery and after, and I learned how they overcame their problems. Reading the history kind of made me proud, and I actually figured out that this is my culture. This is my ethnicity—knowing who I am. So I studied more, and I became even more proud that I was who I was.
> **Interviewer:** So what does being Black mean to you?
> For me it means being hardworking and showing fortitude. Just driving to get the education that we once didn't have. Yeah, you have to have tenacity. Different verbs, or adjectives that describe power and intelligence. Yeah, power and intelligence. I like that combination.

William Cross describes this stage of race identification among adolescents as "immersion," in which there is a desire to learn more about the meaning of racial identification and to provide some detail related to one's origins.[5] Though it is not clear that all individuals follow the stages of racial identity described by Cross and others,[6] it is clear that grappling with the meaning of their racial/ethnic identities was a major concern for many of the students we met. Students like Nestor who actively sought out more information about their identity were common in these schools. In many cases, such students found support among their teachers and others who sought to help them figure out the meaning of their racial identifications.

Allan, an eleventh grader at Thomas Jefferson, also considered his identification and pride toward his group as bound to a historical experience of "tough times":

I'm proud of just the fact that Black people are still here. We have survived through a lot. I learned a lot about history this year. Knowing that White people used to see us as like animals really bothered me. But I also know that the harder we fall, the bigger we come up. We experienced strength and determination because of the tough times we went through. So I feel that our race is strong, that we can do anything because we came through a lot.

Learning about the history of Black people in the United States and the struggles they have faced fostered this student's resilience because he realized that in the face of adversity, "the harder we fall, the bigger we come up."

Efforts to develop a positive racial identity were common and intentional in most of the schools. One of the ways they accomplished this was by inviting prominent African Americans to visit the schools and speak to students about their life experiences. For example, in a visit to Salem in 2006, Sista Souljah, a prominent activist, author, and hip-hop artist, discussed the significance of the boys being in a school that affirmed their identity development as descendants of the African Diaspora. She challenged them in fairly provocative terms: "Understand that you do have enemies . . . people are building cells for you right now with your name on every single one of them . . . The government [wants] to get you [in those cells] so they can make you slaves when slavery is illegal and have you work [for free and so they] can make money off of you . . . My message to Black and Latino people is: Handle your business or you'll be somebody else's business."

This type of identity development work took place at large-scale cultural events and assemblies, and also in the everyday interactions in classrooms, hallways, and afterschool programs. For example, during an observation of a math class at North Star, several students working on percentages got into a conversation during which one of the boys said "my nigga." Without hesitation, two other boys said in almost unison, "That's not right, are you a slave owner? No? Then don't use that language." The fact that the students were learning to challenge each other about the use of the N-word says a lot about the ways in which racial identities were being shaped at some of the schools.

In addition to listening to guest speakers and learning about the history of Black and Latino people in the United States in classes, several students also spoke about what they learned about race from interactions that occurred outside of their neighborhoods. In many cases, students reported that they felt out of place or marginalized because of being Black or Latino in shopping malls and at public events. Some of their heightened sense of awareness seemed to be related to the fact that because they lived in racially segregated neighborhoods and attended segregated schools, they felt awkward and out of place in predominantly White or integrated environments. Similarly, some of the staff we met raised concerns that the racial composition of the single-sex schools did not seem to prepare the young men to attend a postsecondary educational institution in a predominantly White setting.

Some boys reported that they felt scrutinized and uncomfortable with their "color" when interacting "downtown," with White people. One eleventh grader at Jefferson told us,

> To be honest, I'm Black, but I feel like I won't let that get in my way of nothing. Oh, yeah, but those people like at fancy places like downtown and stuff like that, they'd be looking at us all with stares. When people look at me sometimes I think they're staring at me because I'm the only Black person and they think I might do something wrong. I get nervous and all that because I don't want them to call the police because they feel afraid or uncomfortable around me. I have no problem with being this color but sometimes it just feel like I need to be more conscious 'cause I'm being watched. Usually, I'll try to be so perfect so that I don't mess up. I don't want them to think that I don't belong here.

As this student's comment reveals, many of the boys at these schools found themselves negotiating a precarious dichotomy with respect to their racial identities. On the one hand, they were being encouraged by their teachers to embrace a positive sense of Blackness and to develop positive identities, rooted in an understanding of their history and culture. On the other hand, they had a heightened sense of awareness about the broad range of negative stereotypes associated with being Black or Latino, especially in predominantly White settings. They understood that many of the people they interacted with, particularly White people, saw them through these stereotypes, and they experienced some degree of stress in trying not to exhibit traits that confirmed their assumptions.

The Election of a Black President

During the course of our research, Barack Obama was elected president. This proved to be a watershed moment in many of the schools, and we witnessed a number of conversations about the significance of the election during the fall of 2008. In the weeks leading up to the inauguration there was a feeling of excitement present in the conversations teachers were having with the boys, and the boys had a lot to say about how the campaign and the possibility that he might be elected inspired them. During one lunchtime conversation about the presidential campaign in one of the schools, we listened as a student described a news story he watched that morning regarding Obama's campaign stop in the city. The student wondered aloud, "Will he *really* be president?" His question and tone suggested a nervous excitement and nearly an incredulous reaction toward the prospect of having someone in the White House who identified as Black. Another student responded, "I think he might just get it 'cause he's winning the primaries." The first student went back to his doubts: "Do you really think White people will vote for him, especially in the South? It seems too good to be true."

A number of boys spoke about the election process and the feelings they had on the night of Obama's victory. As was true in many Black communities, in these conversations there was unbridled enthusiasm in rooting for him during the debates and a genuine sense of elation over his victory. For instance, Paul, a tenth grader at Thomas Jefferson, told us that he felt a combination of fear and pride watching the election of President Obama:

The night of the election, I actually turned on the TV because there was hype all around the school about it. I felt it too and I was so excited that I went home and turned the television on as soon as I got home. I did not go outside. I wanted to stay home, so I turned on the news, and that was it. You know, I don't usually watch the news. In fact, I never did watch the news like that. But now, I wake up watching the news. I listen to the news now and the radio stations. But the elections, I really watched that. And when they said Barack Obama is the president I got so nervous. I was just scared for some reason. I had a feeling that yeah, our race coming up, that it's good to be Black. And it's good that Obama won the presidential election because if he's running the country, maybe everybody will be better off. It's crazy how one man can make everybody happy.

Despite the joy they felt about the election of Barack Obama, in interviews we learned that the boys did not believe that racism would suddenly come to an end or that the quality of life experienced by Black people would dramatically improve. They were both optimistic about the possibilities for what Black people could achieve but cognizant that racism continued to be a reality for most Black people and that it would not go away even if Obama was the president. For example, Tyrone, a tenth grader at Thomas Jefferson, told us that he felt pride in Obama's election, but also recounted an experience during which his teacher was racially profiled:

We proved ourselves when Barack Obama got elected. He's breaking up the barriers that have been set in front of us. But there are some things we still have to deal with such as police harassment. You know my teacher Mr. C., he said he got stopped for no reason by the police. He was driving home and they just pulled him over. He didn't have anything on him so they let him go. I think things like that will keep happening. In fact, it might happen even more because some White people are mad that Obama won. They may go after us just because we're African American or just because the way we dress draws attention . . . you know, like wearing a hoodie or stuff like that.[7]

Another student, Alex, a tenth grader at North Star, expressed a sentiment that we heard among many of the students in these schools. He described feeling hopeful about the election of Barack Obama, but was cognizant that racism still existed, and the new president would not be able to fix all of the problems that confront black people quickly or easily:

> Now that Barack Obama is elected president, I think it's important for me 'cause it gives me hope but that there will be less racism. The election gives us hope that we can do anything [we] put our minds to but I know he can't solve all of our problems right away. It took us a long time to get to where we are now, so it will probably take a long time for things to get better too.

Another student, Carl, an eleventh grader at North Star, felt the election of Obama gave him hope that a Black man can succeed despite the realities of racism:

> The election shows that people are coming together. It shows that African Americans can do something. I'm excited because it shows that you just have to work hard enough, and you can get what you want. The whole time during the campaign, I was just hoping that he would win. I was just kind of anxious. I always felt like he could make it but I didn't really think he would just because of how some White people think. But when I seen it happen, and when I saw that he had won, I had a real sense of pride. It shows that some White people don't care anymore about race. That makes me feel good. It means they look at more, like what a person is capable of rather than how they look.

Representing Their Identities

Despite the optimism generated by Obama's election, many of the boys remained aware that their racial identities would leave them vulnerable to stereotypes and ongoing discrimination. Several said they felt a particular sense of responsibility to do all they could to combat stereotypes by excelling in school and being aware of how they carried themselves in public. The boys were aware of a range of negative images associated with Black and Latino people, and several of the students spoke about the need to challenge these representations. For instance, Tyler, a ninth grader at North Star, described the images of Black people on television and in the media:

> The stereotypes that are portrayed of Black people on TV and in the media like in the rap videos can have a really bad influence. Younger people see them and they feel as though this is how you're suppose to act. With your pants hanging below your kneecaps, and bandanas, and all this crazy other stuff that they see. And it's like, you know, they act out the stereotypes that other people have created about us. It's like when we drive down the street, my mom and I will look like at a person who is sagging and she'll say, "That can't be comfortable for them to be walking around like that." We just pity them, so to speak. They don't understand the long-term effects of carrying on like that. I realize that I have to represent myself and my people. That's why I'm trying to do my best in school. I want to show the world what we can accomplish just like Obama did.

Tyler's focus on the image of young Black men with "sagging" pants, and the negative feelings he held toward it, was consistent with views expressed by some of the other students we spoke with. Boys often spoke of the need to distinguish themselves from young men in the neighborhood with baggy or sagging pants and other images portrayed on television. Making this distinction was more than a style preference. For many of the students, clothing and personal attire were statements of their worth, their aspirations, and their character. As Tyler states, he and his mother "pity" young men with sagging pants because they believe it is unhealthy to carry yourself in that way. He also expressed a belief that how he carried himself in public and how he performed in school would have some bearing on how Black people were seen by others. Ironically, even though many of the young men we interviewed acknowledged that they wore sagging pants outside of school, they recognized that such styles reinforce native stereotypes and contribute to the negative judgments that others hold toward young Black men.

Another student, Kyle, a seventh grader at Westward, admitted that people think Black boys who wear sagging pants are "bad kids":

People have different views of us because they don't see us for what we see in ourselves. Other people might think we're something that we really aren't. Like when Black boys walk down the street with their pants down they think that's a bad kid. He don't come from a good home, from like a good family. That's what people might think. But that's their opinion. It may not be true at all.

In interviews, some boys told us that because they were attending a school that promotes positive stereotypes and requires a uniform, they were able to project a more positive image of who they were and what they were about. William, a tenth grader at Westward, suggested that his school promotes "positive stereotypes" of Black men and that when he wears the uniform he knows he is also representing the school. He told us that his identity has developed differently because of these positive stereotypes associated with his school:

> Well, the negative stereotypes come from people that don't really know or understand Black people. They want to stay away and don't really care about what happens to Black people. They think [of] us as bad and corrupt. That's where the negative comes from. That's what I like about being at this school. They promote positive stereotypes and it really does affect me right now. The environment that I'm in is all about positive stereotypes: be a man, live up to the creed, be successful. Those are positive stereotypes that positively affect me because they're like told to me every day. And, like, when you hear something repeatedly, it's going to stick to your mind. That's why when I wear this uniform to school in the mornings I feel proud, because I know that this school means something to people when they see it.

Evidence that students are developing a positive sense of their racial and ethnic identity is further supported by our survey data. During the third year of the study, as we learned about this emerging theme of stereotype disruption, we included Claude Steele's Stereotype Threat[8] measure in our research. Steele explores the degree to which a person is aware of stereotypes and is concerned about reinforcing them. Not surprisingly, as shown in table 5.1, boys generally disagreed with stereotypical statements claiming that their ethnic identity was related to

TABLE 5.1

Students' views on stereotype

	Disagree	Neutral	Agree
Ethnicity is related to academic performance.	49%	29%	21%
Members of my ethnic group have trouble performing well in school.	45%	34%	21%
Prejudice has had a big effect on members of my ethnic group.	41%	33%	25%
Prejudice has strongly affected my life.	47%	31%	21%
Prejudice has negatively affected my school experiences.	54%	29%	16%
Teachers often expect lower performance from members of my ethnic group.	61%	26%	13%
Some people think I have less ability because of my ethnicity.	54%	26%	20%
In academic situations I often feel that others look down on me because of my ethnicity.	57%	27%	16%
My ethnicity does not affect other people's perceptions of my academic abilities.	38%	31%	31%
Some academic tasks are more difficult for people of my ethnicity.	50%	32%	18%

Note: Scale includes a 5-point Likert response (strongly disagree, disagree, neutral, agree, strongly disagree). *Agree* combines "agree" and "strongly agree"; *Disagree* combines "disagree" and "strongly disagree."

academic performance, getting good grades in school, and having academic abilities. Interestingly, the boys disagreed most with the statement "Teachers often expect lower performance from members of my ethnic group."

Reproducing Masculine Identities

As we stated in previous chapters, the educators in these schools made it a priority to focus on socializing their male students about what it means to be a man. However, in many cases, the attention given to the two social categories—race and gender—was hard to distinguish because these were, after all, largely Black and Latino male students. For that reason, the intersection of race and gender was often the focus of the socialization efforts that we observed. The educators at these schools were concerned about the character and dispositions of Black and Latino men, and their attention was directed at molding both dimensions of their identities.

In all seven of the schools there was a narrative about Black manhood and masculinity that explicitly suggested they were striving to develop young men who would be honorable, respectful, and resilient. While such qualities were clearly admirable, more often than not the notion of masculinity that was emphasized reflected fairly traditional notions of gender. The young men were being socialized to take on traditional male roles in the context of work, family, and interpersonal relationships. In many cases, this traditional approach to gender socialization proved to be problematic.

Our findings raise important questions about whether or not boys were developing critical perspectives about gender, particularly concerning relationships between men and women, and with respect to issues pertaining to sexuality. In some cases it was clear that the schools were simply reproducing the status quo. The reproduction of traditional forms of masculinity appeared to be predicated on the idea that it would make it possible for the boys to overcome the obstacles confronting men of color within a larger societal context. The goal was to produce strong Black and Latino men who would be able to maintain consistent employment, stable home and family environments, and attain academic achievement.

Data collected from interviews and surveys revealed that many of the boys seemed to embrace the traditional notions of masculinity that the schools were promoting. We administered a survey in the second year of the study that included an adapted masculinity scale. As we analyzed the responses, we detected two consistent dimensions of masculinity—

honor and emotional stoicism—as themes expressed by the boys. This included the notion of "masculine honor" as well as the importance of being responsible, smart, respectful, and firm in one's beliefs. We also sought to understand the degree to which the boys felt comfortable with the emotional or affective dimension of their dispositions, and the degree to which these ideas were compatible with the boys' idea of masculinity and manhood.

The emerging patterns from the survey revealed that most of the boys at the seven schools embraced fairly traditional ideas of manhood and masculinity (see table 5.2). By large majorities—roughly three-quarters in each case—the high school students who took our survey agreed that being respected, making family the most important responsibility, and sticking to beliefs were important elements of being a boy. There was somewhat less agreement on the issue of being smart versus being physically strong; however, a smaller majority of the boys did agree that being smart was better than being strong—a response that seemed to suggest the boys were embracing intellectual ability as being more important than physical prowess.

On items related to emotional stoicism the boys appeared to embrace attributes that are typically considered nontraditional expressions among males (see table 5.3). They were torn on whether it was embar-

TABLE 5.2

Students' views on masculine honor

	Disagree	Neutral	Agree
It is better for a boy to be smart than strong.	10.4%	32.4%	57.2%
It is important for a boy to be respected by others.	6.6%	16.9%	76.4%
A boy's #1 responsibility is his family.	7.4%	22.9%	69.8%
It is important for a boy to stick to his beliefs.	4.8%	21.0%	74.3%

Note: *Disagree* combines "disagree and "strongly disagree"; *Agree* combines "agree" and "strongly agree."

TABLE 5.3

Students' view on emotional stoicism

	Disagree	Neutral	Agree
It's embarrassing for a boy when he has to ask for help.	39.8%	39.8%	20.5%
If a boy tells people his worries, he will look weak.	75.0%	14.8%	10.2%

Note: Disagree combines "disagree and "strongly disagree"; Agree combines "agree" and "strongly agree."

rassing to ask for help, but they overwhelmingly disagreed that telling your worries to another person is a sign of weakness.

While it is not possible to tell from the survey responses the degree to which the boys in the study had moved away from traditional notions of masculinity, our observations and interviews revealed that many of them were doing so. In fact, there was a noticeable disconnect in some of the schools between how the boys perceived themselves in terms of their masculinity and how they were perceived by their teachers.

For example, James Jackson, the principal at Thomas Jefferson, told us that during its first year the school had adopted a number of classroom practices that they had been led to believe would be more effective in promoting achievement among boys. One of these involved the teacher throwing a football to a student when they were called on to answer a question. After a few months of following this practice the principal and teachers realized that the practice often had the effect of embarrassing students who were not particularly athletic and were unable to catch the ball. A year later, Mr. Jackson explained what he learned from this experience:

> We were told that boys were kinesthetic learners and that they would respond well to teachers throwing the football during classroom discussions. I should have known that this wasn't going to work for all of our boys because I wasn't an athlete myself. I was the type of clumsy kid that always embarrassed himself in sports. We have a lot of boys

like that at our school who just aren't into sports, so we dropped it. We want to be inclusive of all of our young scholars so we wouldn't want to do something that would turn some of them off to learning.

Mr. Jackson's willingness to rethink his school's approach to engaging and socializing boys was indicative of a flexibility that we observed at several of the schools. However, on the issue of sexuality, such flexibility was far less common. We learned from our interviews that a significant number of the boys at several schools feared that they would be seen as gay because they went to an all-male school. One boy told us that he was taunted by boys who attended another school within the same building about being gay. Students at Salem reported that they were frequently targeted and harassed by students in the neighborhood for wearing ties and dressing like "nerds and homos."

In our survey, the boys were divided over whether they would have a friendship with a boy who was gay (see table 5.4), with nearly half of them calling themselves neutral on this subject. This suggested they were likely concerned about how such a relationship might affect how others viewed them. But while they were torn on the question of friendship, they clearly agreed that it would bother them if a boy acted like a girl. The boys' responses suggested that even if they were to be friends with boys that were gay, they did not appreciate boys who they believed acted like girls.

TABLE 5.4

Students' views on gender nonconformity

	Disagree	Neutral	Agree
I would be friends with a boy who is gay.	28.3%	44.3%	27.4%
I can respect a boy who backs down from a fight.	9.0%	24.3%	66.7%
It bothers me when a boy acts like a girl.	15.7%	22.4%	61.9%

Note: *Disagree* combines "disagree and "strongly disagree"; *Agree* combines "agree" and "strongly agree."

The educators in all seven schools were aware of the threats their students faced but demonstrated considerably less awareness of the fact that several of their students were struggling to figure out their sexuality. They were even less aware that some of their students identified as gay. The overall culture at all seven schools could be characterized as "hetero-normative," meaning that any student who was gay, bisexual, transgendered, or in the least bit uncertain about his sexual identity was likely to feel out of place. Through both explicit and implicit messages, being a man at these schools clearly meant being heterosexual. It was a message that came through in the way manhood was represented in discussions and lectures. Men are supposed to be strong, smart, good providers, and protectors of women.

Girls as a Cognitive and Sexual Distraction

It was an obvious question to ask all the boys we met: "What's it like to be in a school with no girls?" The themes that emerged from this question allowed us to understand and explore how the boys were defining their masculine identity in relation to what it meant for them to be in an environment apart from girls. A prominent response to this question was, "Without girls I can focus on my grades." A sixth grader at Westward said that if girls were present, "it would change this school because then there would be a lot more fights and a lot less learning in the classroom."

The boys could not explain why they felt girls would be a source of distraction, despite the fact that in five of the seven schools they interacted with or at least saw girls who attended schools that were located in the same building. Nonetheless, the boys repeatedly maintained that if girls were present there would be fights among the boys over them. Such responses suggested that the boys saw themselves as being so preoccupied with their sexuality that they were likely to become aggressive toward each other in the presence of a female. An eleventh grader at Thomas Jefferson explained it in this way:

> If there were girls here, I think it would be even worse. There would have been a lot of fights between boys trying to get girls or whatever.

At my old school, people were like showing off for girls and trying to start fights just to get the attention of a girl. They might try to put someone else down to make themselves look better than they really are. That's why I think that if there were girls here there would be more fights and it would have been even worse.

The boys at Thomas Jefferson, Washington, Salem, and North Star claimed that girls would be a distraction because even the girls at schools that are co-located with other schools are distractions, even though they are not in their classrooms. A tenth grader at Thomas Jefferson said:

It would make most of the guys get sidetracked. We can already see them when we are going to our lockers or in the cafeteria, and the guys get sidetracked. They start taking too much time trying to talk to them and stuff and forget all about getting to class on time. By being late to their classes they end up getting detention, so imagine if they had them in the school. Some guys might not even come to class. They might just be hanging around somewhere talking to the females.

Both of these comments suggest that many of the boys viewed the presence of girls as a sexual distraction, one that could result in uncontrollable behavior. Many of the boys told us that the impact of such distractions would be poor grades and even more disciplinary issues. As stated by a student at Washington:

It would be pretty sad [to have girls in the school] because a lot of kids in my grade, they say they want girls here. I know that if girls were here those people would not study, would not do the work, they wouldn't pay as much attention and some would keep more to themselves. When I was at public school and there were girls there I would really keep to myself because when there are girls around you cannot speak about any guy-ish things. Here you can say, oh well, I'm going to [go] through this, this, and that. We're all boys so we all go through a lot . . . It's a lot easier [without the girls].

The narrative of girls as a sexual distraction suggested that a disturbing characterization of the way interactions between boys and girls occur had been normalized. The idea that boys have sexual urges that cloud their thinking when they are in the presence of girls suggests that boys can't be taught to take responsibility for their behavior. Interestingly, in our focus group discussions we never heard this point of view challenged.

Race and Gender Identities and Their Role in Challenging Adversity

Coming to terms with one's identity—who you are and who you want others to see you as—is an important part of the child development process. It is particularly important to adolescents, who tend to be more strongly identified with their peers than with adults during this crucial stage of development. For children of color, this often also involves constructing a sense of self that places race and ethnicity in a healthy and positive frame. For boys of color, the issue of identity is in some ways even more complex because in addition to figuring out what it means to be a member of a racial/ethnic minority group in American society, they must also figure out what it means to be a male within that group and in relation to other racial/ethnic groups of males. As we've pointed out repeatedly in these chapters, much of that identity construction process involves contending with negative stereotypes that undermine a positive sense of self but may also exert a strong appeal. A young Black man may not want to be seen as a thug or a gangster, but given that such individuals are admired and feared by some, the lure of such a trope cannot be denied. These young men are also constructing a male identity within a larger society that is patriarchal, where men are presumed to be dominant and powerful.

Interestingly, we found that the racial and ethnic identifications the boys embraced included multiple renderings—some that placed race over ethnicity, or ethnicity over race, or even a combination of the two. These expressions of identity support not only what we already know about racial and ethnic identity development, which is that they are integrated processes, but also the notion that they are embedded within the boys' sense of their connections with history and community.

Overall, these findings tell a complicated story about who these boys are and the men they are becoming in schools with a focus on developing resilience. As adolescents, the boys' identities are in flux; they are learning about new aspects of their racial, ethnic, and gender identities that may change over time. They are also being encouraged to draw on the support of their peers or "brothers" if and when it is necessary to support their character development. They are learning about the importance of being creative, studying hard, and giving back to their communities. It could be argued that the boys' sense of masculinity—characterized by being responsible, academically oriented, and goal-oriented—can serve them in knowing how to manage challenging experiences in the wider society. On the other hand, this definition of manhood is predicated on traditional notions of masculinity, which at times many of the boys admitted they were unsure they could ever attain. Embracing these fairly traditional notions of masculinity may very well result in these young men reproducing relations of dominance in their relations with girls and women. Ironically, the educators at these schools hope that they are constructing a new definition of masculinity; however, we found relatively little evidence that this was in fact the case.

6

Resilience and Achievement

Attitudes and Practices That Influence Performance

I'm very biased, but I say a college education is what defines success for boys of color. People define success differently but for me and for our students, success is a college education and I don't ever sway from that. Now, what are some of the other things that they need? I think they need a lot of resilience. They need a great deal of self-confidence. I think they need an incredible amount of persistence and a great deal of courage because these guys for the most part are first-generation college goers and there are a lot of pressures pulling them away from that goal. Even if you don't view going to college as the goal, or equate going to college with success, the other things that you normally equate with being successful—getting a good job, raising a family, being a responsible husband or father, etc.—will require further education. There are a lot of pressures in these communities pulling them away from doing the right thing, so we've got to make sure they have the courage, persistence, and resilience that will make it possible for them to transcend those pressures.

—*Principal, Thomas Jefferson Academy*

The sentiments expressed by the principal of Thomas Jefferson were reinforced by all of the principals at the seven schools studied for this book. Each one defined the success of their schools primarily in terms of getting their boys into college. However, when the question was posed to them, they also acknowledged that just getting to college will not guarantee lifelong success. They were well aware that boys of color will encounter various obstacles—including racism, academic challenges, community pressures, and a host of lowered expectations and negative stereotypes—because of how Black and Latino males are perceived in American society. The educators we met repeatedly emphasized that to overcome these obstacles boys of color will have to become resilient and acquire the kinds of skills and attitudes described in earlier chapters, such as the self-confidence to resist the "pull of the streets," the knowledge of how to "do" school, and the social skills to seek assistance when needed and to establish supportive relationships with adults and peers.

In this chapter we provide a complementary quantitative analysis to examine the degree to which these skills and attitudes were embraced by these students and how they might have influenced their academic performance. In order for us to understand how these attributes related to academic performance, we surveyed the boys at each school annually for three years. As the schools grew in size from one year to the next—from a total enrollment of 844 in Year 1 to 1,632 in Year 3—there was a commensurate increase in the number of students who took part in the survey, from 405 in the first year to 1,038 in the second and 1,056 in the third. (While the number of participating students rose in each of the three years, the response rate actually peaked in Year 2, at 73 percent; the figure for Year 1 was 48 percent and for Year 2, 65 percent.)

Over the three years of our study we developed a variety of survey measures to explore how the skills and attitudes the schools hoped that students were acquiring were connected to particular school practices (e.g., college-going school climate, caring relationships, culturally relevant instruction and curriculum, identity development, etc.). Following

---

This chapter was coauthored by Margary Martin.

are some of the survey measures we used (see appendix 2 for fuller information on survey measures):

- *School climate and culture,* including a sense of belonging to the school environment, a sense of feeling that the school environment is fair, a sense that a multicultural perspective is present, the prevalence of stereotype threats, and the degree of safety perceived in and outside of school.
- *Instructional/academic quality,* including academic press, teacher expectations, peer support, parental expectations, and academic challenge.
- *Academic engagement,* including behavioral, cognitive, and relational engagement.
- *College readiness,* including educational expectations, academic resilience, college pathway knowledge, and career aspirations.

Again, these themes emerged from our efforts to understand the implicit theory of change that was guiding the creation and operation of these schools. By examining the degree to which the schools' goals were embraced by students, our research made it possible to understand whether or not the strategies pursued were indeed contributing to the development of resilience among students. Figure 6.1 provides an outline of the model.

We begin this chapter by using the survey to provide descriptive information on how students perceived the school climate, the quality of instruction, academic engagement, and adult and peer relationships. We explore how each of these perceptions may be influencing achievement and then proceed to a more complicated analysis of how they contribute to academic performance as measured by grades and cumulative GPA. This analysis makes it possible to understand what the previous chapters allude to regarding the interaction between instruction, academic identity development, and school climate. We hope to understand the strength of the relationship between the practices adopted by the schools and the degree to which they foster resilience and

FIGURE 6.1

Resilience skills and attitude achievement model

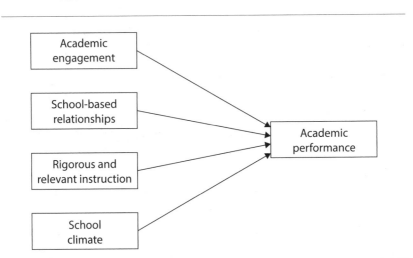

positive identity development that supports improved achievement. In the final section of this chapter, we present findings to explore whether changes in students' perceptions are associated with changes in their academic engagement and achievement as measured by GPA.

Finding Appropriate and Comparable Achievement Measures

A number of factors made it difficult for us to decide which outcome measures would be best to use as indicators of academic success. First, the schools in our study were located in four different states, and each one utilizes a different measure to determine proficiency in math and English language arts (ELA) on standardized assessments. These indicators are not always comparable, and in some states there has been a significant recalibration of scores that eliminated many of the previously recorded gains. Second, students in the study were tested at different times—and in high school some students were not tested every year. This too made comparisons of achievement across schools difficult. Finally, the one private school in the study used a different measure for assessing student performance, utilizing standardized tests (though their tests were different than those used by other schools in the same state) and a fundamentally different grading system.

To address the first two problems, we determined that course grades were the best common measure to use as our outcome variable for each year, specifically cumulative GPA. With this decision, we were able to include six of the seven schools in the study, but were not able to include the private school for these particular sets of analyses. In addition, for the purpose of our analysis we were concerned less with student performance on a particular test than with the extent to which their grades changed over time. We were particularly curious about how the school interventions that were implemented may have been associated with these changes.

The primary data for this chapter comes from the Year 2 sample of 1,038 students (drawn from students at six of the seven schools) who completed the student survey in a single academic year. It consisted of 725 high school students and 313 middle school students, with an average age of 15.7 years old ($\underline{SD}$ = 2.5). The survey data we are using also represented Years 2 to 3 of the schools' operation and demonstrate greater levels of program maturation.

Factors Impacting Academic Performance

Recent research reports[1] and several recent studies[2] have suggested that acquiring certain "noncognitive skills" is essential to ensuring academic achievement and advancement. More specifically, the research has shown that the social and emotional dimensions of development have great bearing on academic performance. These dimensions have been described as "noncognitive" because they include personal attributes such as self-regulation, impulse control, perseverance, and grit.

In our own research we have found the term "noncognitive skills" to be problematic and incongruent with the strong and ongoing relationship between social, cognitive, and behavioral factors and their interaction with academic performance. Furthermore, several relevant studies have found that variability in the academic performance of students of color is highly correlated with beliefs and perceptions of the social, cognitive, and behavioral supports available within the learning environment.[3] As our model (see figure 6.2, discussed later in this chapter) suggests, the academic growth of students, particularly boys of color from marginalized communities, is also influenced by environmental conditions within the local social context. Several researchers have documented how environmental conditions can affect learning conditions within schools as well as student outcomes.[4] For example, several researchers have explored how academic performance is correlated with perceptions of racial bias, stereotype threats, and an assortment of variables related to school conditions.[5] For this reason, as we explore the relationship between the "noncognitive" skills and the academic orientation of students, we do so with an awareness of how the social context may influence perceptions. With this theoretical framework in mind, we begin to explore how these perceptions of school climate, instruction, and adult-peer relationships may have influenced conditions for academic achievement and growth.

School Climate

Given that all seven of the schools in our study placed considerable importance on developing a school climate that was supportive of the academic and social development of students, we decided to measure how students perceived these efforts using four dimensions: 1) sense of fair treatment, 2) school cohesion, 3) sense of belonging to school, and 4) peer academic support. The compilation of these measures provides a comprehensive way of understanding how students perceived the school climate, culture, and ethos that existed at their school (see appendix 2 for reliability and validity of measures).

Fairness

The construct of fairness explores the extent to which students reported that they believed they were being treated fairly by adults at school. As seen in table 6.1, a large majority of students agreed with all four statements assessing fairness in their relationships and interactions, in interactions they perceived as "race-based," in grade distribution, and in the application of school rules.

School Cohesion

We used the construct of cohesion to measure how students perceived the degree of unity and cohesion among students. Table 6.2 presents respondent percentages for all school cohesion items. On each of these items except for "getting along in school," the students overwhelmingly considered group cohesion to be present in their school.

Sense of Belonging

The sense of belonging construct was designed to measure the degree to which students felt as though they belonged in their school. Table 6.3 presents percentages for items in this category. For both middle and high school youth, the majority claimed to fit with other students at their school. However, there were significant numbers of students who

TABLE 6.1
Perception of fairness

To what extent do you agree with the following statements about your school?	Disagree	Agree
Administrators treat students with respect.	24.2%	75.8%
Teachers treat students from different backgrounds in the same way.	26.3%	73.4%
In my school, everyone has the same opportunity to get good grades.	17.7%	82.3%
The punishment for breaking school rules is the same no matter who you are.	32%	68%

Note: *Disagree* combines "disagree" and "strongly disagree"; *Agree* combines "agree" and "strongly agree."

TABLE 6.2

Perception of cohesion

To what extent do you agree with the following statements about your school?	Disagree	Agree
Everyone gets along in this school.	70.4%	29.7%
In my school, students make friends with students from different countries or cultures.	19%	81%
In my school, students from different racial, ethnic, or cultural backgrounds treat each other with respect.	33.2%	66.9%
Students from different religious backgrounds treat each other with respect.	26%	74%

Note: Disagree combines "disagree" and "strongly disagree"; Agree combines "agree" and "strongly agree."

did not think of other students and teachers as family, and who thought that others might not care if or when they were not at school.

Peer Academic Supports

As part of the degree to which students felt supported by their peers, we thought it would be important to probe the concept of brotherhood that many of the educators at these schools claimed was central to their mission. Table 6.4 shows the percentages of students who agreed or disagreed with statements relating to peer academic support. On each item except for "helping each other prepare for tests," from two-thirds to three-quarters of the boys identified peer academic support as an element of the climate at their school.

The patterns revealed on these four measures of school climate add a degree of complexity to the issues discussed in chapter 4. While the educators at these schools thought they were succeeding in creating a climate that fostered resilience, the development of skills and attitudes that promoted academic success, the development of bonds of "brotherhood," and strong relationships between students and school staff, the survey reveals that this may not have entirely been the case. While

TABLE 6.3

Perception of belonging

To what extent do you agree with the following statements about your school?	Disagree	Agree
I fit in with the students at this school.	29.1%	70.9%
People at this school are like family to me.	49.6%	50.4%
People care if I'm not at school.	35.6%	64.4%

Note: *Disagree* combines "disagree" and "strongly disagree"; *Agree* combines "agree" and "strongly agree."

a majority of the boys identified the dimensions of climate fairness, belonging, cohesion, and peer academic support as being present at these schools, significant numbers stated that they did not help each other prepare for tests or discuss what happened in class.

To further understand whether these patterns were significant to academic performance we analyzed the correlation among a number of different variables. As expected, perceptions of fairness [.043, $p < .01$] had a positive association with grades, while belonging [–.043, $p < .01$] and cohesion [–.004, $p < .01$] were negatively associated with grades. It could be that feelings of cohesion and belonging to school develop

TABLE 6.4

Peer academic support

	Agree	Disagree
My friends try hard in school.	73.5%	26.5%
My friends and I talk about what we did in class.	64.4%	35.6%
My friends and I help each other prepare for tests.	57.5%	42.5%
My friends and I help each other with homework assignments.	70.5%	29.5%
My friends and I think it is important to attend every class.	73.5%	26.5%

Note: *Agree* combines "agree" and "strongly agree"; *Disagree* combines "disagree" and "strongly disagree."

quickly, while improving academic performance takes more time. Many of these boys were coming from school environments that were not meeting their academic needs. Hence, while they may have begun to make a connection to their new schools relatively quickly, they may have needed more time to adjust to the academic demands placed on them. It is also important to point out that while these associations suggest a relationship, they should not be interpreted as implying causality. Later in this chapter we will look more closely at whether and how these measures of skills and attitudes contribute to academic performance.

Perceptions Related to Instruction

Due to the variation in the approach taken to instruction by teachers within these schools, it seemed inappropriate to try to capture perceptions of instruction schoolwide. However, because literacy is such an important indicator of competency and college readiness, we decided to focus on ELA grades for Year 2 of our study when conducting our analysis (see chapter 3, table 3.3). The activities we selected were generally seen as related to college preparation. Given that the schools all placed a major emphasis on college preparation, we decided to collect data on the types of instructional activities being employed in classrooms in Years 2 and 3 of the study. The majority of middle and high school students identified the following activities as occurring at least once a week: explaining what you've read in a class discussion; discussing how something you read connected to real life; studying something that is about an issue you care about; and explaining in writing how you solved a math problem. Meanwhile, a minority of students reported that they wrote a three-page paper, worked in groups on a big class project, or made an oral presentation in class more than once a week. The infrequency of some of these activities raises questions concerning the relationship between these activities and the grades students received.

Though the frequency of demanding literacy activities for high school students was not as great as one might expect at a school that is committed to preparing its students for college, the majority of students did report that their teachers, and at times the material, were challenging. Table 3.4 (see chapter 3) illustrates responses to indicators on ELA course challenge. We sought to understand whether middle and high school students perceived their ELA courses as rigorous and demanding. A little over a quarter of middle (29.5%) and high school (25.2%) students reported that they never found the work in their ELA classes difficult. The remainder of students reported that they found the work they received to be difficult at least once a month. An overwhelming majority of middle (79.3%) and high school (76%) students reported that they had to work hard at least once a week to do well. While it is not possible to determine whether student perceptions of rigor are a relevant indicator of how well they were being prepared for college, the fact that more students did not feel challenged may be a cause for concern. We will return to this point later.

Another important perception is the degree to which the boys felt that their teachers held high expectations of them. As discussed previously, raising academic expectations was a critical part of the change in school climate that each of the schools was trying to bring about. The vast majority of boys felt their teachers held high expectations of them and their classroom peers (see table 3.1 in chapter 3). This is significant because it points to the possibility that high expectations are not simply reserved for the higher performing students.

Additionally, we analyzed the correlations between course challenge, teacher expectations, high-impact literacy activities, and cumulative GPA based on prior analyses of linear association. We define high-impact literacy strategies as courses that were set up (some of which lasted for ninety minutes or more) to address the literacy needs of students. In some cases, these were specifically designed for students who were behind academically. However, some of the schools required all of their students to take these intensive reading and writing courses. We found that high-impact literacy activities maintained a negative correlation with cumulative GPA [−.116, p < .01] which we found to be highly significant. Ironically, this means that literacy activities and academic growth are associated in negative ways. However, perceptions of course challenge had a positive and significant correlation with cumulative GPA [.202, p < .01].

This means that the greater the degree of course challenge as perceived by students, the more likely that this would be associated with higher cumulative GPA. Though correlations only spell out an association between variables and not causality, this finding helps to establish that the perception of instruction as challenging (i.e., feeling challenged by coursework, tests, and content) by students is significantly related to better grades. Further, it establishes the significance and relevance of the focus adopted by these schools on resilience, relationships, and cultural relevance, and on how these are related to the academic performance of students.

The Three Dimensions of Academic Engagement: Behavioral, Cognitive, and Relational

Behavioral Engagement

Increasingly, researchers who study learning and the factors that influence academic achievement have identified the importance of engagement.[6] In this study we analyzed three dimensions of academic engagement: behavioral, cognitive, and relational. At each of the schools in this study, the practitioners we met, observed, and interviewed discussed the importance of students' acquiring the skills and attitudes associated with being a good student. These include such behaviors as paying attention in class, participating in class discussions, turning in homework, punctuality, and good attendance. We defined these skills and attitudes as behavioral engagement, and we adopted a scale to assess whether students were completing the behavioral tasks the school deemed necessary for success in school. In each of the schools, we were told that building a supportive and responsive school environment was essential for getting students fully engaged. While administrators spoke about the behavioral expectations they had of their students—adhering to the dress code, getting to school on time, holding individuals accountable for their actions, and so forth—many also told us that they had to meet their students halfway, offering them a level of active support that most of them, having never been held to such high expectations before, were unaccustomed to.

Table 6.5 presents the students' responses on all of the behavioral engagement items we measured. The great majority of them reported positive classroom behaviors—finishing their schoolwork on time, paying attention to the teachers, following rules, and asking questions when they didn't understand something. While roughly a third admitted that they had disrupted class more than once a week, and similar percentages said they sometimes came to class without pen and paper, were late to class, or forgot to take the assigned books home, only one in ten reported skipping classes once a week or more. The extent to which these behavioral skills and attitudes had been embraced is hardly surprising,

TABLE 6.5

Students' behavioral engagement

In the first semester or term of this year, how many times did any of the following occur?	Never	Less than once a week	Once a week or more
I finished the schoolwork assigned to me.	2.4%	6.3%	91.4%
I paid attention in class.	2.4%	4.6%	93%
I tried to do my best in school.	3.1%	7.7%	89.1%
I followed the rules in school.	3.7%	9.6%	86.7%
If I didn't understand something, I asked questions.	7.7%	15.8%	76.5%
I disrupted the class.	29.5%	34.5%	35.9%
I turned in my homework.	3.1%	10.7%	86.1%
I did not bring a pen/pencil or paper to class.	33.7%	28%	38.2%
I forgot to take home books needed to complete an assignment.	42.3%	32.5%	25.3%
I was late to class.	44.2%	31.6%	24.1%
I skipped or cut classes.	79.3%	10.3%	10.3%

Note: Less than once a week combines "less than once per month" and "less than once per week"; Once a week or more combines "once or twice a week" and "every day or almost every day."

given the emphasis each school placed on conformity with school rules and norms. Conversely, students who have not adopted these behaviors may be at even greater risk of failure or of being identified as problem students because of their deviation from school norms.

Cognitive Engagement

Whereas behavioral engagement can be observed through a student's comportment in the classroom and adherence to school rules and norms, cognitive engagement can only be detected by talking directly to students about what they are learning. In our focus groups and interviews with students, teachers, and administrators, three conditions for cognitive engagement emerged: the need for real-world applicability of what was being learned, cultural relevance, and the need to address the various learning styles of students. Additionally, all three groups mentioned the need for high expectations in the classroom that could be actualized through in-depth, challenging work. The educators also spoke of the challenges that they encountered in their efforts to produce a high level of cognitive engagement. Primary among these was the fact that many students were not accustomed to inquiry-based work that required problem solving and higher-order thinking skills. When we asked the educators how they knew whether or not their students were cognitively engaged, they told us that when students feel enthusiastic about the material and actively engage in the work assigned, teachers have greater confidence that genuine learning is taking place.

The cognitive engagement construct that we adopted was tied to the findings we generated from our focus group interviews. We developed questions designed to measure the degree to which students were interested and intellectually engaged. Table 6.6 presents respondent percentages for all cognitive engagement items. The majority of students expressed an affirmative response to items related to materials that they were able to identify with. This was particularly the case when the work assigned was difficult for them.

The results seem to indicate a generally high a level of cognitive engagement among students; however, two items give cause for concern.

TABLE 6.6
Students' cognitive engagement

	Agree	Disagree
I get bored with my schoolwork.	59.6%	40.4%
I feel good when I learn something new, even if it's hard.	84.5%	15.5%
I listen carefully when others talk about topics I'm interested in.	90.5%	9.5%
I like new challenges.	84.5%	15.5%
When I'm working on something I care about, nothing can distract me.	62.2%	33.8%
When I have a clear goal, I can really focus.	85.5%	14.5%
I'm a curious person.	79.1%	20.9%
When my schoolwork is too difficult, I give up.	27.7%	72.3%
When I encounter a new problem, I first think about the strategies that I've used to solve similar problems in the past.	76.8%	23.2%
I like it when teachers help me think about things that I'd never thought of before.	85.8%	14.2%

Note: Agree combines "agree" and "strongly agree"; Disagree combines "disagree" and "strongly disagree."

Over a quarter of the respondents stated that they were likely to give up when the work was difficult, and one-third admitted that they could be distracted while working. Given that not all of the students at these schools were performing at proficiency levels or higher, these items may suggest areas of engagement that the educators will need to focus on to a greater degree than they have up to now.

Relational Engagement: School-Based Relationships
During our first year of data collection, the various schools described the need for relationship building between teachers and students and among students themselves, which they hoped would serve as a critical mediator of academic success. In effect, teachers and student support

staff were considered the "front line" in this work, and much of it was occurring in classrooms. In our examination of administrator interviews, teacher interviews, and student focus groups, there were several descriptive characteristics used to define the type of adult who fosters positive relationships with students. For example, accessibility was mentioned most frequently as the quality students valued in administrators, staff, and teachers. Across schools, participants stressed the importance of teachers and administrators making themselves available to students at virtually any time of day.

The relational engagement construct that we adopted was designed to assess the degree to which students felt that they had supportive relationships with adults or peers and whether or not this led them to feel connected to school. Table 6.7 presents respondent percentages for all

TABLE 6.7
Supportive relationships at school

	Agree	Disagree
There is at least one adult in school I can always count on.	81.8%	18.2%
I feel that there is no one in school who can help me.	16.6%	83.4%
Teachers do not treat me with respect.	27.1%	72.9%
I have at least one friend at school that can help me figure out my homework.	83%	17%
If I have a problem at school there is someone I can count on.	79.1%	20.9%
Teachers do not care about my future.	16.6%	81.1%
There is someone at school who makes me who feel like a successful student.	82%	18%
School is a lonely place where no one cares about me.	16%	83.8%
If I have questions about schoolwork, I can count on someone there to help me.	87.5%	12.5%

Note: Agree combines "agree" and "strongly agree"; Disagree combines "disagree" and "strongly disagree."

relational engagement items. The boys reaffirmed the adult support re-lationships we described in chapter 4. Not only did the majority of the boys say they had adults to go to, but they also felt these adults cared about their future and academic progress.

With the exception of the item pertaining to perceptions of respect from teachers, it appears that the vast majority of students felt con-nected and supported by school staff. We also analyzed the correlations among these variables to understand whether these engagement com-ponents were associated with grades. All three engagement measures were positively associated with grades: behavioral [.373, $p < .01$], cogni-tive [.125, $p < .01$], and relational [.095, $p < .01$]. As stated earlier, this does not mean that engagement causes higher academic performance, rather it points to a positive association in which more engagement oc-curs in concert with growth in academic performance as measured by grades.

Putting the Secret Sauce Together: How Do Climate, Instruction, and Engagement Influence Achievement?

As we described in chapter 1, a majority of the boys enrolled at these schools were at least one grade level behind when they arrived. When we looked at the academic performance of the students during the three years that we carried out our research, the average performance was at best in the C range. Calculated as a percentage, average cumulative grades were around 71.5% in both Year 1—the baseline year—and Year 2. The distribution of grades for our sample by percentile is represented in figure 6.2 below. The lowest performing students (20th percentile) had extraordinarily low grades, averaging just over 60 percent or in the D to D– range. The highest performing students, in the top 20 percent of the sample or 80th percentile, earned on average 82.4 percent. It is also apparent that from Year 1 to Year 2 students demonstrated limited growth in GPA. However, they did not experience a downturn in per-formance as is often observed in other research studies on Black and Latino boys.[7]

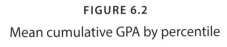

FIGURE 6.2

Mean cumulative GPA by percentile

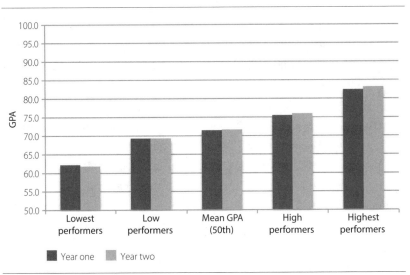

Though on average there was relatively little growth in academic performance (as measured by grades) experienced by students, we wanted to probe whether there might have been other changes occurring that were not revealed in grades. For example, we wanted to know whether students were developing skills and attributes associated with resilience, and if they were acquiring the attitudes and motivation that might eventually contribute to their academic performance. In other words, given that the qualitative data collected for the study among the practitioners led us to believe that all students were being taught skills that theoretically should lead to higher levels of academic engagement, we wondered whether this would be revealed through the survey data. The implicit theory of change that was operational at each of these schools was premised on the idea that through better instructional quality, strategies that positively affirm identity, higher expectations, and a school climate and culture focused on mitigating identity struggles, student performance would improve. We sought to use our qualitative and quantitative analysis of the data we collected to see if these factors did indeed contribute to academic performance. Using multiple regression predictive analysis, we specified a model where each factor of this protective environment was entered into the model to determine the relative influence of each on students' grades. Figure 6.3 provides a visual representation of our practice-based hypothesis.

Our process involved conducting various statistical analyses in a series of steps. When entered into a multiple regression model, and controlling for where they attended a middle school or high school, the model was found to be statistically significant, with a moderate amount of the variation explained (r^2 = 30%, p < .0001). Table 6.8 (see chapter appendix) provides an overview of the regression model. We found the ways in which the students perceived the interaction of instruction,

FIGURE 6.3

Model of academic performance in single-sex schools

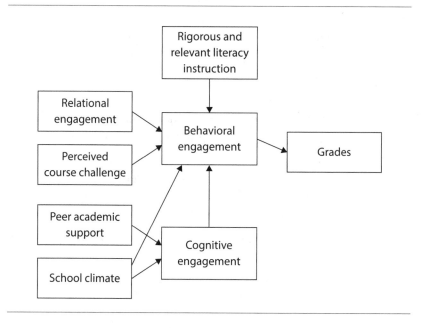

relational engagement, school climate, and behavioral and cognitive engagement explained 30 percent of their grade patterns. Looking more closely at these emerging patterns, behavioral engagement and exposure to rigorous and relevant literacy instruction were found to be significant, and most importantly they were unique predictors of grades as well. These initial findings suggest that, while the schools espoused the importance of getting their students cognitively engaged and exposing them to a rigorous and responsive curriculum, the grades their students actually earned were largely predicted by factors associated with behavioral engagement (see figure 6.3). Behavioral engagement—which is based on the extent to which students exhibit behaviors associated with high performance, such as turning in their homework, participating in class discussions, and so forth—was the single strongest predictor of student grades. Though it is expected that instruction plays a significant role in the academic performance of students, from a student perspective, it is the degree to which they understand how to conduct themselves in school that appears to be most predictive of academic success.

This finding regarding the importance of behavioral engagement is consistent with other research that has found it to be a primary predictor of academic engagement in the United States.[8] Interestingly, while perceived exposure to rigorous and relevant literacy instruction was indeed predictive of grades, it contributed very little (only .3%). This finding does not necessarily suggest that exposure to such curriculum hurts or is of little value to students' performance, but rather that the grading system itself may be, in many cases, more oriented toward rewarding behavior as opposed to the quality of the work that students actually produce. Of course grades are a crude predictor of academic performance because research has shown that they are frequently influenced by highly subjective factors from teachers. However, as we pointed out earlier in the chapter, we were not able to use test scores as the basis for comparison, so we were forced to rely upon grades as a proxy for academic performance.

Despite these limitations the question remains: what are the factors that influence whether or not the students at these schools adopt the skills and embrace the norms related to behavioral engagement? We employed a hierarchical multiple regression to test the relationship between school climate and perceptions of instruction on academic engagement. These regressions were performed to predict the unique influence of school climate and instruction variables on aspects of academic engagement and the relationship between cognitive and relational engagement, and to further predict how these in turn influence behavioral engagement.

The model of best fit was a four-step one that included the control variables, engagement subscales (behavioral, cognitive, and relational), instructional variables, and school climate variables (see table 6.9 in the chapter appendix). Since behavioral engagement accounted for a large percentage of academic performance, we looked at which factors significantly predicted behavioral engagement. Our results showed that school climate and relational (e.g., school-based adult supports) and cognitive engagement were unique predictors of behavioral engagement (see figure 6.3). In other words, **the degree to which students conform to the behavioral expectations of their school is predicted by their sense of fairness, safety, and belonging in the school setting, their intellectual interest in school, and the feeling that they have supportive adult relationships in school.** In particular, a sense of fair treatment accounted positively while a lack of a sense of belonging accounted negatively for behavioral engagement.

We then explored how cognitive engagement was contributing to grades (see table 6.10 in the chapter appendix). Of the individual school climate variables, fair treatment was significant and a positive predictor of cognitive engagement, as were relational engagement and academic peer support. On the other hand, the degree of challenge in ELA courses was a small but significantly negative predictor of cognitive engagement, perhaps suggesting a weak but fragile balance between course content being challenging versus being too difficult as related to students' cognitive engagement. **Thus the degree to which students were intellectually interested in school was determined by the degree to which they felt supported by teachers, perceived the quality of instruction to be challenging, and experienced the school environment as fair.**

Relational Engagement

As we have already stated, our measure of relational engagement is based on the degree to which students perceive themselves as supported by adults in and out of their school. In our single-sex schools, high relational engagement was predicted by feelings of belonging, fair treatment in school process, interest in school, and instructional quality. Cognitive engagement (see table 6.11 in the chapter appendix) added 17.4 percent, while school climate accounted for the largest addition to the variance, adding 25.2 percent to the model on factors predicting relational engagement. **Thus the degree to which boys in these single-sex schools felt that the educators supported them influenced how intellectually interested they were in school. This in turn is also related to feelings of safety, fairness, and belonging that they perceived in school.** This is an important finding because it situates the importance of school-based adult supports as strongly tied to the state of the school climate (e.g., safety, fairness, and belonging).

While only behavioral engagement was found to be directly and uniquely predictive of student grades, upon further examination we found that strong relationships with staff and peers and a supportive school climate, as shown in figure 6.3, were also positively associated with higher student outcomes. School climate and adult-student relationships did not directly influence student grades, but they were found to have indirect influences through their effect upon academic engagement. That is, certain factors relating to climate (peer support, fairness, etc.) and instruction (engaging instruction, etc.) influenced aspects of academic engagement, which in turn influenced the cumulative GPA of students.

Since behavioral engagement was the biggest factor related to students' grades, we also looked at what other factors might significantly predict behavioral engagement. This was done through mediation analysis,[9] a statistical procedure that allows one to examine how behavioral engagement interacts with socioemotional factors, and in turn, with GPA. Our analysis revealed that climate (sense of belonging, fairness, and connectedness), course challenge (perception that teachers hold high expectations, supportive behaviors from adults), and engagement (cognitive and adult supports) were all factors that influenced a student's behavioral engagement. Specifically, our results found that students who reported having supportive and caring relationships with adults, who found their coursework challenging, and reported that their level of cognitive engagement was high, also reported higher levels of behavioral engagement. These findings are consistent and support what we discussed in chapters 3 and 4, where we found that students responded well to being challenged, to feeling connected to adults, and to the college readiness activities available at school. Together, these factors provided students with a concrete sense of what to do in school.

Likewise, both school climate and the degree of course challenge were predictive of cognitive engagement. However, the effect of relationships on cognitive engagement was not the same as on behavioral engagement. Whereas supportive and caring relationships with adults were an important predictor of behavioral engagement, the role of peers—specifically having friends who provided academic support—was important for cognitive engagement, which in turn predicted behavioral engagement. **In other words, students who reported that they surrounded themselves with academically oriented peers also reported higher levels of cognitive engagement.** Additionally, the middle school students who participated in the survey reported significantly higher levels of cognitive engagement than students attending the high schools in our study. It is unclear why such a pattern of cognitive engagement emerged among middle and high school students. However, what is most important to note is the significance of peer influences on cognitive engagement. This is a finding that is reinforced by several research studies.[10]

The Effect of School Climate, Engagement, and Instruction Attitudes on Academic Performance

In this chapter we have presented findings from our analysis of the factors identified in the theory of change. We grounded our analysis on the data collected in our fieldwork to identify the factors that may be contributing to academic achievement (as measured by GPA) in these single-sex schools for Black and Latino boys. We found that academic engagement, relationships, school climate, and factors related to the quality of instruction, were key contributors to academic performance. Among these factors, behavioral engagement was the single most important contributor to academic performance. We also found that being exposed to literacy instruction that is more associated with passive learning and test preparation (e.g., not much writing or personalized instruction) was negatively associated with grades. This suggests that while compliant behavior may contribute to higher grades, the absence of rigorous instruction may undermine them.

Furthermore, we found that school climate and relational factors were indirectly predictive of grades in the following ways: cognitive engagement and supportive and caring relationships with adults emerged as key factors that contributed to behavioral engagement, along with a sense that the coursework they received was challenging. As one would expect, the perception that coursework was challenging contributed to cognitive engagement, but the roles of school climate and peer relationships also emerged as particularly predictive of cognitive engagement.

If students surrounded themselves with peers who provided each other with academic support and reinforced the importance of academic success, and if this occurred in a climate where students felt they belonged to the community and were being treated fairly, the result would likely be higher levels of engagement—the factor that is most strongly associated with positive learning outcomes. These patterns point to a strong relationship between academic performance and school climate are not entirely surprising given prior research on engagement and school performance.[11] The intentional effort on the part of these schools to impart skills and strategies that reinforce norms associated with successful school performance seem to have the effect of producing better academic outcomes for some students and disrupting the stereotypes typically associated with young men of color.

Overall, our statistical analysis and the findings they yielded confirm that the theory of change employed by these schools may in fact be contributing to student success. The socioemotional factors play a very important role in influencing the engagement and performance of the boys. However, the findings also show that the schools have not been successful in reaching all the boys or sustaining socioemotional mechanisms over time. Obviously, producing positive academic outcomes for the majority of students requires ongoing effort. Moreover, these schools (the five that haven't closed) are still relatively new, and while they seem committed to finding ways to meet the needs of all their students, this will clearly require more time to achieve. Despite their commonalities, young men of color are not monolithic; they have diverse needs, learning styles, and sources of motivation. These schools are committed to finding ways to connect with the boys they serve. Clearly it will not be accomplished through a one-size-fits-all approach.

Chapter 6 Appendix

TABLE 6.8

Hierarchical multiple regression of academic engagement, school climate, and instruction challenge on cumulative GPA

	Dependent measure		
	Cumulative GPA, spring semester, 2008		
	R^2 change	*F-value*	*Standardized β*
Step 1: Control variables			
School attended			.429***
Student grade level			−.008
R^2 change (Baseline)	18.2%***	141.4	
Step 2: Engagement predictors			
Behavioral engagement			0.311***
Cognitive engagement			−0.40
Relational engagement			0.077**
R^2 change	10.2%***	60.4	
Step 3: School climate variables			
Sense of fair treatment			.076**
Sense of belonging to school			−.148***
Sense school cohesion			−0.065*
Perceived safety			0.004
Peer support			−.100**
R^2 change	1.9%***	6.9	
Step 4: Instructional challenge			
Course challenge			.054**
Exposure to high literacy			.021
R^2 change	.3%***	2.9	
R^2 total	**30.7%*****		

*Correlation is significant < 0.05 level (2-tailed).

**Correlation is significant < 0.01 level (2-tailed).

***Correlation is significant < 0.001 level (2-tailed).

TABLE 6.9

Hierarchical multiple regression of relational/cognitive engagement and school climate on behavioral engagement

	Dependent measure		
	Behavioral engagement		
	R^2 change	F-value	Standardized β
Step 1: Control variables			
School attended			−0.43
Student grade level			.116***
R^2 change (baseline)	1.3%	8.31	
Step 2: Engagement predictors			
Cognitive engagement			.407***
Relational engagement			.124***
R^2 change	21.9%***	95.51	
Step 3: School climate variables			
Sense of fair treatment			.196***
Sense of belonging to school			−.217***
Sense school cohesion			.136
Perceived safety			−.059
Peer support			−.01
R^2 change	3.7%***	51.6	
R^2 total	26.9%***		

***significant < 0.001 level (2-tailed).

TABLE 6.10

Hierarchical multiple regression of relational engagement, school climate, and perceptions of instruction on cognitive engagement

	Dependent measure		
	Cognitive engagement		
	R^2 change	*F-value*	*Standardized β*
Step 1: Control variables			
School attended			−.120***
Student grade level			.110***
R^2 change (baseline)	2.0%**	13.1	
Step 2: Engagement predictors			
Relational engagement			.436***
R^2 change	18.0%***	105.7	
Step 3: School climate variables			
Sense of fair treatment			.231***
Sense of belonging to school			−.183***
Sense school cohesion			.034
Perceived safety			−.025
Peer academic support			.406***
R^2 change	16.1%***	89.05	
Step 4: Instructional predictors			
ELA course challenge			−.046*
Exposure to instruction related to high literacy			.028
R^2 change	.2%	71.8	
R^2 total	**36.3%**		

*significant < 0.05 level (2-tailed).

**significant < 0.01 level (2-tailed).

***significant < 0.001 level (2-tailed).

TABLE 6.11

Hierarchical multiple regression of cognitive engagement, school climate, OST, and instruction on relational engagement

	Dependent measure		
	Relational engagement		
	R^2 change	F-value	Standardized β
Step 1: Control variables			
School attended			−.228****
Student grade level			.123***
R^2 change (baseline)	5.4%**	36.2	
Step 2: Engagement predictors			
Cognitive engagement		124.5	.421***
R^2 change	17.4%***		
Step 3: School climate variables			
Sense of fair treatment			.269***
Sense of belonging to school			.249***
Sense school cohesion			.09***
Perceived safety			−.011
Peer academic support			.083**
R^2 change	25.2%***	145.7	
Step 4: Instructional predictors			
ELA course challenge			.090***
ELA exposure to literacy instruction			.090***
R^2 change	1.6%***	124.0	
R^2 total	**49.6%**		

*significant <0.05 level (2-tailed).

**significant < 0.01 level (2-tailed). .

***significant < 0.001 level (2-tailed).

7

Creating Protective
School Environments

A Framework for Reform

For those who are advocates of single-sex education, who see separating boys, especially Black and Latino boys, as a solution to the critical social problems they face in American society, this book may be a disappointment. Rather than a ringing endorsement and resounding affirmation of the value they add and of their potential to serve as a "silver bullet" solution to the problems facing Black and Latino boys, our research shows that the issues related to the education and social development of boys are too complex to lend themselves to simple solutions. The findings from these seven carefully examined schools do provide insights into the strategies that seem to be effective at addressing the academic and social needs of young men of color, but they have not yielded clear, positive evidence that single-sex education is the most effective way to protect Black and Latino boys.

In many important respects, that is not what our exploration into these single-sex schools has been about. Though we started our study with the goal of trying to understand whether or not single-sex education held the potential for ameliorating some of the hardships confronting males of color in the United States, we soon realized that what we were really learning about was how groups of educators who were committed to this goal undertook the task of designing and administering schools to protect boys of color. More specifically, we learned quickly that our study needed to unpack the theory of change guiding the development of these schools so that we could understand how the practitioners sought to understand and address the structural and cultural realities confronting this marginalized population.

We were surprised to find how similar the approaches adopted by these seven schools were as they devised strategies to create a protective environment that would develop the resilience of young men of color. While many of the educators did in fact attend conferences together where they spoke to others about single-sex education, they never met during the early years when their schools were being established, and never came together to share ideas about curriculum, teaching, school culture, youth development, or student support; nevertheless, they ended up designing schools that were remarkably alike in many important ways.

To those familiar with the history of educational opportunity policy in the United States over the last forty years, this finding might not seem surprising. As we pointed out in chapter 1, the problems confronting Black and Latino males, in schools and in society, have been well known for some time. Even though single-sex schools may be a relatively recent intervention designed to address those challenges, other interventions have been around for much longer. Mentoring programs like the Omega Boys Club in San Francisco[1] and Archbishop Malloy High School's leadership program[2] have been around for many years. So too have community-based interventions like Beacon schools, Boys Clubs, and Big Brothers/Big Sisters of America, as well as rites-of-passage programs like Simba. These community-based programs and interventions, which in many ways are the precursors to the single-sex schools and the strategies they have employed, are well known to educators and youth service providers who focus on serving the needs of Black and Latino males.

However, creating a school that can meet the academic and social needs of young men of color is far more challenging than merely establishing a community program. For this reason, while some of the new schools that we examined in this study are exemplary and clearly better than many of the traditional public schools where so many Black and Latino males experience failure, others have struggled in delivering quality education to the young men they serve. In fact, two of the schools that were originally part of this study have since been closed by the districts they were part of due to poor academic performance.[3] While the decision to close these schools may not have been based on sound policy nor even have been fair to the schools and the students they served, the fact is that the schools that were closed were struggling. With graduation and achievement rates that were below 50 percent, low levels of proficiency as measured by student performance on state exams, and a lack of demand for enrollment as measured by the number of applicants received, these schools clearly were not thriving.

For this reason, we maintain that despite their strengths and the good intentions of the educators who are advocates of this model, our findings do not suggest that single-sex schools should necessarily be embraced as models for educational intervention. If state and federal laws continue to uphold their creation, single-sex schools may be an option that should be made available to parents who believe their sons will benefit from such an alternative, but it should not be held up as a panacea. While it is clear that something must be done to address the pervasive failure among Black and Latino males in American public schools, it is not clear that this is the intervention that will solve the broad array of problems they face.

A Targeted Approach to School Reform to Address the Needs of Boys of Color

Despite their struggles, what we learned about the experience of these schools and the boys attending them is relevant to any educators, parents, or community groups interested in creating protective school environments that intend to foster resilience and improve opportunities for academic success among boys of color. Since the passage of the Elementary and Secondary Education Act (ESEA) in 1965 by President

Lyndon Johnson, school reform in the United States has been characterized by a series of sweeping initiatives that have been offered periodically as a means to overhaul and elevate American education to new heights. In most cases, reforms have been promoted by advocates and elected officials as a means to improve the academic performance of American students and make it possible for the nation to maintain (or reclaim) its competitive advantage. These reform moments have been marked by bold promises such as those that accompanied Goals 2000, adopted by President Bill Clinton, and No Child Left Behind, by President George W. Bush. Education historians David Tyack and Larry Cuban have characterized such efforts and the letdown that has inevitably accompanied them "as an elusive march toward utopia"[4] and point out that the grand promises of reform are typically issued each time a new administration, at the state or federal level, assumes office.

More often than not, the school reform strategies promoted by policy makers, foundations, and many educators have ignored the underlying social and economic challenges that impact education, and, consequently, an important dimension of America's educational challenges have not been addressed. Tyack and Cuban argue that the reforms promoted by elected officials have typically "avoided intractable problems such as social inequality and racial discrimination and placed unrealistic expectations upon schools."[5] For this reason, most of the reforms adopted over the last forty years have done little to improve schools in low-income communities, and the schools that have needed help the most have proven to be the hardest to help.[6]

The single-sex schools we examined in this study were created with the explicit purpose of serving a segment of the population that has been historically underserved and whose needs for effective educational interventions were glaring and obvious. Unlike most reform initiatives, these schools adopted strategies that were explicitly designed to protect the young men of color from the hardships they frequently encounter in the low-income urban communities where they reside, and they sought to promote resilience and academic success so that those students would have an alternative to traditional schools where failure was normalized.

Even though these schools lacked the resources to meet the social and emotional needs of their students or to truly mitigate the harm present in the local context, they went to great lengths to protect and shield them from harm, and when we found areas where they clearly fell short, there was no doubt that their efforts were genuine and sincere.

The strategy that most of these schools relied on to protect young men from environmental harm consisted of efforts to promote resilience and self-esteem through a culturally relevant curriculum, positive adult relationships, peer academic support, concrete efforts at planning for college, the development of a school climate that encouraged fairness and belonging, and a relentless focus on academic press. All of the schools attempted to provide their students with access to adult mentors who could provide guidance and support, but they could not ensure access to trained professionals such as social workers, psychologists, dentists, or nurses, who could address more complex needs. Educators that we interviewed acknowledged that many of the students had a broad range of psychological and health needs that were not being met. However, they also acknowledged the limitations of what was possible with the resources at their disposal. As the principal at Thomas Jefferson put it:

> Of course we would like to do more for these young men. So many of them come to us needing counseling, or needing to get their teeth or eyes examined. I wish we could help, and sometimes we provide referrals to health centers, but there's only so much we can do. Besides, the most important thing for us is to stay focused on the academics because that's what they need to insure their future and that's how we will be judged.

The need to focus narrowly on academic achievement at the expense of other important developmental needs, acknowledged with some regret by the principal, is common to many schools in urban areas, but it is actually a fairly recent development. During the 1960s and 1970s much of the effort to reform urban public schools in the United States focused on desegregation and the need to reduce the effects of poverty on children.[7] School busing initiatives, Head Start programs, magnet schools, and TRIO college preparation programs (e.g., Upward Bound, McNair Scholars, and Talent Search), were designed to counter the pernicious effects of racial segregation and concentrated poverty in inner-city communities.[8] The thinking guiding these initiatives was that by deliberately addressing the lack of opportunity and social issues related to poverty, improved academic outcomes for students could be obtained.[9] It was in effect a very different theory of change than the one adopted by the seven schools in our study or by many others that operate in urban areas today. There is evidence that to some degree the strategy worked, and several researchers have found that considerable progress was made during this period in reducing disparities in achievement and increasing graduation rates as a result of these broader social reforms.[10]

However, following the release of *A Nation at Risk* in 1983, the educational reforms that were pursued in the 1980s and 1990s—such as those called for in the 1994 Goals 2000 act, a blueprint for reform initiated under the first Bush administration and passed into law under President Bill Clinton—have placed greater emphasis on raising academic standards and increasing the accountability of educators and students. Increasingly, reformers have downplayed the importance of addressing social needs or ameliorating the effects of poverty. With the adoption of No Child Left Behind in 2001, school reform efforts have concentrated to an even greater degree on raising academic standards and increasing accountability through the use of high-stakes testing. More recently, under the banner of "No Excuses," a new generation of reformers, many of whom are ardent supporters of charter schools, have gone even further in narrowing the focus of school reform to strategies that boost student achievement (as measured by performance on standardized tests) and derided those who suggested that poverty is an obstacle to student achievement.[11] Instead, the new reformers call for strict discipline and a highly regimented form of teaching that writers such as Doug Whitman have described as a new form of paternalism.[12] Such approaches have supplanted the context-focused reforms of the previous era such as the full-service schools championed by the

Children's Aid Society and scholars like James Comer in the 1990s.[13] The assumption guiding the new wave of reform is that improved student academic outcomes can be obtained by altering conditions within schools, in effect ignoring the social and economic circumstances of the homes and communities where students live.

This is the reform context in which the new single-sex schools have been created. Given the persistence of high levels of academic failure among African American and Latino males,[14] and given that so many of the challenges they face lie outside of school—gangs, drug trafficking, interpersonal violence, and high arrest and incarceration rates[15]— it would be truly remarkable if a narrow focus on raising academic achievement could positively alter their life outcomes. This is not to suggest that the schools we've profiled were mistaken to focus their efforts on social and emotional development, adult support networks, peer academic support, a school climate of fairness and belonging, or the quality of teaching their students received. The findings from this study suggest that the schools that have done the most to create a clear and coherent strategy for delivering instruction, and that have succeeded in creating a safe and orderly learning climate, are doing a far better job in meeting the needs of the young men they serve than traditional schools in the same neighborhoods. However, the data on outcomes for Black and Latino males suggests that more is needed and that good intentions and heroic efforts to create good schools will not be enough.

Advocates of single-sex schools for African American and Latino boys would do well to learn from the experience of past reforms that promised a great deal but largely failed to deliver the improved academic outcomes that had been sought. As is true with many of the new single-sex schools, it would be unfair to characterize all of the past reform initiatives as failures. In fact, it could be argued that many of the reforms that were heralded as breakthrough innovations in the past—site-based management, small schools, block scheduling—were not given enough time to take hold before being scrapped and replaced by something new. In fact, several scholars have argued that our nation's inability to stick with a reform strategy long enough to see if it bears fruit is a major part of the reason we aren't making more progress in the effort to improve schools.[16] As Tyack and Cuban point out, many reforms have been scrapped without ever being evaluated simply because of changes in political leadership. Cynical observers have argued that school reform itself has become a multibillion-dollar industry comprised of think tanks, consultants, and a variety of nonprofits. Like other industries that have sprung up in response to pressing social problems, critics charge that the reformers actually have been complicit in school failure because success would effectively end their *raisons d'être* and drive them out of business.[17] Taking a less cynical perspective, Hess[18] has argued that the tumultuous nature of educational politics at the local level—contentious battles over school governance and protracted conflicts over wages and work rules with labor unions, to name just two of the more common conflicts—have been the major factors contributing to the lack of progress in the nation's efforts to improve public education. Finally, several critics have argued that the reforms have failed because in many cases the theory of change guiding them has been weak and has not taken into account all of the related changes that are necessary for a particular reform to yield positive results.[19] There have also been several cases in which those who legislated a reform were unaware of the adverse and unintended consequences that might result if a particular reform (e.g., smaller class size) were pursued.[20]

Critical Education Reform

For the reasons detailed above, it is important for those who have embraced single-sex schools as a solution to the numerous challenges and hardships confronting Black and Latino boys to learn lessons from the recent history of school reform, or they may be doomed to repeat the mistakes of the past. Many of the educational reforms implemented over the last forty years have not succeeded in bringing about higher levels of achievement for the most-at-risk students, especially young men of color, nor have they resulted in improvements in the most disadvantaged schools. Unlike other reforms, the current effort to create single-sex schools has most frequently been promoted by Black and Latino educators and community leaders. They have done so out of a genuine desire to do something to "save boys" from the hardships that destroy the lives of so many. This study clearly shows that some of the measures they have adopted are effective, while others have had more limited impact. The advocates of single-sex education would therefore do well to learn from the mistakes of past reforms and continue to search for ways to solve the large and complex problems they have chosen to address rather than to simply embrace single-sex education as a panacea.

This study also suggests that the educators who are creating these new single-sex schools should be guided by clear thinking based on sound educational practices. Clearly, Black and Latino boys need what every student in America needs—excellent, caring teachers, a supportive learning environment, access to a rigorous and engaging curriculum, and a safe school led by a committed and visionary educational leader. Some of the schools in this study had all of these ingredients to varying degrees, and not surprisingly their students excelled. These schools and others like them located in communities scattered throughout the country remind us that *the problem is not who we serve but how they are served*. This point must be impressed upon educators who have lapsed into blaming the students they serve, who perceive them through their deficits and regard their families as broken and pathological. Poverty, crime, gangs, and other social problems that are endemic to many low-income neighborhoods are real and pose formidable challenges to educating children of all kinds, but they do not negate the ability of children to learn when schools can mitigate some of the adversity.[21] Such obstacles are especially dangerous to boys of color. When the pull of the streets is more powerful than the lure of the classroom, and when constant bombardment by negative stereotypes results in a distorted image of who they are and what they can be, young African American and Latino males can be drawn onto a path of failure and delinquency at an early age. However, the successful schools that exist show us that these obstacles can be countered and even overcome by educators who work closely with parents and communities to design positive learning environments that meet the needs of the children they serve.

Of course, creating such schools is not easy. If it were, the problems facing Black and Latino males would have been solved long ago. This book was written as a call to action for educators, parents, and policy makers to address the issues confronting young men of color with a sense of urgency, and to treat those issues as an *American problem*, rather than as an African American or Latino problem. The continued failure of so many young men increases the likelihood not just that they will end up permanently unemployed, in prison, or dead at an early age, but that our society will accept such conditions as normal. To the degree that we accept these disastrous trends as inevitable, all of us are endangered.

APPENDIX 1

Descriptions of the Schools

Thomas Jefferson Academy for Young Men
History and Community Context

Thomas Jefferson Academy is located in a large Midwestern city, a predominantly Black community that historically served as an early beacon of hope for African Americans escaping racial segregation in the South. This legacy is a source of inspiration for school officials because it links the school's present goals to its past legacy. At the time of the study, Thomas Jefferson was the city's first and only public charter high school for young men.[1] The school was founded in 2002 by a group of African American education, business, and civic leaders and is part of Cross Plain, a nonprofit organization that manages and operates the school.

According to the school's official public relations packet, "Thomas Jefferson was born out of this group's experience of working with, and supporting, an independent high school serving young African American men." The success experienced at the independent private school inspired the group to attempt to apply the model in a public setting. The founder and CEO of Thomas Jefferson, James Jackson, has a history of working with African American boys in urban settings from his previous experience as head of a Catholic high school primarily serving Black boys.

Jackson's vision had been influenced by his prior experience at the private school. He wanted to take the best elements from that model and apply them to a public school in a setting for families who could not afford private education.[2] This vision, as we had learned over the course of our four years at the school, included replicating the model to eventually create five Thomas Jefferson Academy campuses.

The school officially opened in September of 2006. Mr. Jackson described its creation as "a direct response to the urgent need to reverse abysmal graduation and college completion rates among young men in urban centers, particularly African American males." With such ambitious goals, the mission of Thomas Jefferson is to provide its young men with a rigorous college preparatory education and the social skills they will need to succeed. The school is not only focused on preparing students to enter college, but is committed to supporting them through college as well.

Throughout the period when we carried out research at the school (2006–2009), we noticed many large, empty lots of land in the neighborhood surrounding the school, some with unfinished construction. The main street leading up to the school contained a combination of boarded-up buildings, liquor stores, pawnshops, and the occasional fast-food place. On our way to the school, we frequently spotted several police cars making stops throughout the community. There is a public library that appears to have been recently constructed. The neighborhood itself appears to have once been a stable working-class community that has recently been in decline.

Within three of the blocks adjoining the school, we counted twelve houses that were boarded up. There is a mix of apartment buildings and dwellings that contain multiple units.

Thomas Jefferson is located on the third floor of the Landing High School Campus building—a block-long structure with enormous pillars lined across the front entrance and an adjacent running track. The third floor, where Thomas Jefferson is housed, has a large rectangular shape. Each side of the rectangle contains classrooms and offices. In the center of the school there is a glass enclosure that makes it possible for you to look down to the second floor and into the library. The hallways are lined with college banners and artifacts from college fraternities. The walls hold displays of "Intriguing African Americans," from Louis Farrakhan to Oprah Winfrey, and to sports icons such as the Williams sisters. There are posters of "African American Firsts" showing great inventors, astronauts, athletes, and artists. There is also some artwork on a door depicting young African American heroes.

Student Recruitment and Demographics

Thomas Jefferson had approximately 150 Black boys in its inaugural ninth-grade class and expanded until reaching their full cohort of 565 students attending ninth through twelfth grades (see chapter 1, table 1.1). According to the director of development and recruitment, students are heavily recruited from the local elementary and middle schools. During recruiting visits, information cards are passed out to interested parents and students. The cards are returned to Thomas Jefferson, after which each interested household is contacted to encourage them to consider choosing the school and to answer any additional questions.

Thomas Jefferson also holds an open house so that parents and potential students can meet teachers and get more information about the school. It is at this point where the admissions process begins and students and parents fill out applications. The boys are randomly chosen from the pool of applicants, with a wait list created for those students who did not get selected in the initial lottery. In the first lottery, 160 students were selected.

Once admitted, the boys are then required to attend a summer program to prepare for the academic demands of the school. If the selectees do not come to the summer session, they lose their spot at the school and one of the boys on the wait list is admitted.

Organizational Structure

Thomas Jefferson operates using a shared leadership approach. The school's CEO is more than merely the educational leader. He is also responsible for public relations and fundraising. Mr. Jackson takes this responsibility very seriously, speaking about his school with a passion and enthusiasm that is more like one might expect from a moral leader than from a typical school principal.

In addition to Mr. Jackson, several individuals serve as administrators at the school, managing different components of school operations. For example, the director of development and recruitment focuses on student recruitment, the vice president of academic affairs focuses on academic activities such as curriculum support and professional development, the vice president of student programs focuses on nonacademic activities such as discipline and community service activities, and the vice president of finance and facilities focuses on budgetary operation of the school. Thomas Jefferson also has a board of directors and several councils that assist in the expansion of the school.

In 2006–2007, the staff at Thomas Jefferson consisted of twenty-three employees (including administrators and assistants), the majority of whom were Black males. Eleven of the staff members were teachers, including a special education coordinator; of these, two were White male, one was a Black female, and eight were Black males (an additional female teacher left the school in the middle of the year for personal reasons).

The teaching staff had an average of six years of experience. Five of the teachers had master's degrees. In addition to teaching in their subject areas, many of the teachers served as Pack leaders, meeting with students twice a day during the Pack periods which serve as a time for counseling and academic support. Teachers also assisted in organizing the students during the daily morning community meetings. Moreover, several of the teachers led afterschool and extracurricular activities, as well as providing extra help to students before and after school.

In the student handbook, all of the faculty e-mail addresses were listed along with their phone extensions. Staff meetings and professional development were held every Wednesday after the end of the early release. These professional development sessions varied in topic. During some of our observations, the sessions focused on differentiated instruction, analyzing recent assessment data, and discussions of upcoming events such as college road trips and special guest speakers to the school. In addition, throughout the school year the staff attended longer professional-development workshops and an annual retreat.

Curriculum

The school's public-relations packet describes the curriculum in the following way: "The Thomas Jefferson approach to education is to encircle the student with four connecting arcs that provide a comprehensive educational experience." The four arcs are: Academic, Activity, Service, and Professional. The Academic curricular arc corresponds to rigorous college-preparatory curriculum and instruction that focuses on reading, writing, and public speaking. The Activity curricular arc includes participation in a variety of extracurricular activities. Each student is required to participate in at least two extracurricular activities (credit and grades are given). The goal is to use these activities to develop their confidence, interpersonal skills, leadership qualities, and respect for others. The purpose of the Service curricular arc is to develop students' sense of responsibility to community through service learning projects. To this end, students work in groups to identify a problem in the community and then design a project to address or fix the problem. The Professional curricular arc aims to develop students' vocational goals and sense of professional possibilities.

Toward these ends, once a week during their junior and senior years, students participate in year-long internships with corporations and businesses. The internships are designed to provide an opportunity for students to increase their understanding of the business world, reinforce character and leadership development, and serve as a means for students to gain valuable work experience.

School Climate, Extra- and Co-Curricular Programs and Activities

In addition to the curricular arcs, other aspects of the curriculum are designed to create a culture of academic seriousness at the school. This includes providing students with their own Apple laptop computers. Students receive their laptops in the morning, carry them throughout the school day in a compact, over-the-shoulder carrying case, and return them at the end of the day, where they are locked up in a storage cart.

The school has a strict uniform policy. The boys wear khaki pants, dress shoes, a belt, tucked-in white dress shirts, red ties, and black blazers. Compliance with the uniform policy is checked every morning during the ritual of the daily community meeting, called Community Time. The computers and the uniforms are symbols that convey the high expectations the school holds toward the students. It also sends the message that the school is willing to invest in making sure they succeed.

During Community Time, students line up in rows by their "Packs" (advisory-like groups whose lead teacher stays with the group for all four years). The students line up by height within each Pack. Every staff member, including members of the office staff, joins in the ritual. The community meeting includes celebrations of individual student success, Pack group victories, whole-school accomplishments, and general announcements of upcoming events. This time is also used to address shortcomings and infractions that may be prevalent among the student body, such as arriving late to school, taking too long to get in line, missing assignments, and so forth. Community Meetings are a time when student council speeches are made and students who have been exceptionally hardworking are acknowledged with gold ties that they wear all week long. During the meeting, the students in gold ties are asked to come to the stage and lead the school in reciting the school's creed:

We Believe.
We are the young men of Thomas Jefferson.
We are college bound.
We are exceptional—not because we say it, but because we work
    hard at it.
We will not falter in the face of any obstacle placed before us.
We are dedicated, committed and focused.
We never succumb to mediocrity, uncertainty or fear.
We never fail because we never give up.
We make no excuses.
We choose to live honestly, nonviolently and honorably.
We respect ourselves and, in doing so, we respect all people.

We have a future for which we are accountable.
We have a responsibility to our families, community and world.
We are our brother's keepers.
We believe in ourselves.
We believe in each other.
We believe in Thomas Jefferson.
WE BELIEVE.

Another significant element of the extracurricular experience at Thomas Jefferson is the exposure to well-known artists, politicians, and intellectuals that these boys are not accustomed to meeting or interacting with. For example, during one of our visits Harvard University Professor Henry Louis Gates was a featured speaker at the school. On another occasion, Spike Lee was the invited speaker. One administrator described the need for these events as opportunities for the boys to see successful African Americans who were raised in communities like their own. The school administrators hope that such exposure will inspire their students to succeed and to believe that they can overcome the obstacles that they may encounter. One staff member explained the purpose behind these events in this way:

> To succeed in life, one, they need the basics of education, they need an opportunity to go on to college, they need an opportunity to be successful when they get to college. And two, they need to have the doors open up for them, they need some doors to some places that they've never been, begin to open up for them. One of the things that we've been doing so far in this freshman year is making sure that our guys get some exposure that they normally wouldn't have. We've taken our guys to some Urban League dinners; we took a lot of our guys down to see Barack Obama when he announced his presidential candidacy. And that's just the sort of thing that would usually be outside of their reach. We want to make sure that they see that these are many people, who in many respects come from where you come from, these are people who can relate to what you go through on a day-to-day basis and they have these personal success stories, and so can you. If

Barack can be a success, then so can you. If you can meet these people who had similar experiences to you and they overcame those challenges, then you can do the same thing.

The final component of Thomas Jefferson's extracurricular program is the afterschool program. The school operates from 8:30 a.m. to 4:30 p.m., with afterschool enrichment activities offered until 6:00 p.m. During many visits, we would find a significant proportion of the student body still in the school after 4:30 p.m.

The afterschool activities include basketball, football, track, choir, and student council, to name a few. Though these clubs are based on faculty interest and availability, students also have the opportunity to start their own clubs if they get enough signatures on a petition. The goal is to provide the boys at Thomas Jefferson with an enhanced educational experience, one that is so positive and compelling that it makes it possible for the students they serve to succeed in school and in life.

North Star Academy for Young Men
History and Community Context

North Star Academy for Young Men, a high school in a large Northeastern city, was created in 2004. The group 100 Black Men, Inc., a national organization formed for the purpose of organizing successful Black men to support other Black men and boys, played a key role in its creation of the school. The organization was central in shaping the school's focus on character development and mentoring, and it provides ongoing support to the school.

According to Principal Darrell Trust, North Star Academy was developed out of conversations among leaders of 100 Black Men, Inc., that he and other members of the organization held to discuss the "national crisis that is impacting young men of color" and the need for a school in their metropolitan area that better served young Black men. In explaining the idea behind the development of the school, Principal Trust articulated the rationale with a sense of urgency: "We wanted to create a public school where young men would have an opportunity to come and be exposed to a level of expectation around character development and leadership that would really help to shape the future of this city and this nation."

North Star Academy's promotional materials distinguish the school from other urban high schools. The glossy promotional materials feature young men in ties and blazers and describe the safety and orderliness of the school environment, as well as the high level of student "Pack and fraternity" evident among students. The materials also emphasize the school's focus on college preparation and "academic excellence" that is achieved through the academic rigor of the curriculum, the school's discipline and dress codes, and the special programs, including the mentoring program, Saturday Institute, and the mandatory two-hour extended day program.

Principal Trust stated that he aimed to create a "professional environment" at the school, but also one that is a "small family environment" where staff "feel very comfortable, enjoy coming to work every day, and are prepared to just work very, very hard to make things happen for our young men." The school's promotional material also emphasizes leadership, teamwork, and community service as character traits promoted among students. According to the school's mission, members of the school community aim to "be citizens of integrity who will become lifelong leaders through team building and servicing our community." North Star Academy is not reticent about proclaiming that its core values are "academic excellence, leadership, character development, mentoring, integrity, and community service."

During the 2006–2007 school year, North Star Academy was housed within two separate neighboring school facilities. North Star South was housed in a separate school, referred to as the Math and Science Building, while North Star North shared space with a middle school in a facility referred to as the Humanities Building. North Star Academy cafeteria, Town Hall, library, and afterschool program activities were housed in the Math and Science Building. This disjointed arrangement, while common among schools throughout the city due to space shortages, was not ideal for the type of learning environment the school was trying to create. Fortunately, the school was able to move into a brand-new facility in the fall of 2009.

North Star Academy is located in a residential area made up of large and small apartment buildings, including public housing apartments. It is situated just a few blocks away from a major boulevard and an interstate highway. The school is approximately five blocks from a well-known sports complex, which provides close and easy access to trains and buses that service the area. More than 90 percent of residents of the immediate neighborhood around the school are renters, and in 1999 the median household income of $24,802 was about 65 percent of the annual household income in the metropolitan area. The poverty rate in the neighborhood was 25 percent—approximately 4 percentage points higher than the rate for the city as a whole. The racial makeup of the surrounding neighborhood is nearly evenly divided between people identifying themselves as Black (52%) and Latino (49%).

Student Recruitment and Demographics

During the 2006–07 school year, North Star enrolled 269 students in the ninth, tenth, and eleventh grades and added an additional 125 ninth-graders in the fall of 2007—growing to serve approximately 400 students. The school is made up almost exclusively of boys who self-identify as Black or Latino, with nearly two-thirds of the school's population identified as Black and one-third as Latino.

According to the school guidance counselor, the majority of students at North Star live in the neighborhood in the general vicinity of the school, but students also come from other areas of the city. North Star Academy is designated as a "limited unscreened program" in which admission priority is given to students who attend school information sessions. Principal Trust stated that the school holds a series of open houses each year so that students and their parents can see the school and learn about the academic program and the school's special programs and policies.

Parents complete a North Star Academy application and are asked to provide student records, including eighth-grade report cards and attendance reports. Parents and students are also encouraged to return to the school to speak with teachers and other staff in order to "see if they think it's a good fit." The process, according to Principal Trust, also allows school staff to determine who they believe would be a good match for their school. Administrators often encourage those students to select North Star Academy as their first option on the high school application. Both Principal Trust and the guidance counselor stated that they work to enroll students who know about the school program and want to attend an all-male school. The guidance counselor stated that approximately 60 percent of the students assigned to the program had been interviewed at the school and that the administration hoped to reach a point in the future where all admitted students had been interviewed.

Organizational Structure

North Star Academy for Young Men "is the result of an ongoing partnership between 100 Black Men, Inc. and the district Department of Education." The school has a board of directors and is also supported by the North Star Academy Foundation, a nonprofit, 501c(3) foundation, which was established to provide support for the Academy as well as other educational initiatives like it. The foundation raises supplemental resources to support the school and has a full-time executive director.

Principal Trust was the founding principal of a nearby high school, a position he held for seven years. He left this post to be the founder of North Star Academy for Young Men. Mr. Trust sees his role as "half principal, half national spokesman." About the latter he stated, "This is a much larger vision and beginning of what I see as a real national movement to say that our boys can make it, and a call to action to men all around this country to get up off their butts and to get involved and to do something about [it]."

Mr. Trust is a charismatic figure who has been very successful in generating financial and political support for the school. An assistant principal, Mr. Galloway, supports Principal Trust by overseeing the day-today operation of the school and the teacher recruitment committee. In addition to the assistant principal, the school has a well-rounded staff including a second assistant principal, two directors of mentoring/dean of students, a director of student life, director of college planning, coordinator of student services, director of internships and community service, a social worker, and a guidance counselor.

Curriculum

North Star Academy divides the academic year into two semesters with six-week marking periods. Parents are informed of their child's academic progress through progress reports that are distributed six times a year. In addition, parents have access to their sons' grades online throughout the semester. School begins at 8:15 a.m. and ends at 3:45 p.m.—a total of seven and a half hours. This is significantly longer than the typical six-hour school day at traditional public high schools.

North Star Academy emphasizes academic rigor as part of its mission. Some of the courses offered at North Star Academy are listed in the following table:

School Climate, Extra- and Co-Curricular Programs and Activities

The disciplinary rules at North Star are extensively outlined in the Student Handbook. Discipline is tracked through the use of the Discipline for Character (DFC) card, which records any infractions its holder may have committed. Students must have their DFC card at all times and must relinquish it to any school administrator at his/her request. If any student does not have his DFC card, he will receive an automatic detention. Each infraction counts for one point. After six points, its cardholder will receive an automatic detention.

Detention is served in the school during lunch or after school from 4:30 to 6:30 p.m. If a student fails to complete an assigned detention, he receives a one-day in-school suspension. Infractions are categorized into four levels depending upon their severity. They range from receiving a point against the student on his DFC card to an automatic Super-

TABLE A.1

Course selections at North Star Academy

Core four year subjects	Electives or additional requirements
Living Environment	French I, II
Earth Science	Music
Spanish I, II, Native Spanish Language Arts	Writing/Public Speaking
Physics	U.S. Government/Economics
Chemistry	Global History I, II
Concepts in Chemistry	U.S. History
Algebra II/Trigonometry	Health
Intermediate Geometry	Physical Education
Geometry	Accounting
Pre-Algebra	
Algebra	
Pre-Calculus	
English I, II, III, IV	

intendent suspension, which may be accompanied by police involvement for criminal offenses and/or parental notification. The Student Handbook informs students that they "must always bear in mind that any conduct that is harmful to the good name of the school or the good of the community will be subject to disciplinary action. The North Star discipline is self-discipline."

The school uniform consists of "scholastic" gray pants, black belts, and a long- or short-sleeved light blue dress shirt. The shirts are to be "tucked in" at all times. In addition, students must wear "dress shoes or black boots." The school has a dress-down version of the uniform, which can be worn on Fridays. This version includes construction-style boots, tan khakis, and a blue North Star polo shirt. The school does not allow headgear, including hats, combs, brushes, berets, or do-rags, nor any visible piercings. The Student Handbook asserts that these regulations "are made to encourage habits of neatness, order, good taste, and professionalism."

North Star Academy provides an Extended Day program that includes activities in martial arts, trumpet instruction, debate team, poetry enrichment, and chess. In addition to their Extended Day programs, North Star also offers a Saturday Institute. The Institute's focus is on the social development of the young men. Activities include financial literacy, health and wellness, and cultural literacy. The structure of this program varies by grades: ninth graders are required to attend, but for tenth and eleventh graders attendance is voluntary, though highly encouraged. SAT preparation and other extracurricular activities are offered for all students.

Among the special events that North Star offers is the end-of-year welcome for new (incoming) students and their parents, called Celebrating Fathers and Mentors, at which students who have just completed the academic year are acknowledged for their accomplishments and special praise is meted out to students who have demonstrated improvement. The event involves a college fair for students and their parents.

The school provides a Summer Bridge program. This program is designed to assess students' skill levels and to address deficiencies before they enter the ninth grade. North Star has an impressive parent outreach program as well. On one Saturday per month, parents are invited to attend workshops at the school focused on issues related to parenting and providing academic support to their sons. On each of the occasions when we attended these workshops, turnout was high (300 to 400 parents were present) and parents were effusive in their praise for the school.

Westward Leadership Academy
History and Community Context

Westward Leadership Academy opened in 2005–2006 in a large Northeastern city, with a mission to develop boys of color, grades six through twelve, into urban leaders by preparing them for success in college, advanced studies, and a professional career. "Strong, Capable, and Conscious" are the words featured in school brochures to describe the kind of leaders Westward works to cultivate. As future leaders, students are encouraged to be morally strong so they can do what is right no matter how hard it might be. They must be capable so that they can do whatever is required, both with respect to their academic performance but also regarding their ability to exercise good judgment outside of school.

The principal of Westward, Clem Carver, developed the mission based on his participation in the district's principal training program. Principal Carver explained that several of the themes that are central to his vision were inspired by his participation in a fraternity conference in early 2005.

Westward is located inside a middle school building with four floors. The school occupies the top two floors of the building, while another middle school occupies the lower two floors. Its students have two entrances from the street that they may use to access the school. The current layout has the school shaped like a T, with one long corridor leading to two shorter "wings" at one end of the school. The two wings are organized by grade (6th graders on one side and 7th graders on the other). At the end of each wing are stairwells that are not utilized. In addition to housing the seventh graders, the southern wing contains the main office (which is a converted classroom) and an elevator shaft. On the northern side, the sixth-grade wing includes a small storage room and a bathroom used by the staff and adult visitors.

The isolated nature of the school's space allows it to create its own physical identity that the educators believe is important to give the school its character. Despite sharing the space with other schools, there is no observed cross-flow of students from the other schools. There is also a visible presence of security, both at the entrance to the school and in the hallways. To the observer, safety within the school does not seem to be a problem.

Westward is located in a low-income neighborhood that has gradually been experiencing gentrification. The gentrification process is changing the residential and business landscape of the area. The 2000 census reports that the community surrounding Westward is 45 percent male and 55 percent female, with a median age of 32.6 years. Eighty-nine percent of the residents are identified as Black, 2 percent White, and 8 percent Latino (of all races). For the 2000 census, 83.8 percent of neighborhood residents reported their race/ethnicity. Of those responding, 18.2 percent identified as West Indian (excluding Hispanic Groups), 4.4 percent as Sub-Saharan African, and 56.2 percent as Other.

The median income of neighborhood residents was only $25,135, with 26.3 percent of families and 29.0 percent of individuals earning incomes that placed them below the poverty level. This compares to the national averages of 9.2 percent for families and 12.4 percent for individuals below the poverty level, and a citywide average of 20.3 percent. Finally, for the 2000 census population that was twenty-five and over within the census tract area, only 67.0 percent had a high school degree or higher, and only 12.7 percent had a bachelor's degree or higher. Thirty-three percent had less than a high school degree.

Student Recruitment and Demographics

As a new school, the population of Westward was relatively low at the beginning of the study. The school enrollment for 2006–2007 was 120 students. At the time it consisted of 70 sixth graders and 50 seventh graders. The ethnic/racial background of the student population is 98 percent Black, 1.5 percent Latino (2 students), and .5 percent Other (1 student). By 2009–2010, the school enrollment had not grown beyond the initial 120 students. Part of the problem was marketing.

Unlike schools such as Thomas Jefferson and North Star, Westward had little in the way of supplemental resources and therefore was not able to promote its existence with glossy brochures. As a result, most of the students who enrolled at the school during its first year were not there by choice. Instead, because space was available, students were assigned to the school. As we would learn over the course of the three years that we carried out our research at Westward, lack of choice would prove to be a major challenge for the school as well as the significant isolation of low performing students. (Westward was one of the two schools mentioned in chapter 7 that was closed subsequent to our study due to persistent low academic performance.)

Student recruitment materials indicate the four factors essential for incoming sixth graders: 1) academic ability and potential for improvement; 2) regular attendance and preparedness; 3) adherence to school rules and adult direction; and 4) respect for self and others, including peers and adults. The admissions process consists of two rounds of interviews. During the first interview, the school is interested in learning about the applicant's preference of academic subjects, any conflict situations with a peer, and the conflict resolution process used by the student. Students are also asked what they believe is the meaning of respect. In the second round, students participate in a school tour and an additional interview. Prospective students also attend an English language arts class at the school so that they can get of sense of the academic expectations. During this process, special attention is given to how students transition from one room to another.

Organizational Structure

Westward is headed by a principal, but many administrative decisions are made by a Cabinet comprised of the principal, two assistant principals, a dean, two department chairs, two grade chairs, coaches, the parent coordinator, the guidance counselor, the school safety officer, and the school secretary. The Cabinet is responsible for the daily governance of the school and meets on a weekly basis. The principal, along with the two assistant principals, is responsible for the coordination of the Cabinet. The assistant principals and the dean are in charge of the monitoring the academic progress of students and making sure that students who are foundering receive timely support.

The department chairs, grade chairs, and coaches work closely on the curriculum and instruction, and the parent coordinator represents the needs and interests of families. This is often the person that parents speak to if they have concerns about their child or something that has occurred at the school. The guidance counselor adds pertinent background information about students and families during discussions about matters at the school, when appropriate. The secretary is the liaison for the support staff, including school aides. The partner coordinators, positions held by a math lead teacher and ELA lead teacher, work with the school's academic, business, community, and data institutional partners.

Westward also maintains a School Leadership Team that meets once a month to discuss a variety of matters that are relevant to the operation of the school. The parents and families, teaching staff, partners, and students are well represented at these meetings. Westward is organized around the theme of business, and students are organized into four phases of the corporate ladder. As students move from one grade to the next, they "climb the corporate ladder" and assume increasing and varying levels of responsibility.

Student representatives from each of the four Business Phases are elected by their peers to serve on the School Leadership Team. A major initiative of the School Leadership Team is the development of the Comprehensive Education Plan of the school. There are also department meetings specifically geared toward the monitoring and improvement of Westward's curriculum and instruction. Coaches play an integral role in these meetings because they often have strong relationships with the students and know them well.

Finally, the Pupil Personnel Team meets to discuss what is happening to the students who are most in need of social interventions such as counseling, home visits, and health services. This team is chaired by the guidance counselor and consists of the parent coordinator, the two assistant principals, the two deans, the attendance officer and school safety officer, the school nurse, and the school psychologist.

The staff of Westward is predominantly Black, but not predominantly male. There is an equal balance of male and female teachers, and although the founding principal Clem Carver is a Black male, his replacement three years later is a Black woman. Each staff member maintains several roles. For example, each of the humanities and math/science teachers and the business education teacher is a community group advisor. Community group advisors are mainly responsible for tracking students' growth and progress using their Programs for Learning, Assessment, and Nurturing (PLANs). The dean handles discipline and guidance, and implements the sports program and other co-curricular activities after school. The business education/research skills teacher teaches technology courses and also develops the middle school business curriculum.

Curriculum

At Westward, the schedule operates on an extended day from 8:00 a.m. to 4:00 p.m. Monday through Thursday. On Fridays the school day ends at 3:15. To minimize disruption, the students travel to all classes with their grade teams, and though their teachers change over the course of the day, the grade team stays together. Each class period is forty-five minutes. Class size ranges from fifteen to twenty students.

With its focus on business, economic development, and community, Westward aims to offer a rigorous academic program, professional experiences, and leadership development. Each of these features of the school is regarded as a requisite for college success. The business education classes begin in the sixth grade with a semester-long course in Fundamentals of Business. In this course, students explore the components of a business and examine neighborhood businesses. The business focus for the seventh and eighth grade is on local businesses and the business needs of the local community. Students undertake an economic-needs assessment of the community and an analysis of needs for which businesses can be created and/or attracted to the area.

During the ninth and tenth grades students conduct a regional and national analysis of businesses with a focus on historical and emerging trends. As eleventh- and twelfth-graders, students explore business through an international lens. In addition to the business curriculum, students complete a course on research skills in grades six through ten to assist them in the two-year Action Research Project they complete during the eleventh and twelfth grades. This component of the curriculum is still under development.

As part of its curriculum, Westward partners with various organizations in order to further the curricular focus on business and community development. Table A.2 below provides an overview of these partnerships.

School Climate, Extra- and Co-Curricular Programs and Activities

Westward boasts a range of extra- and co-curricular programs and activities designed to support the school's overall focus on business and community development. For example, like many single-sex schools, Westward has a dress code, consistent with the business theme, which consists of a "business casual" and "business formal" uniform. The

TABLE A.2

Westward partnerships

Organization[3]	Involvement
Organization 1	Community development corporation; assists students with local business mapping and improvement.
Organization 2	Provides Geographic Information System (GIS) training and information on community mapping.
Organization 3	Provides mentors, tutors, and speakers as well as assistance with development of the business curriculum.
Organization 4	Provides field trips, speakers, and presentations on concepts of city planning.
Organization 5	Nation's largest publicly traded commercial real estate development company; hosts visits to their offices, speakers, and business curriculum development work.
Organization 6	Coordinates early literacy based community service activities.
Organization 7	Black male initiative: hosts Career and Exploration Day.
Organization 8	Organizes service learning projects, assists with CiviConnections project, and coordinate Youth Service Club.
Organization 9	Academic center; develops research curriculum and host college tours.

business casual outfit consists of a purple-collared pullover polo shirt, khaki pants, and black shoes. The business formal uniform, required on only certain occasions, is a dress shirt, tie, dress pants, and shoes.

Westward also offers a nationally recognized student support program called Advancement Via Individual Determination (AVID). This program was developed by middle and high school teachers and professors to impact student success and college preparation. The model seeks to engage students who are in the academic middle (B, C, and even D students) in enrichment and motivational activities. The curriculum, used in content-area classes and in the AVID elective, is based on the WIC-R method: writing, inquiry, collaboration, and reading. Students enrolled in the AVID elective focus on organization and study skills along with critical thinking and questioning techniques, and receive academic help from peers and college tutors.

Another important co-curricular program is College Connections. This program offers a variety of college-themed experiences in and out of the classroom. Each homeroom, for example, is named after local colleges or universities. During the school year, the students in the homerooms visit their respective colleges and make presentations about their trips to students in their grade level. In each classroom, banners from each teacher's college expose students to additional colleges. The note next to each banner reads, "This is where I went to college. Where will you?" This message also seeks to inspire students to pursue a college education.

In addition to trips associated with College Connections, students engage in myriad of field trips to educational organizations, cultural institutions, and private corporations including a stock exchange, arts society, Citibank local branch, and local newspaper offices. Field trips have also included cultural events such as the Bodies Exhibit at the local museum, King Tut exhibit, and the Underground Railroad.

In addition to trips, the school's Friday Speaker Series brings professionals in business and community development and college students to share their experiences in the workforce and in college. It is anticipated that the speakers will inspire students to excel in school and beyond, as well as serve as role models for students. Past speakers include Kevin Powell, activist and poet, and local real estate developers. Presentations by college students have addressed "What Is College Like?" and "What Is It Like to Go Away to College?"

Service learning activities supplement the trips offered and build on the school's theme of community development. Through the Youth Service Club, established in collaboration with a local environmental organization, students have participated in a variety of projects, including:

- *City Day:* a schoolwide, day-long volunteering event dedicated to revitalizing public schools.
- *Hands-on Local City Day:* a citywide parks revitalization event.
- *Martin Luther King Day Service Project:* students visit day-care centers and afterschool programs and read to younger children about Dr. King's dreams and legacy.
- *Penny Harvest:* students collected $325 (2006).
- Philanthropy Roundtable: students learn about the grant process and work on distributing $1,000 to local community organizations.
- Local Community Pantry: students help bag food for needy families.
- Nursing Home Visit: games and conversations with residents.
- Reading Buddies Program: reading with younger children at local day-care centers and elementary schools.
- Civic Project: in conjunction with local art center, students advocate literacy for homeless and displaced youth in the school's neighborhood. The Civic Project involves teachers and students nationwide in linking community history with local service-learning activities.

Salem Academy on Culture and Justice
History and Community Context

Jared Franklin and Kofi Lewis, former colleagues and history teachers at a local charter school focused on law, founded Salem Academy on

Culture and Justice in a large Northeastern city. During the four years they taught together, they frequently discussed "doing something big" for young men in education, birthing the vision of Salem. When Jared was accepted to the local city leadership training program and given the opportunity to develop his own school, he reconnected with Kofi and asked him to be the school's program director. Together they began planning to actualize their vision; the resulting creation was Salem, which opened in September of 2004.

The Salem theme is succinctly expressed by their motto: "Retrieve the Past in Order to Create the Future." With an emphasis on history and civic engagement, the Salem mission "is to nurture, educate, and graduate young men who are civic-minded, critical thinkers, skillful problem solvers and of exemplary character . . . [who] will become college-bound, family and community leaders; concerned for the rights and welfare of others, socially responsible, confident in their capacity to make a difference, and ready to contribute personally to civic and political action." As articulated by the school administrators themselves, this mission includes preparing young men for life beyond high school and providing them with the tools to succeed in college and in society—to defy statistics and cultivate identities of success and achievement.

In order to capture the vision of Salem, the founders adopted and modified Haki Madhubuti's poem, *The Book of Life*, to describe the nature and character of the young men they hoped to graduate. Through interviews with both leaders, we learned that their goal is to produce young men who will exude confidence, respect, and responsibility. They also want to educate young men who will be distinguished by the way they interact with others—men, women, and children—and they want their students to be role models of excellence and initiators of positive social change in their own lives, in the lives of their families and communities, and in the world.

In addition to the mission and vision set forth by the Salem leadership, the school is founded upon the *Nguzo Saba*—the seven principles of Kwanzaa. These principles are: *Umoja* (Unity), *Kujichagalia* (Self-Determination), *Ujima* (Collective Work and Responsibility), *Ujamaa*

(Cooperative Economics), *Nia* (Purpose), *Kuumba* (Creativity), and *Imani* (Faith). The Nguzo Saba principles are geared toward cultivating character and building community for all members of the school family. The seven core principles also undergird the culture of the school and infuse the academic curriculum and co-curricular activities. The culmination of the mission, vision, and core principles is expressed in the Salem school oath written by Kofi Lewis:

> I am a Salem Scholar.
> In my actions, words and deeds I journey the path of a Warrior.
> When I am present I exude brilliance, character and an awesome
> power.
> Just look at my impeccable attire.
> Prepared for my rendezvous with destiny, I take full advantage of all
> opportunities.
> Like the Sankofa Bird, I reach back for my legacy, ushering in a new
> reality.
> The Nguzo Saba—the keys to unlock the mysteries to building
> community.
> Each breath of my life, I create a rich history.
> I pledge my entire being to live with self-love, respect and integrity.
> Today, I claim victory over the forces that attempt to destroy me.
> I possess self-control, moving toward self-mastery.
> Executing my educational master plan, I am striving to become a
> responsible Salem man.

Salem is housed on the campus of what used to be a large comprehensive high school. During a school tour, the principal described the neighborhood as one that has a history of violence, where gang-related activity is commonplace both out in the community and within the schools. According to the census tract data from 2000, the residents of neighborhood are ethnic minorities—Black (40%) and Hispanic (60%)—and nearly all of them (96.4%) rent their residential space. Only 50 percent of the residents are employed in the labor force, and nearly half (44%) of the families reside below the poverty line. Located within a ten-minute walk of public transportation and near various retail businesses, the facility is home to six public high schools.

The detailed cement structure, resembling ancient Greek architecture, spans two city blocks in length and one full block in width and includes a multi-sport athletic field enclosed by a chain-link fence. The school building stands significantly higher than the residential and retail complexes that surround it—most of which are marred with graffiti and secured with iron bars—and is surrounded by a seven-foot black cast-iron fence. Through the gates, three cement staircases pave the way to the school's main entrance.

Student Recruitment and Demographics

When Salem opened in 2004–2005, it began with about 100 students and steadily grew to 324 students by 2007–2008. However, by 2009–2010, Salem's enrollment had declined to 253 young men in the ninth through twelfth grades. Racially/ethnically, 54 percent of Salem students identify as Black of African, Caribbean, and U.S. descent, and 42 percent identify as Latino (primarily Dominican and Puerto Rican). The majority of the students live within the surrounding community, although some students commute from nearby neighborhoods.

According to school administrators, the enrollment process for Salem is traditional in the sense that students select the school; the school does not select them. Students complete the regular New York City high school application and have the option to select Salem as one of their twelve school choices. The Salem staff also participates in recruiting students by attending high school fairs, hosting open houses, and giving presentations at neighborhood middle and junior high schools. Like Westward, Salem does not have much in the way of supplemental financial resources, and so the school is not able to market its existence to attract students or parents who are looking for the type of all-male learning experience it offers. (Along with Westward Academy, Salem was one of the two schools mentioned in chapter 7 as designated to close after our study was completed, due to persistent low academic performance.)

Organizational Structure

The core leadership team at Salem is comprised of Jared Franklin, the principal and cofounder, Kofi Lewis, program director and cofounder, and an assistant principal. In addition to managing the school budget and other administrative tasks, the assistant principal's role includes supervising daily life at the school and ensuring the overall safety of the school environment. Although Principal Franklin is ultimately responsible for overseeing the delivery of the school's mission, he relies on Program Director Kofi Lewis, who brings fifteen years of teaching experience to Salem, to monitor the academic program on a day-to-day basis.

As program director, Mr. Lewis's primary responsibility is to engage the community and provide professional development that emphasizes connecting the staff to the school's mission and vision and fostering an understanding of how historical knowledge is used to cultivate positive identities for their students. For example, Mr. Lewis conducts a Rites of Passage Program for the boys and the teachers attending Salem.

Assistant Principal Forester also contributes to the development and support of teachers. Transitioning from the classroom after ten years of teaching to his first year as assistant principal at Salem, Mr. Forester's role encompasses a multiplicity of duties including special education, ESL education, technology support, classroom instruction assistance, and teacher professional development. In addition, he plays a central role in upholding the attendance policy, which is an integral component of the Salem school culture.

The thirty-six-member teaching staff of Salem includes the Administrative Leadership Team, content area teachers, guidance counselors, and support staff. The support staff includes: three school aides, two secretaries, one dean, one paraprofessional, and one community assistant. Most teachers (22) in the school identify as Black or African American. Eight teachers identify as Latino. There are also six staff members who identify as White. The staff is almost evenly split between men (19) and women (17).

Curriculum

The curriculum is intended to actualize the Salem mission and vision. Kofi Lewis describes the school's approach to curriculum as "thematic and interdisciplinary" yet centered on the study of history, law, civics, and the arts. Teachers work collaboratively to develop innovative interdisciplinary units within and across grade levels. According to school documents, the goal of this approach is "to produce young men who possess the skills and qualities of a college-bound historian, an independent thinker, investigator, problem-solver, activist, and a master of acquiring and synthesizing multiple strands of information."

In order to attain the Salem standard of achievement, Salem students follow a course sequence that is aligned with its state's mandates. In addition, students are required to produce portfolios consisting of assignments and major pieces of work from each class, including elective courses and additional work completed during co-curricular activities. Table A.3 shows the four-year academic plan and lists the elective courses that are available to Salem students.

School Climate, Extra- and Co-Curricular Programs and Activities

The school day begins at 8:46 a.m. each morning and classes are conducted in seven 44-minute blocks, with an equally long lunch period prior to the final academic period. Students are released from the regular school day at 2:56 p.m. While on school grounds, students must comply with the behavior conduct standards set forth by Salem administration and staff. The Salem scholarly conduct states: "All scholars should conduct themselves in an appropriate and civil manner, with proper regard for the rights and welfare of other scholars and other members of the school community, and for the care of school facilities and equipment." Disciplinary action will be taken if a scholar's conduct is "disorderly, insubordinate, disruptive, violent, endanger[ing] the safety, morals, health, or welfare or others, [and] any form of academic misconduct." Furthermore, there is a zero tolerance policy toward drugs

TABLE A.3

Courses of study at Salem

Course (number of years)	Electives
English (4)	Ancient African History
Mathematics (4)	Art Appreciation
Social Studies (4)	Civil Law
Science (4)	Constitutional Law
Foreign Language (3)	Drama
Art Electives (2)	Government and Citizenship
Physical Education (2)	History of African- and Latin-Based Music
Health (1)	Indigenous Latino History
Internship (1.5)	Jewelry Making
	Law and Dispute Resolution
	Law and Social Problems
	Law and the Criminal Justice System
	Music Industry
	The African and Latino Experience in the 20th and 21st Centuries

or weapons allowed on campus at any time. If these standards of conduct are broken, students are subject to disciplinary action, which may include an oral or written warning up to school suspension.

The key to enforcing the guidelines for scholarly conduct is the transformation room. Located in a space at the end of the side corridor of the fourth floor, the transformation room is used for handling anything from in-school behavior problems to tardiness. Principal Franklin described it as a place where students go when they need to transform their behavior, appearance, or attitude. For instance, if a student is tardy to school he cannot disrupt his first period class by entering late. Instead, he must proceed to the main office to obtain a note and then go to the transformation room until the end of first period. Similarly, if a student arrives to school out of dress code he must report to the transformation room to correct his appearance prior to participating in the school day.

Another important aspect of the school climate is student attendance, which includes two general policies. First, as is true for other schools in the State, students at Salem are required to maintain attendance of at least 80 percent in order to receive academic credit for a course. Secondly, the Salem attendance policy requires students to maintain a minimum of 80 percent attendance each marking period to remain "on track."

Student attendance is monitored by the administration through meticulous record keeping whereby the administrative support team works to maintain accurate records of student tardiness and absenteeism each morning. In addition, Salem administrators utilize a tracking system that sorts students based on their attendance and credit accumulation. Students' names are written on index cards and hung in the administrators' offices according to their attendance group. This system allows administrators to note immediately if a student's attendance drops below the minimum so they can intervene with closer monitoring or other assistance services, if necessary. Likewise, if a student is not on track to graduate based on the accumulated number of credits, their progress is carefully monitored. Members of the administrative staff hold regular follow-up meetings with students who are not on track to graduate.

In addition to the guidelines for scholarly conduct, students must also comply with the Salem dress code, which requires a dress shirt tucked into dress or casual slacks, a tie, and shoes (no tennis shoes). Students have flexibility in the colors and designs they choose to wear, but must stay within these additional dress code guidelines: "Clothing must be safe, appropriate, and not be disruptive or interfere with the educational process; safe footwear must be worn; vulgar, obscene, libelous, or denigrating items must not be worn; clothing that promotes and/or endorses the use of alcohol, tobacco, or illegal drugs and/or encourages illegal or violent activities or pornographic/sexual overtones must not be worn." Again, failure to observe these guidelines merits disciplinary action.

Beyond the traditional academics offered during the school day, students are encouraged to participate in Salem's co-curricular activities, which are structured in two programs: Saturday Academy and Extended Day. Saturday Academy operates from 10:00 a.m. to 12:00 p.m. and targets students who are struggling in the areas of English and mathematics, specifically. In addition to academic assistance, students participate in recreational and cultural activities, including athletics, field trips, African drumming, songwriting, and self-defense classes.

The Extended Day Program is offered on Tuesdays, Wednesdays, and Thursdays after school from 3:30 to 5:30 p.m. During the first hour, teachers provide students with homework assistance and offer tutoring or other academic services. The second hour of the Extended Day Program utilizes Giant Thinkers, one of Salem's youth organization partners, to "facilitate youth-centered workshops on identity, self-esteem, manhood, values, overcoming obstacles, life skills, substance abuse, health, and fitness."

Besides co-curricular activities, Salem organizes monthly grade-level meetings called Town Hall Meetings. These meetings provide an opportunity to recognize and celebrate the scholars' achievements, motivate and encourage them, and simply communicate announcements relevant to each particular grade. It is also a time for students to share experiences from school field trips or events with their classmates. In addition to the Town Hall Meetings, the administration utilizes all-school assemblies to invite inspirational speakers and special guests that emulate the core values of Salem.

Washington Academy for Boys
History and Community Context

Washington Academy for Boys, a private elementary school in a large Northeastern city, opened its doors in 2003 when it welcomed its first class of fifty-two boys in fourth and fifth grades. The Academy has expanded one grade per year since its inception and now offers grades four through eight. The school was developed with the purpose of "helping bright boys from low-income families identify and celebrate their gifts in a community that will teach them to be successful men." To this end, the boys are engaged in the pursuit of academic excellence, courage, and personal honor. The goal is to focus both on the development of the intellect and the spirit.

Washington Academy is located in a neighborhood that has gained a reputation for being the center of the City's counterculture. Small boutique clothing shops, tattoo parlors, nightclubs, and restaurants line the streets and give the neighborhood an artistic sensibility. Although in recent decades gentrification has changed the character of the neighborhood, it still has a vibrant, youthful character that makes it attractive to tourists.

Like many schools in the city, the school occupies a tall, multilevel structure and does not have a large playing field or parking space. Administrative offices are located on the first of three levels, while classrooms are located on the second and third levels. The cafeteria is in the school's basement. Students utilize the local Boys' Club for physical education, as well as parks and recreational spaces available in the neighborhood.

Modeled after independent private schools that serve boys from affluent backgrounds, Washington Academy seeks to instill in its students an appreciation for learning. It does this by challenging and engaging the students, helping them think critically about their world and applying what they learn from a moral and ethical standpoint in a collaborative and safe learning environment. Each of the classrooms are arranged in "seminar style," with tables and chairs in a U or board-table formation facing the teacher. In so doing, the school envisions that each student is encouraged to take risks and tests his own limits, meeting and going beyond what he thought he could do on the way to achieving his maximum potential.

In addition, Washington Academy aims to provide a safe learning environment, where "community, integrity, care, personal honor, emotional courage, and mindfulness" are celebrated. Such practices are designed to help the boys define themselves as young men. According to the school's Web site, "Graduates will be prepared to attend selective independent day and boarding schools in the Northeastern United States as well as the city's competitive parochial and public schools."

Student Recruitment and Demographics

Since opening, Washington Academy has sustained its enrollment. In 2009–2010, it had 116 boys in fourth through eighth grades. In this cohort, there are eighteen eighth graders, nineteen seventh graders, thirty-two sixth graders, twenty-seven fifth graders, and twenty fourth graders. Administrative records indicate that 51 percent of students identify as Black, 33 percent as Latino, and 16 percent as Asian. There are no special education or English language learners students, and all students qualify for free lunch.

In order to be considered for Washington Academy, the student and parent or guardian must each fill out an application, and the student's current teacher must complete a recommendation form. The parent/ guardian form asks questions about home and family, while the student application asks the student about extracurricular activities, his strengths, the type of reading he enjoys, his favorite book, favorite school subjects, and a word that describes him. The teacher recommendation asks questions about the student's behavior, personality, and academic skills. In addition, a student transcript must be submitted.

Organizational Structure

The primary administrators for the school are Brother Brendan Flessa and Mr. Dominic Spencer. Brother Flessa is the president, founder, and chairman of the board of trustees of Washington Academy. He graduated from a Catholic university in 1966 and has graduate degrees in counseling and social work. The principal, Dominic Spencer, has both undergraduate and graduate degrees from an Ivy League university. He also has extensive independent school leadership experience.

Principal Spencer oversees a staff of twenty highly skilled administrators, teachers, and staff, including an assistant head of school for curriculum and faculty development and an assistant head of school for administrative operations. He also has two master's degrees with concentrations in the science of teaching and educational administration. The Leadership Team itself brings a wealth of experience and success working with lower-income students and with bright students making the transition to the nation's most competitive and elite high schools. Together President Flessa and Principal Spencer set a tone for the school.

Washington Academy has twelve teachers in total for the fourth through eighth grades, covering the core classes of language arts, physical and life science, mathematics, and history (social studies), as well as grammar, keyboarding, public speaking, civics, music, drama, art, and logic. While some teachers teach only a single subject or field, several teachers teach multiple subject areas. For example, one teacher teaches sixth- and seventh-grade math as well as seventh-grade civics, while another teacher teaches fourth-, fifth-, sixth-, and eighth-grade art as well as fourth- and fifth- grade Spanish.

Most of the teachers are male (10), but are mixed in terms of racial/ethnic identity (4 identify as Black/African American, 3 as Latino, 6 as White, and 1 as East Asian). The background of the teachers differs from the other single-sex schools because of the hiring process Principal Spencer describes in selecting them: "I can't always afford the most experienced teachers but I can hire the smartest, that's why I hire from Ivy League schools."

Curriculum

The curriculum at Washington Academy emphasizes critical thinking and moral and ethical development. In addition to the core subjects of language arts, physical and life sciences, mathematics, history, and Spanish, students learn social studies in combination with language arts coursework, music, drama, art, logic, and public speaking. The grade-level course sequence for students involves a combination of departmental and self-contained classes. Fourth grade is self-contained. Co-curricular classes include visual arts and Spanish. Fifth grade is partially self-contained and students have separate math/science, language arts, social studies, visual arts, and Spanish teachers. Students in the sixth through eighth grades have separate language arts (reading, writing, and grammar/usage), social studies, Spanish, mathematics, and science classes, with electives in keyboarding, public speaking, philosophy, great books, economics, yoga, art history, social justice (for 8th graders), and civics.

School Climate, Extra- and Co-Curricular Programs and Activities

Washington Academy has a daily schedule that features an 8:00 a.m. to 3:30 p.m. day, with the fourth and fifth grades beginning their day at 8:30 and the middle school at 8:00. The schedule includes an hour for lunch, gym three times a week, advisory/homeroom meetings four days a week, and a community meeting once a week. There are no study halls. All classes are sixty minutes long. Like most single-sex schools we studied, Washington Academy has a dress code that consists of a dress shirt, tie, slacks, and dress shoes.

According to Principal Spencer, there are only minor discipline issues to address that occur fairly infrequently. The students and faculty work together to mediate any issues, concerns, or minor conflicts that may arise during the school day. The school also has a code of conduct in which the students and their parents must sign off. In terms of extra- and co-curricular programs, the school currently participates in a premedical program offered to especially gifted math/science students who are of African American or Latino descent, and a local community program, which is a one-week historical immersion program for students who qualify through their character and contributions to the school.

Washington Academy offers a guest lecture series and a "great books" elective held after school for the eighth graders. Fellows from a local prestigious performing arts school have also been working with students, teaching them a classical string instrument as well as instructing them on music history. Students are encouraged to attend concerts once per month as part of this program. In late October, Washington

Academy hosts a Community Week centered on events designed to build a sense of community. All students are encouraged to participate in the Mentoring Partnership and attend school-sponsored retreats and community service projects throughout the year, including fourth- to eighth-grade Mentoring Partnerships and seventh- and eighth-grade retreats.

Kennedy College Preparatory Academy
History and Community Context

Kennedy Academy, founded in 2007, is a college preparatory charter middle school (grades 5 to 8) located in a large Southwestern city. The school offers a rigorous academic program along with a structured disciplined environment. As testament to the school's attempt at promoting academic rigor, students and parents are required to sign an agreement that mandates attendance from 7:15 a.m. to 5:00 p.m. each school day. Students are also required to complete two hours of homework each day during the week. There are two half days of Saturday school each month and approximately four weeks of summer session. The school's academic plan and calendar follows a model that has been recognized for its success in educating low-income students of color.

Kennedy is part of a network of schools run by a large national charter management organization and foundation dedicated to training outstanding school leaders to open and operate high performing schools. In addition, the foundation is responsible for supporting excellence and sustainability across all of the schools in its network and leading network-wide innovation efforts to leverage its growth.

The foundation provides a variety of supports and services to all of the schools in its network, including legal support, assistance in acquiring and financing real estate, technology and other infrastructure needs, financial management, corporate governance, operations, communications, marketing, and development. The foundation, however, does not manage the schools in its network. Rather, each school is run by a leader who has received training from the network but has flexibility and autonomy in managing the school's affairs.

Additionally, the school is governed by a local board of directors, and the charter is held by a local 501(c)3 organization. Schools in the network share a core set of operating principles that include a focus on high expectations, choice and commitment, more time (to succeed in academics and life), power to lead, results, and a commitment to excellence. Kennedy is the only all-male schools in the charter network, and its approach to serving its students differs in a number of significant ways from other schools in the network.

The Academy is located on a strip mall that the charter management organization and foundation purchased in order to create a K–12 school campus. In order to accommodate new students as it has expanded, the school facility has been renovated each year upon adding a new grade level. The space is organized into a U shape with large classrooms, a cafeteria, a greeting area for the receptionist, and a playground area in the back of the strip mall that was still under construction at the time we carried out our research. The walls of the school are lined with posters of colleges and prominent African American figures. The highlight of the space is an expansive mural in the entryway of the school with a portrait of Frederick Douglass painted by a local artist, along with the quote "It is easier to build strong children then to repair broken men."

Student Recruitment and Demographics

Kennedy began serving approximately 100 students in 2007–2008, and by 2009–2010 the enrollment was 252 students. The summer before the school opened, the principal and other staff walked the neighborhood and distributed flyers about the school to community members. The principal's intent was to introduce himself to the community and for the community to see beyond the charter network—particularly given the proliferation of schools opened by the same charter network throughout this district.

Most students at Kennedy identified as African American (86%), although the school also served Mexican students (12%) and a small number of White students (2%). When students register for Kennedy, they sign a contract that obliges them to commit to "work, think, and behave in the best way I know how and do whatever it takes for me and my fellow students to learn." Parents are also required to sign a contract and make a commitment to "make sure our child arrives to school every day by 7:15 a.m. (Monday–Friday) or boards a Kennedy bus at the scheduled time, help our child in the best way we know how, make ourselves available to our children and the school, and address any concerns they might have." Likewise, teachers commit to "teach in the best way we know how, do whatever it takes for our students to learn and make ourselves available to students and parents." According to the school principal Steve Howard, such commitments are designed to "create a sense of mutual accountability. We want everyone who is part of this community to understand the role they must play to insure success."

Organizational Structure

Kennedy's administrative team is comprised primarily of the principal and the budget manager. Due to Kennedy's support from the charter management organization, the school has received IT, budget, data analysis, and professional development support. This makes it possible for the principal to serve as an additional instructional guide in most of the classrooms. The teaching staff consisted of four teachers during the first year. By 2009–2010, there was a total of ten teachers.

Principal Howard is originally from the Northeast and had been in public education for twelve years, beginning as a middle school teacher. He became fascinated with the idea of 90/90/90 schools (school that are demographically 90 percent free and reduced priced lunch, 90 percent minority, and 90 percent proficient and above on state exams), which led him to want to assume a leadership position that would allow him to build a 90/90/90 school from the ground up. With training from the national foundation under his belt and a new school opening in the southwestern United States, Principal Howard was lured away from the Northeast to become the first principal of Kennedy. He explained why he felt that creating such a school for boys of color was particularly important to him: "When I see these young men I see my-self. I grew up just like most of them, in a poor family attending pretty bad public schools. I got lucky because of education. I had teachers who cared about me. That's why I know education can make a difference and that's what we intend to do here."

Curriculum

Kennedy's curriculum reflects the academic guidelines for the state's department of education (literacy and numeracy, geography, science and social science). In addition, the school's goal is to facilitate learning in subjects that are relevant to the lives of students while providing them with knowledge and skills that can help them be successful. The school aims to expose students to learning materials that are culturally relevant and to utilize challenging activities that will prepare them for the social, cultural, and academic obstacles they might encounter in the future.

Lessons at Kennedy follow the rubric developed by Greg Lemov in his book *Teach Like a Champion*. Upon entering the classroom, students are required to complete a "Do Now" assignment designed to prepare their minds for the day's work and to insure that no time is lost in the transition. Generally, twenty to thirty minutes are reserved for some form of direct instruction that is followed by an equal amount of time for students to work on activities relating to the material that has been introduced. During this part of class, students also complete a "Home-work Review," designed to show where they still need help, and a "Skill of the Day/Essential Question/Exit Ticket," which focuses on the over-arching question that guides that day's lessons. The goal is for students to experience a high degree of consistency in the classroom with respect to the format and pace of lessons. Students receive homework daily and are expected to begin working on it during study hall. Additionally, stu-dents receive 135 minutes each week of physical education.

Principal Howard developed the instructional program, and he visits classrooms throughout the day to insure that the plan is followed. For the first three years that the school was in operation, the major focus of the curriculum was on reading. The principal established reading groups each week based on reading skill areas of focus. For example, fifth graders struggling around word recognition work with a teacher who targets that skill for the entire week. At the end of each week, the students participate in an online diagnostic assessment. The results of the assessment frame the next series of reading groups.

The principal and teachers each lead a weekly reading group. These groups involve guided reading, reading aloud, and peer group reading. Principal Howard explains the school's focus on reading in this way: "Many of our students came to us as low readers. We know from the research that if they don't develop their literacy skills they will struggle through high school. Our goal is to lay a foundation for success and hopefully to cultivate a genuine love of reading."

School Climate, Extra- and Co-Curricular Programs and Activities

Kennedy students are also expected to positively contribute to the school community as citizens. To that end, as at Salem Academy, the school's administration established a set of values based on the seven principles of Kwanzaa (the Nguzo Saba) that were reflected in the life of Frederick Douglass. These values guide the decisions that adults make in the school as they model how they would like students to make decisions in their lives:

- *Unity:* We work to create unity (togetherness and harmony) within our family, our school, and our community. We seek peace.
- *Self-Determination:* We work to define ourselves, to know who we were, who we are, and who we will become. We determine for ourselves what we will be called and how we will be known. We seek ourselves.
- *Collective Work and Responsibility:* We work to make the problem of our brother a problem of our own. If there is a problem, we look for a solution. If there is a better way, we find it. We seek solutions.
- *Cooperative Economics:* We work to make sure that there is enough for everyone. If a teammate needs help, we give. If we need help, we ask. We seek to share.

- *Purpose:* We work with urgency and intent. We understand that each one of us is here for a reason and that reason is to better ourselves and our community, and in doing so, leave a mark. We seek our destiny.
- *Creativity:* We work to leave the place where we are better than the way we found it. We seek service.
- *Faith:* We believe in ourselves, our parents, our teachers, our leaders, and our community. We believe in the good intent that they have for us and the hard work they do for us. We believe it is the right work. We believe we will win. We seek the best in everyone.

Bethune Academy
History and Community Context

Bethune Academy serves students in grades six to eight from a low-income community in a large Southeastern city. Bethune, like other single-sex schools in the region, was founded to address the historically low levels of achievement among African American boys in the community. The school seeks to accomplish this goal by employing gender-based teaching strategies geared to what they regard as "boys' learning styles." The mission of the school is to develop globally competitive leaders by providing a rigorous college preparatory curriculum utilizing gender-based strategies in a safe and nurturing learning environment. The school's creed, which students are required to memorize, is:

> I am a young man,
> growing strong
> using my mind
> to create words, to fashion images, and to perform deeds,
> that will uplift my present, past, and future.
> I will respect myself and others.
> I promise to be and do my best.
> Some days I may land short of my goals

But I will not fall . . .
With the guidance of my teachers, family, friends and community
I will rise like the Eagle and soar.
I will live diligently each day knowing
I owe it to myself and to the world to take full advantage of
the vast opportunities presented before me
that will shape my very existence
to continue to be the very best I can be.

In 2007 the school was temporarily housed in a building often used when other schools in the district are in development or undergoing renovations. The school is located in a middle-class, mixed-race community. Since most of the students do not reside in the neighborhood, bus transportation is provided. School buses pick up students from several sites throughout their community and drop them back at their stops in the afternoon after school and extracurricular activities have ended. The school also provides transportation for parents to attend the annual Open House and other school-sponsored events.

At the main entrance of the school there are metal detectors and uniformed security personnel, including a uniformed police officer. The principal of the school, Clayton Brown, was recruited from a Southeastern city. When we asked Principal Brown why he was recruited, he explained, "I suppose it's because I have a deep passion and commitment to educating Black boys. I had a reputation back in his former district as an effective principal. I hope to bring what I learned there to this school."

The neighborhoods where students from Bethune are drawn have the highest crime and the highest incarceration rates in the state. Principal Brown stated that he believes that nine out of ten of the students' fathers are incarcerated. From his perspective, the school is an opportunity to establish a culture of high expectations and give students a "fighting chance." He is interested in rallying the community around the school and moving illegal activities away from the students' local community. "We are in a mission to save these boys. We know that if we do not succeed many of them will turn to a life of crime. We are doing everything we can to give these young men a positive alternative."

Student Recruitment and Demographics

The school officially opened its doors in August 2007, admitting over a hundred sixth-grade students with plans to expand to twelfth grade by 2013. In 2009–2010, the student population was 253. Nearly all (99%) of Bethune students identify themselves as Black. Based on the National School Lunch Program, over 90 percent of Bethune students are eligible for free or reduced price lunch programs. The school district Bethune is part of has a choice plan that allows parents to select which middle school their students will attend. Most students end up in their neighborhood middle schools, but parents are expected to apply to a small number of specialized magnet schools. Bethune is one of these schools, but because it is new and has not had funds to advertise, the school district has assisted in recruiting students to enroll.

The vast majority of students that have enrolled at Bethune are behind academically. In many cases, the school district got their parents to enroll their children into the school by convincing them that they had a greater chance of being successful in a small, nurturing environment. However, the fact that many of the boys did not choose to attend Bethune on their own and, in some cases, did not realize they would be attending an all-male school until they got there, has proved to be an additional challenge for the school.

Organizational Structure

The administrative staff of Bethune Academy consists of a principal, vice principal, counselor, and social worker. Principal Brown was formerly a principal of a precollege academy for boys in a nearby Southern state. His former school was converted from a comprehensive high school into two gender-based academies. Under Principal Brown's direction, students were exposed to a college preparatory curriculum including advanced placement and dual-enrolled college-level courses. Principal Brown is a strong believer in gender-based learning strategies for boys, and he believes that a focus on technology, kinesthetic activity, and cooperative learning will produce higher levels of achievement.

In addition to the administrative staff, Bethune employs nine core teachers and three specialist teachers. Three teachers of electives are shared with a nearby single-sex school for girls. All of the teachers identified as either Black or White, and equal numbers identified as male and female.

Curriculum

The school day is organized into forty-five-minute periods, beginning with an advisory period that starts at 8:30a.m. Periods five through eight are longer—seventy-five minutes—and scheduled as blocks. The idea is to provide teachers with more time for hands-on learning activities. The formal curriculum is described as college preparatory and aligned with state performance standards that define clear expectations for instruction, assessment, and student work. The curriculum is thematically focused on business, engineering, science, and technology. According to Principal Brown, the thematic focus is intended to provide students with "real-world knowledge and skills that could lead to real jobs."

Teachers at Bethune have been trained to deliver content through gender-based teaching strategies that emphasize kinesthetic learning, active use of technology, and cooperative learning. For example, a teaching strategy available via the school's website that was derived from a professional publication on teaching strategies for secondary boys and girls is "Pass it Back." For this strategy, students create a fill-in-the-blank sheet of statements using the material to be covered on the quiz/test, then answer the questions in teams by having individual students complete one answer and then "pass it back" to a teammate (students are in rows). Members of the faculty learned these and other strategies through professional development sessions provided to the staff by the Gurian Institute.

According to its Web site, the Gurian Institute is an organization "committed to helping boys and girls reach their full potential by providing professional development on gender-based strategies." The staff has also participated in professional development focused on inclusive teaching, differentiated instruction, technology integration, reading and writing across the curriculum, and teaching higher-order thinking.

In addition to the formal curriculum, the school boasts a number of academic enrichment activities including an advisory curriculum focused on Making All Learning Exciting. The goal of the advisory is to provide students with activities that will elevate their self-esteem, instill a sense of personal responsibility, and promote academic engagement. Students also have the opportunity to participate in the 100 Book Challenge, a school-wide program designed to encourage reading.

School Climate, Extra- and Co-Curricular Programs and Activities

Bethune provides all incoming students with a uniform free of charge. The uniform consists of beige slacks, white button-down dress shirt, and dark or white sneakers or black shoes. The uniform is mandatory, but Mr. Brown indicated that the students could wear a white polo shirt with school logo on Fridays.

The school also boasts an active mentoring program made possible through a partnership with a Boys Scouts of America chapter. There is also a popular robotics club, an afterschool All Stars Club linked to a national organization that provides comprehensive afterschool programs primarily to middle schools. The All Stars Club incorporates activities that provide academic support, enrichment opportunities, and health and fitness activities. Bethune leverages a number of partnerships with the district Communities in Schools office, the local chapter of 100 Black Men, Inc., and local colleges and universities.

APPENDIX 2

Survey Measures and Instructional Action Codes

Cumulative Grades: Grades were collected from administrative records each year provided by each of the participating schools.

Engagement

Behavioral Engagement

This 7-item scale was adapted from the LISA student interview (Suarez-Orozco 2001) and focuses on the behaviors of academic engagement reported by students. This scale assesses whether the students were completing the tasks necessary to be successful in school, including attending and participating in class and completing homework and course assignments. Respondents were asked to determine the frequency of behavioral engagement occurrences from "never" to "every day or almost every day." Scores ranged from 0 to 3, with higher scores indicating higher levels of engagement (Cronbach's α=.73).

Cognitive Engagement

This 9-item scale (Martin and Suarez-Orozco, unpublished) measures the degree to which students are interested and intellectually engaged in what they are learning (e.g., "I enjoy learning new things"). Responses were coded on a 4-point scale ranging from 1 = Strongly Disagree to 4 = Strongly Agree (Cronbach's α=.75).

Relational Engagement

This 9-item scale was adapted from the LISA student interview (Suarez-Orozco 2001) assesses the degree to which students felt that they had a supportive relationship with an adult or a peer that helped them feel connected to school (e.g., "There is at least one adult in school I can always count on"). Responses were coded on a 4-point Likert scale ranging from 1 = Strongly Disagree to 4 = Strongly Agree (Cronbach's α=.79).

Peer Academic Support

This 5-item scale, developed by the Chicago Consortium, measures the extent to which students have friends who support their doing well in school. Support includes such items as valuing education ("My friends think it's important to do well in school") and tangible help ("My friends and I help each other prepare for tests"). Items are measured on a 4-point Likert scale where 1 = Strongly Disagree and 4 = Strongly Agree). (Cronbach's α=.83)

School Climate

School Climate consists of 4 subscales to gain a comprehensive sense of the school ethos or positive climate that exists at the school (Cronbach's α=.86). While the alpha for the entire scale was quite high, in our testing a counterintuitive pattern emerged that suggested that climate, while not significant or large, contributed negatively to achievement, including:

1. *Sense of Fair Treatment, Sense of School Cohesion, Sense of Belonging to School, and Perceived Safety.* Items are measured on a 4-point Likert scale where 1 = Strongly Disagree and 4 = Strongly Agree. (Cronbach's α=.79).

2. *Sense of Fair Treatment.* This 4-item scale, developed by Fergus and Martin (unpublished), measures the extent to which students

report feeling that students are treated fairly by school adults, both generally ("The punishment for breaking school rules is the same no matter who you are") or by group ("Teachers treat students from different backgrounds in the same way"). Items are measured on a 4-point Likert scale where 1 = Strongly Disagree and 4 = Strongly Agree. (Cronbach's α=.79)

3. *Sense of Belonging to School.* These three items taken from the Chicago Consortium measure the extent to which students feel like they belong in their school ("I fit in with the students at this school"). Items are measured on a 4-point Likert scale where 1 = Strongly Disagree and 4 = Strongly Agree. (Cronbach's α=.69)

4. *Sense of School Cohesion.* This 4-item scale measures the extent to which students report that students and adult respect and get along with each other, regardless of differences in their backgrounds ("Everyone gets along in this school"). Responses were coded on a 4-point Likert scale ranging from 1 = Strongly Disagree to 4 = Strongly Agree (1). (Cronbach's α=.75)

Exposure to Rigorous and Relevant Literacy Instruction

This 7-item scale is adapted from items developed by the Chicago Consortium and further developed by Martin (forthcoming), based on the college readiness research literature. This scale measures the extent to which students report exposure to instruction related to preparedness for university studies and consists of items related to higher-order thinking such as presenting or discussing literature, collaboration, and extended critical writing. Scores ranged from 0 to 4, with higher scores indicating higher levels of exposure or participation in the instructional activities. (Cronbach's α=.75)

ELA Teacher Quality

This 5-item scale from the Chicago Consortium measures the extent to which students report that teachers have high expectations of students' schoolwork, believe in their ability to achieve, and are attentive to their learning needs. Items are measured on a 4-point Likert scale where 1 = Strongly Disagree and 4 = Strongly Agree). (Cronbach's α=.90)

ELA Course Challenge

This 5-item scale from the Chicago Consortium measures the extent to which students report instruction as academically challenging ("In this class, how often do you find the work difficult?"). Respondents were asked to determine the frequency of challenging occurrences from "never" to "every day or almost every day." Scores ranged from 0 to 4 with higher scores indicating higher levels of challenge. (Cronbach's α=.79)

Exposure to Instruction Related to High Literacy

This 7-item scale is adapted from items developed by the Chicago Consortium and further developed by Martin (forthcoming), based on the college readiness research literature. It measures the extent to which students report exposure to instruction related to preparedness for university studies and consists of items related to higher-order thinking such as presenting or discussing literature, collaboration, and extended critical writing. Scores ranged from 0 to 4 with higher scores indicating higher levels of exposure or participation in the instructional activities. (Cronbach's α=.75)

Instructional Action Codes for Analysis

Interaction

    T: Teacher
    S: Student
    C: Class

    T-S: Individual interaction between teacher and student
    T-SS: Teacher-students (small group—2–6)
    T-C: Teacher-whole class
    T-1/2C (or 1/3C, etc.): Teacher-group interaction when class is divided into large groups

S-S: Student-student (pairs)

S-SS: Student-students (small group—2–6)

SS-SS: Students to students (small groups—3–6)

S-C: Student-whole class

S-1/2C (or 1/3C, etc.): Student-group interaction when class is divided into large groups

Instructional Actions

Discussions

DI1: Discussion of the substance of a topic being taught

DI2: Discussion to brainstorm ideas/reasons around a topic/theme

DI3: Discussion to discuss opinions about an idea or topic/theme

DI4: Discussion to problem solve

DI5: Debate

DIO: Discussion Other

Question and Answer

QA1: Information questions (QRE): Teacher asks questions, students respond, teacher evaluates

QS1: Information questions: Student(s) ask questions(s), teacher answers question

QS2: Information questions: Student(s) ask questions(s), teacher probes with question (e.g., asking leading questions to help students come to the answer)

Listening

LI1: Lecture by teacher

LI2: Instructions/directions

LI3: Students listen to CD/cassette

LI4: Guest visitor/presenter lecture or presentation

TR1: Listening to music to denote transitions between activities

SP1: Speech/Presentation

SP2: Performance

LIO: Listening Other

Note-taking

   NT1: Students take notes from the board
   NT2: Students take notes from oral story/lesson
   NT3: Students take notes from reading passage
   NTO: Note-taking Other

Reading

   Aloud
   RA1: Directions
   RA2: From book/text
   RA3: Student work

   Independent
   RI1: Directions
   RI2: Tests, problems etc. (e.g., on worksheets)
   RI3: Textbooks
   RI4: Self-selected text
   RI5: Other teacher-selected text
   REO: Reading Other

Research

   RCH1: Self-selected/initiated research
   RCH2: Assigned research
   RCHO: Research Other

Writing Activities

   Prompted
   WP1: Students respond to writing prompt selected by teacher
   WP2: Students respond to writing prompt in text book/classroom
      material
   WP3: Students respond to writing prompt in test preparation
      booklet/material
   WP4: Essay writing

Writing Process
WP5: Drafting
WP6: Revising
WP7: Editing
WP8: Finalizing/word processing

Unprompted
WU1: Students write freely on topic they select
WU2: Students write in journals (e.g., reading response)
WU3: Students write to explain solution to a problem (e.g., math journaling)
WAO: Writing Other

Worksheets
WS1: Students complete graphic organizer
WS2: Students complete equation-based (math) worksheet (fill-in response)
WS3: Students complete multiple-choice worksheet
WS4: Gap fill
WS5: Short answer response
WS6: Essay response
WSO: Worksheet Other

Hands-on
EX1: Students conduct experiments
BU1: Students build/cut or construct something with their hands
DR1: Assigned free-drawing/painting/drafting/tracing, etc.
DR2: Self-selected free-drawing/painting/drafting/tracing, etc.
DR3: Diagramming/plotting/mapping, etc.
HOO: Hands-on Other (dramatic activities here)

Physical Action
TPR: Total physical response (teacher speaks, students mimic—think Simon Says)

PA1: Physical mnemonic (e.g., clapping hands to remember iambic pentameter)

TR2: Physical movement for transitions between activities

PAO: Physical Activity Other

Visual/Multimodal Learning

VM1: Students watch a film or animated media

VM2: Look at nonanimated visual media such as paintings, drawings, diagrams, or charts with overhead projector/slides/PowerPoint

VM3: Look at printed media such as poems, slogans, or any other writing with overhead projector/slides/PowerPoint

VM4: Students conduct observations

Recordings

RC1: Students listen to recorded music

RC2: Students listen to recorded speech

Internet

IN1: Use of Internet for research

IN2: Use of Internet to communicate (officially)

IN3: Use of Internet for other reason (note reason)

Computer

CO-XXX: Playing a *computer game* related to learning (add specific code related to what they are doing from above; e.g., if they are doing an on-SAT prep game with multiple choice = CO-WS3; if drafting on the computer it would be CO-WP5)

VMO: Visual/Multimodal Other

Behavior/Discipline

Praise

PR1: Teacher privately praises student (takes aside or in 1-1 discussion)

PR2: Teacher publicly praises student or students

Discipline

DS0: Silent disciplinary action—a look, tap on desk, etc.

DS1: Teacher privately addresses student behavior—student stays where he his

DS11: Teacher privately addresses student behavior—takes student aside, or out of room

DS2: Teacher publicly addresses student behavior in front of other students

Discipline TONE: Add one to the end

"+" denotes a positive orientation (e.g., an invitation to discuss, such as "Tell me what's going on", or a smile, etc.)

"–" denotes a negative orientation such as a reprimand (e.g., DS2– means *Reprimands student in front of class*)

Notes

Chapter 1

1. In this book we use the term *Black* to include individuals who are so identified by others due to their skin color and physical features, and who identify themselves as being of African or Caribbean descent; this includes students who identify as "African American."

2. We define *Latino* as individuals who identify as being of Cuban, Mexican, Puerto_Rican, Dominican, South or Central American, or other Latin American cultural origin regardless of race.

3. Schott Foundation, *Yes We Can: The Schott 50 State Report on Black Males in Education* (Cambridge, MA: Schott Foundation, 2010); P. Noguera, *The Trouble with Black Boys* (San Francisco: Jossey-Bass, 2008).

4. Noguera, *Trouble with Black Boys*; R. Mincy, *Black Males Left Behind* (Washington, DC: Urban Institute Press, 2006).

5. A. M. Miniño, *Mortality among teenagers aged 12–19 years: United States, 1999–2006* (NCHS data brief no. 37, Hyattsville, MD: National Center for Health Statistics, 2010).

6. Centers for Disease Control, *FactSheet on HIV and African Americans*, http://www.cdc.gov/hiv/topics/aa/.

7. K. D. Kochanek, J. Q. Xu, S. L. Murphy et al., *Deaths: Preliminary data for 2009* (National vital statistics reports, vol. 59, no. 4, Hyattsville, MD: National Center for Health Statistics, 2011).

8. Phillip Moss and C. Tilly, "Raised Hurdles for Black Men: Evidence from Interviews with Employers" (working paper, Department of Policy and Planning, University of Massachusetts–Lowell, 1993); W. J. Wilson, *More Than Just Race: Being Black and Poor in the Inner City* (New York: W. W. Norton, 2009).

9. M. Torres and E. Fergus, "Social Mobility and the Complex Status of Latino Males: Education, Employment and Incarceration Patterns from 2000–2009," in *Invisible No More: Understanding the Disenfranchisement of Latino Men and*

Boys, ed. P. Noguera, A. Hurtado, and E. Fergus (New York: Routledge, 2011); R. Fry and M. Lopez, *Hispanic New Largest Minority in College Enrollment* (Washington, DC: Pew Hispanic Center, 2012).

10. Torres and Fergus, "Social Mobility"; B. Meade, F. Gaytan, E. Fergus, and P. Noguera, *A Close Look at the Dropout Crisis: Examining Black and Latino Males in New York City* (New York: Metropolitan Center for Urban Education, 2009).

11. Torres and Fergus, "Social Mobility."

12. P. Gandara and F. Contreras, *The Latino Education Crisis* (Cambridge, MA: Harvard University Press, 2010); P. Noguera, A. Hurtado, and E. Fergus, eds., *Invisible No More: Understanding the Disenfranchisement of Latino Men and Boys* (New York: Routledge, 2011).

13. E. Fergus, P. Noguera, M. Martin, and L. McCready, *Theories of Change Among Single-Sex Schools for Black and Latino Boys: An Intervention in Search of Theory* (New York: Metropolitan Center for Urban Education, 2010).

14. http://www2.ed.gov/nclb/landing.jhtml.

15. National Association for Single-Sex Public Education Web site, http://www.singlesexschools.org/schools-schools.htm.

16. F. Mael et al., *Single-Sex versus Coeducational Schooling: A Systematic Review* (Washington, DC: U.S. Department of Education, Office of Planning, Evaluation, and Policy Development, 2005); F. Mael, "Single-Sex and Coeducational Schooling: Relationships to Socioemotional and Academic Development," *Review of Educational Research* 68 (1998):101–129.

17. Mael, "Single-Sex and Coeducational Schooling."

18. Claude Steele, *Whistling Vivaldi: And Other Clues to How Stereotypes Affect Us.* (New York: W.W. Norton, 2010).

19. William Julius Wilson, "Cycles of Deprivation and the Underclass Debate," *The Social Service Review* 59, no. 4 (1985): 541–559; Sheldon H. Danziger and Robert H. Haveman, eds., *Understanding Poverty* (Cambridge, MA: Harvard University Press, 2001).

20. Jean Anyon, "Social Class and School Knowledge," *Curriculum Inquiry* 11 (1981): 2–42; H. Giroux, *Theory and Resistance in Education* (New York: Bergin and Harvey, 1983); Douglas Massey, "Latinos, poverty, and the underclass: A new agenda for research," *Hispanic Journal of Behavioral Sciences* 15 (1993): 449–475.

21. S. Danziger, G. Sandefur, and D. Weinberg, *Confronting Poverty* (Cambridge, MA: Harvard University Press, 1994).

22. Nathan Glazer and Daniel Moynihan, *Beyond the Melting Pot* (Cambridge, MA: MIT Press, 1970); O. Lewis, *The Children of Sanchez* (New York: Random House, 1961).

23. John Ogbu, "Variability in Minority School Performance: A Problem in Search of an Explanation," *Anthropology and Education Quarterly* 18 (1987): 312–334.

24. Lewis, *Children of Sanchez.*

25. Ogbu, "Variability in Minority School Performance," 312–334.

26. J. Hoberman, *Darwin's Athletes* (New York: Houghton Mifflin, 1997).

27. James Diego Vigil, *Barrio Gangs: Street Life and Identity in Southern California* (Austin, TX: University of Texas Press, 1988).

28. Signithia Fordham, *Blacked Out: Dilemmas of Race, Identity, and Success at Capital High* (Chicago: University of Chicago Press, 1996).

29. Michelle Fine, *Framing Dropouts: Notes on the Politics of an Urban Public High School* (Albany, NY: State University of New York Press, 1991); J. MacLeod, *Ain't no makin' it: Leveled aspirations in a low-income neighborhood* (Boulder, CO: Westview Press, 1995).

30. R. Morrow and C. Torres, *Social Theory and Education* (Albany, MA: SUNY Press, 1995); M. B. Spencer, "Social and cultural influences on school adjustment: The application of an identity-focused cultural ecological perspective," *Educational Psychologist* 34 (1999): 43–57; M. B. Spencer, D. Dupree, and T. Hartmann, "A phenomenological variant of ecological systems theory (PVEST): A self-organization perspective in context," *Development and Psychopathology* 9 (1997): 817–833.

31. P. Bourdieu, "Cultural Reproduction and Social Reproduction," in *Power and Ideology in Education* (London: Oxford University Press, 1977); S. Bowles and H. Gintis, *Schooling in Capitalist America* (New York: Basic Books, 1976); Paul Willis, *Learning to Labor: How Working Class Kids Get Working Class Jobs* (London: Saxon House, 1977).

32. L. Althusser, "Ideology and Ideological State Apparatuses," in *Lenin and Philosophy and Other Essays* (New York: Monthly Review Press, 1971); J. Anyon, "Social Class and the Hidden Curriculum of Work," *Journal of Education* 162 (1981):67–92; Anyon, "Social Class and School Knowledge," 3–41; M. Apple, "The new sociology of education: Analyzing cultural and economic reproduction," *Harvard Educational Review* 48 (1978):495–503.

33. M. B. Spencer, D. Dupree, and T. Hartmann, "A phenomenological variant of ecological systems theory (PVEST): A self-organization perspective in context," *Development and Psychopathology* 9 (1997): 817–833; M. B. Spencer, "Social and cultural influences on school adjustment: The application of an identity-focused cultural ecological perspective," *Educational Psychologist* 34 (1999): 43–57.

Chapter 2

1. Sample books are Peg Tyre, *The Trouble with Boys: A Surprising Report Card on Our Sons, Their Problems at School, and What Parents and Educators Must Do* (New York: Crown, 2008), and Niobe Way, *Deep Secrets: Boys' Friendships and the Crisis of Connection* (Cambridge, MA: Harvard University Press, 2011).

2. E. Fergus and P. Noguera, "Doing What It Takes to Prepare Black and Latino Males in College," in *Changing Places: How Communities Will Improve the*

Health of Boys of Color, ed. C. Edley and J. Ruiz (Berkeley, CA: University of California Press, 2010); J. Greene and M. Winters, *Leaving Boys Behind: Public High School Graduation Rate* (New York: Manhattan Institute, 2006); P. Noguera, A. Hurtado, and E. Fergus, eds., *Invisible No More: Understanding the Disenfranchisement of Latino Boys and Men* (New York: Routledge, 2011).

3. M. Gurian, *The Minds of Boys* (San Francisco: Jossey-Bass, 2007); Leonard Sax, *Boys Adrift* (New York: Basic Books, 2009).

4. Lise Eliot, *Pink Brain, Blue Brain: How Small Differences Grow into Troublesome Gaps—And What We Can Do about It* (Houghton Mifflin Harcourt, 2009).

5. Beth C. Weitzman, Diana Silver, and Keri-Nicole Dillman, "Integrating a Comparison Group Design into a Theory of Change Evaluation: The Case of the Urban Health Initiative," *American Journal of Evaluation* 23 (2002): 371–385.

6. Anthony Bryk and Barbara Schneider, *Trust in Schools* (New York: Russell Sage Foundation, 2002).

7. Nel Noddings, *The Challenge to Care in Schools* (New York: Teachers College Press, 2005); Angela Valenzuela, *Subtractive Schooling: U.S.–Mexican Youth and the Politics of Caring* (Albany, NY: SUNY Press, 1999).

8. C. Suarez-Orozco, M. Suarez-Orozco, and T. Todorava, *Learning a New Land* (Cambridge, MA: Harvard University Press, 2008).

9. Oscar Lewis, *The Children of Sanchez* (New York: Random House, 1961).

10. Signithia Fordham, "Racelessness as a Factor in Black Students' School Success: Pragmatic Strategy or Pyrrhic Victory?" *Harvard Educational Review* 58 (1988): 54–84; S. Fordham and John Ogbu, "Black Students' School Success: Coping with the Burden of Acting White," *Urban Review* 18 (1986): 176–206.

11. J. S. Eccles and A. Wegfield, "Teacher Expectations and Student Motivation," in *Teacher Expectancies*, ed. J. B. Dusek (Hillsdale, NJ: Erlbaum, 1985), 185–220; J. S. Eccles-Parson, T. F. Adler, and C. M. Kaczula, "Socialization of achievement attitudes and beliefs: Parental influences," *Child Development* 53 (1982): 310–321; J. S. Eccles-Parsons, J. L. Meece, T. F. Adler, and C. M. Kaczula, "Sex differences in attributions and learned helplessness," *Sex Roles* 8 (1982): 421–432.

Chapter 3

1. College Board, *Reaching the top: A report of the national task force on minority high achievement* (New York: College Board Publications, 1999), http://research.collegeboard.org/sites/default/files/publications/2012/7/misc1999-3-reaching-the-top-minority-achievement.pdf; Michael T. Nettles, Catherine M. Millett, and Douglas D. Ready, "Attacking the African American–White Achievement Gap on College Admissions Tests" (Washington, DC: Brookings Papers on Education Policy, No. 6, 2003), 215–252.

2. http://www.avid.org.

3. Gloria Ladson-Billings, *Dreamkeepers* (New York: Jossey-Bass, 2009).

4. Ladson-Billings, *Dreamkeepers*.

5. L. Delpit, *Other People's Children: Cultural Conflict in the Classroom* (New York: New Press, 2006).

6. T. Perry, C. Steele, and A. Hilliard, *Young, Gifted, and Black: Promoting High Achievement Among African-American Students* (Boston: Beacon, 2003).

7. J. J. Irvine and D. E. York, "Learning styles and culturally diverse students: A review of literature," in *Handbook of Research on Multicultural Education*, ed. J. A. Banks and C. A. Banks, 484–497 (San Francisco: Jossey-Bass, 2001); G. Ladson-Billings, "Preparing teachers for diverse student populations: A critical race theory perspective," *Review of Research in Education* 24 (1999): 211–247; Ladson-Billings, *Dreamkeepers*.

8. G. Gay, *Becoming Multicultural Educators: Personal Journey for Professional Agency* (San Francisco: Jossey-Bass, 2003).

9. Gay, *Becoming Multicultural Educators*; Ladson-Billings, *Dreamkeepers*.

10. James A. Banks et al., *Democracy and Diversity: Principles and Concepts for Educating Citizens in a Global World* (Seattle: University of Washington, Center for Multicultural Education, 2005); Geneva Gay, *Culturally Responsive Teaching: Theory, Research and Practice* (New York: Teachers College Press, 2000); Ladson-Billings, *Dreamkeepers*; Christine Sleeter, *Culture, Difference and Power* (New York: Teachers College Press, 2001).

Chapter 4

1. J. D. House, "Self-Beliefs as Predictors of Student Grade Performance in Science, Engineering and Mathematics," *International Journal of Instructional Media* 27, no. 2 (2000): 207–220; G. Evelyn LeSure-Lester, "Effects of Coping Styles on College Persistence Decisions among Latino Students in Two-Year Colleges," *Journal of Student Retention* 5, no. 1 (2003–2004): 11–22; S. B. Robbins, K. Lauver, Huy Le, D. Davis, Ronelle Langley, and A. Carlstrom, "Do Psychosocial and Study Skill Factors Predict College Outcomes? A Meta-Analysis," *Psychological Bulletin* 130 (2004): 261–288.

2. Wayne K. Hoy, C. John Tarter, and Anita Woolfolk Hoy, "Academic Optimism of Schools: A Force for Student Achievement," *American Educational Research Journal* 43, no. 3 (Fall 2006): 425–446.

3. Huy Le, Alex Casillas, Steven Robbins, and Ronelle Langley, "Motivational and Skills, Social, and Self-Management Predictors of College Outcomes: Constructing the Student Readiness Inventory," *Educational and Psychological Measurement* 65, no. 3 (2005): 482–508; Veronica Lotkowski, Steven Robbins, and Richard Noeth, "The Role of Academic and Non-Academic Factors in Improving College Retention: Act Policy Report," ACT, 2004.

4. Le, Casillas, Robbins, and Langley, ibid.; Lotkowski, Robbins, and Noeth, ibid.

5. K. A. Griffin and W. R. Allen, "Mo' money, mo' problems?': High achieving Black high school students' experiences with resources, racial climate, and resilience." *Journal of Negro Education*, 75 no. 3 (2006), 478–494.

6. R. Mickelson, "The Attitude-Achievement Paradox among Black Adolescents," *Sociology of Education* 63 (Jan. 1990): 44–61.
7. Ibid.
8. E. Fergus, *Skin color and identity formation: Perceptions of opportunity and academic orientation among Puerto Rican and Mexican youth* (New York: Routledge, 2004); Carla O'Connor, "Making sense of the complexity of social identity in relation to achievement: A sociological challenge in the new millennium," *Sociology of Education*, Extra Issue (2001): 159–168; Carla O'Connor, "Race, Class, and Gender in America: Narratives of opportunity among low-income African American youths," *Sociology of Education* 72 (1999): 137–157.
9. Theresa Perry, C. Steele, and A. Hilliard, *Young, Gifted and Black: Promoting High Achievement among African American Students* (Boston: Beacon, 2004).
10. National Center on Education Statistics, *Postsecondary Expectations and Plans for the High School Senior Class of 2003–04* (Washington, DC: NCES, 2010).
11. J. Weissman, Bulakowski, and Jumisko. "Using research to evaluate developmental education programs and policies." In J. M. Ignash (ed.), "Implementing effective policies for remedial and developmental education," *New Directions for Community Colleges*, No. 100 (1997), 73–80.
12. Founded in 1989, Posse identifies public high school students with extraordinary academic and leadership potential who may be overlooked by traditional college selection processes. Posse extends to these students the opportunity to pursue personal and academic excellence by placing them in supportive, multicultural teams—Posses—of 10 students. Posse partner colleges and universities award Posse Scholars four-year, full-tuition leadership scholarships; see www.possefoundation.org.
13. Jacquelynne S. Eccles, Carol A. Wong, and Stephen C. Peck, "Ethnicity as a Social Context for the Development of African-American Adolescents," *Journal of School Psychology* 44, no. 5 (Oct. 2006): 407–26.
14. C. Midgley, H. Feldlaufer, and J. S. Eccles, "Student/Teacher Relations and Attitudes toward Mathematics Before and After the Transition to Junior High School," *Child Development* 1, no. 60 (1989): 981–992.
15. Midgley, Feldlaufer, and Eccles, ibid.; Meredith Phillips, "What Makes Schools Effective? A Comparison of the Relationships of Communitarian Climate and Academic Climate to Mathematics Achievement and Attendance During Middle School," *American Educational Research Journal* 34 (Winter 1997): 633–662.

Chapter 5
1. Lisa Delpit, *Other People's Children: Cultural Conflict in the Classroom* (New York: The New Press, 2006).
2. Geneva Smitherman, *Talkin That Talk: Language, Culture and Education in African America* (New York: Routledge, 2000).

3. The total responses for this cohort of survey respondents was 1,056; however, only 1,007 identified a racial or ethnic identification.

4. E. Fergus, P. Noguera, and M. Martin, "Construction of Race and Ethnicity for and by Latinos," in *Handbook on Latinos in Education*, ed. E. Murillo et al. (New York: Routledge, 2010).

5. W. E. Cross Jr., *Shades of Black: Diversity in African-American Identity* (Philadelphia: Temple University Press, 1991).

6. Ibid.; J. S. Phinney, "The multigroup ethnic identity measure: A new scale for use with diverse groups," *Journal of Adolescent Research* 7 (1992): 156–176.

7. This statement further highlights the hyperawareness boys of color maintain about being profiled in ways that mirror the 2012 murder of Trayvon Martin.

8. Claude M. Steele and Joshua Aronson, "Stereotype threat and the intellectual test performance of African Americans," *Journal of Personality and Social Psychology* 69, no. 5 (1995): 797–811.

Chapter 6

1. C. A. Farrington, M. Roderick, E. Allensworth, J. Nagaoka, T. S. Keyes, D. W. Johnson, and N. O. Beechum, *Teaching adolescents to become learners. The role of noncognitive factors in shaping school performance: A critical literature review* (Chicago: University of Chicago Consortium on Chicago School Research, 2012).

2. P. Tough, *How Children Succeed* (New York: Mariner Books, 2013); L. A. Blackwell, K. H. Trzesniewski, and C. S. Dweck, "Theories of intelligence and achievement across the junior high school transition: A longitudinal study and an intervention," *Child Development* 78 (2007): 246–263; A. L. Duckworth, C. Peterson, M. D. Matthews, and D. R. Kelly, "Grit: Perseverance and passion for long-term goals," *Journal of Personality and Social Psychology* 92 (2007): 1087–1101.

3. A. Bandura, *Social learning theory* (Englewood Cliffs, NJ: Prentice Hall, 1977); A. Bandura, *Social foundations of thought and action: A social-cognitive theory* (Englewood Cliffs, NJ: Prentice Hall, 1986); A. Bandura, "Social cognitive theory of self-regulation," *Organizational Behavior and Human Decision Processes* 50 (1991): 248–287.

4. R. Rothstein, *Class and Schools* (New York: EPI and Teachers College Press, 2004).

5. P. Carter, *Stubborn Roots: Race, Culture and Inequality in US and South African Schools* (New York: Oxford University Press, 2013);

6. W. Boykin and P. Noguera, *Creating the Opportunity to Learn: Moving from Research to Practice to Close the Achievement Gap* (Alexandria, VA: ASCD, 2011); C. Suarez-Orozco, M. M. Suarez-Orozco, and I. Todorova, *Learning a New Land: Immigrant Students in American Society* (Cambridge, MA: Harvard University Press, 2008).

7. M. Martin, R. Mincy, E. Fergus, and P. Noguera, *A Trajectory Study of Black Boys in NYC Public Schools* (New York: Metropolitan Center for Urban Education, 2011).

8. J. A. Fredricks, P. C. Blumenfeld, and A. H. Paris, "School Engagement: Potential of the Concept, State of the Evidence," *Review of Educational Research* 74, no. 1 (2004): 54–109; Suarez-Orozco et. al, *Learning a New Land*.

9. R. M. Baron and D. A. Kenny, "The moderator-mediator variable distinction in social psychological research: Conceptual, strategic and statistical considerations," *Journal of Personality and Social Psychology* 51, no. 6 (1986): 1173–1182; D. A. Kenny, D. A. Kashy, and N. Bolger, "Data analysis in social psychology," in *The Handbook of Social Psychology*, vol. 1, ed. D. Gilbert, S. Fiske, and G. Lindzey (Boston: McGraw-Hill, 1998), 233–265.

10. Boykin and Noguera, *Creating the Opportunity to Learn*; Suarez-Orozco et. al, *Learning a New Land*.

11. A. S. Bryk and B. L. Schneider, *Trust in schools: a core resource for improvement* (New York: Russell Sage Foundation, 2002); Fredricks, Blumenfeld, and Paris, "School Engagement," 54–109; N. Noddings, *The Challenge to Care in Schools: An Alternative Approach to Education*, 2nd ed. (New York: Teachers College Press, 2005); R. W. Roeser, J. S. Eccles, and A. J. Sameroff, "School as a context of early adolescents' academic and social-emotional development: A summary of research findings," *Elementary School Journal* 100, no. 5 (2000): 443–471; Suarez-Orozco et. al, *Learning a New Land*.

Chapter 7

1. http://stayaliveandfree.org.

2. http://www.molloy.edu/molloy-life/campus-life-and-activities/student-leadership/leadership-conferences.

3. A study carried out by the Metropolitan Center of Urban Education at New York University showed that while the two schools were objectively "low performing," when the performance of Black and Latino males at these schools was compared to the performance of Black and Latino males at other secondary schools, students at these "failing" schools were performing at higher levels.

4. David Tyack and Larry Cuban, *Tinkering Toward Utopia: A Century of Public School Reform* (Boston: Harvard University Education Press, 1997).

5. Ibid., 46.

6. C. Payne, *So Much Reform, So Little Change* (Boston: Harvard University Education Press, 2008); G. Orfield, *Hard Work for Good Schools: Facts, Not Fads, in Title I Reform* (New York: Century Foundation, 1996).

7. C. S. Jencks, S. Bartlett, M. Corcoran, J. Crouse, D. Eaglesfield, and G. Jackson et al., *Who gets ahead? The determinants of economic success in America* (New York: Basic Books, 1979); C. Jencks, *Inequality: A reassessment of the effect of family and schooling in America* (New York: Basic Books, 1972); C. Jencks and M. Phillips, *The black-white test score gap* (Washington, DC: Brookings Institution Press, 1998); P. Barton and R. Coley, *The black-white achievement gap: When progress stopped* (Princeton, NJ: Education Testing Service, 2010).

8. J. S. Coleman, *Equality and achievement in education* (Boulder, CO: Westview Press, 1969); Orfield, *Hard Work for Good Schools*.

9. Tyack and Cuban, *Tinkering Toward Utopia*; A. LaShaw, "The radical promise of reformist zeal: What makes inquiry for equity plausible?" *Anthropology and Education* 41, no. 4 (2010): 323–340.

10. Barton and Coley, *The black-white achievement gap*; Richard Rothstein, *Class and schools: Using social, economic, and educational reform to close the black-white achievement gap* (Washington, DC: Economic Policy Institute, 2004); Jencks and Phillips, *The black-white test score gap*; Barton and Coley, *The black-white achievement gap*.

11. A. Thernstrom and S. Thernstrom, *No Excuses: Closing the Racial Gap in Learning* (New York: Simon and Schuster, 2003).

12. D. Whitman, *Sweating the Small Stuff* (Washington, DC: Fordham Institute, 2003).

13. J. P. Comer, "Educating poor minority children," *Scientific American* 259, no. 5 (1988): 24–30; J. G. Dryfoos, J. Quinn, and C. Barkin, *Community Schools in Action: Lessons from a Decade of Practice* (New York: Oxford Press, 2005); H. S. Adelman and L. Taylor, "Mental health in schools and system restructuring," *Clinical Psychology Review* 19, no. 2 (1999): 137–163.

14. M. Martin, R. Mincy, E. Fergus, and P. Noguera, "Trajectory Study of Black Males in NYC Public Schools: 1998–2007." An examination of 10,000 Black Males entering NYC public schools as fourth graders and followed until 12th grade (2011); http://steinhardt.nyu.edu/scmsAdmin/media/users/eaf7/BMDC_Black_Male_Education_Trajectory_Report-FULL.pdf; B. Meade, F. Gaytan, E. Fergus, and P. Noguera, *A Close Look at the Dropout Crisis: Examining Black and Latino Males in New York City* (New York: NYU Metropolitan Center for Urban Education, 2009).

15. M. Greenberg and D. Schneider, *Environmentally devastated neighborhoods: Perceptions, policies, and realities* (New Brunswick, NJ: Rutgers University Press, 1996); Richard Rothstein, *Class and schools: Using social, economic, and educational reform to close the black-white achievement gap* (Washington, DC: Economic Policy Institute, 2004).

16. Tyack and Cuban, *Tinkering toward Utopia*; R. F Elmore, *School Reform from the Inside Out* (Cambridge, MA: Harvard Education Press, 2004).

17. LaShaw, "Radical promise of reformist zeal."

18. F. Hess, *Spinning wheels: The politics of urban school reform* (Washington, DC: Brookings Institution, 1999).

19. Elmore, *School Reform from the Inside Out*; M. Fullan, *Leading in a culture of change* (San Francisco: Jossey-Bass, 2007); P. A. Noguera, "Transforming High Schools," *Educational Leadership* 61, no. 8 (2005).

20. Perhaps the clearest example of an adverse, unintended adverse consequence of a reform was seen in California in 1992 after Governor Pete Wilson mandated that class sizes in kindergarten and first grade be lowered to no more

than 20 students per class. Policy makers had not anticipated that lowering class size would require them to create more classrooms and hire more teachers.

21. D. Kirp, *Kids first: Five big ideas for transforming children's lives and America's future* (New York: Perseus, 2011).

Appendix 1
1. School public relations packet.
2. Individual interview with Troy King.
3. Names of organizations are not provided in order to maintain anonymity of schools.

Acknowledgments

This book would not have been possible without the support and participation of countless individuals. First, we acknowledge the students, principals, teachers, school resource officers, school aides, social workers, guidance and college counselors, and other school staff who must remain nameless for the sake of confidentiality. We are grateful for your willingness to allow us to visit your schools and we deeply appreciate your candor as you shared with us your thoughts, concerns, and perceptions regarding the important work you are doing.

We also acknowledge the Bill and Melinda Gates Foundation and thank them for their generous support in funding this exploratory study. We are particularly grateful to Melissa Chabran and Jana Carlisle, the two program officers at Gates Foundation who provided us with insightful feedback during the data collection and report phases of the study.

The process of data collection involved countless hours of protocol development, field-testing, data collection, entry and analysis, and final report writing. This part of the project involved collaboration with colleagues, multiple graduate students, undergraduate students who were paid through work-study, and research staff who contributed a great deal to this endeavor. We are particularly appreciative of Laura Torres, Katherine Scuirba, Mellie Torres, Onnie Rogers, Anne Beitlers, Carolyn

Strom, Joseph Nelson, Alexandra Cordero, Lois Goddard, and Roey Ahram, whose dedication in carefully collecting and analyzing data for this study was essential. During the writing of this book specific individuals played a key role in contributing analysis and/or writing to some of the chapters, including: Professor Lance McCready (University of Toronto), Dr. Joseph Nelson, Anne Beitlers, Dr. Mellie Torres, and Dr. Katherine Scuirba.

Additionally we are thankful for the continuous feedback from the editorial team at Harvard Education Press. In particular we appreciate the hours of reading and conversation with Caroline Chauncey—your feedback was very helpful.

Finally, we are extremely grateful for the unwavering support of our respective family members. Their love and understanding was essential throughout the study and while we were writing this book.

About the Authors

Edward Fergus is assistant professor of educational leadership at Steinhardt School of Culture, Education, and Human Development at New York University. Dr. Fergus is a practitioner and researcher whose work explores the effects of educational policy and practices on the lives of people living in vulnerable conditions. More specifically, his current work is on the educational outcomes of boys of color, disproportionality in special education and suspensions, and school climate conditions for low-income and marginalized populations. His work is intended to provide ways in which practitioners can develop schools as protective environments for low-income and marginalized student populations. Dr. Fergus has been a secondary school history teacher, evaluator of state and federal programs, and program director of out-of-school-time programs. Since 2004, he has been the coprincipal investigator of a multimillion-dollar state contract with the New York State Department of Education on disproportionality and has served as coprincipal investigator of a study on single-sex schools for boys of color (funded by the Bill and Melinda Gates Foundation). Dr. Fergus was also appointed in 2011 to the Yonkers Public Schools Board of Education and currently serves on the Governor's New York State Juvenile Justice Advisory Group. He has published numerous articles on disproportionality in special education and on race/ethnicity in schools; he is the author of *Skin Color and Identity Formation: Perceptions of Opportunity and Academic Orientation* *among Mexican and Puerto Rican Youth* (Routledge, 2004), and coeditor with A. Hurtado and P. Noguera of *Invisible No More: Understanding the Disenfranchisement of Latino Men and Boys* (Routledge, 2011).

Dr. Fergus received a bachelor's degree in political science and education from Beloit College and a Doctorate in Education Policy and Social Foundations from the University of Michigan.

Pedro Noguera is the Peter L. Agnew Professor of Education at New York University. He holds tenured faculty appointments in both the department of Teaching and Learning and the department of Humanities and Social Sciences at the Steinhardt School of Culture, Education, and Human Development at NYU. He is also the executive director of the Metropolitan Center for Urban Education and the codirector of the Institute for Globalization and Education in Metropolitan Settings (IGEMS). Dr. Noguera is the author of seven books and over 150 articles and monographs. His most recent books are *Creating the Opportunity to Learn*, with A. Wade Boykin (ASCD, 2011) and *Invisible No More: Understanding the Disenfranchisement of Latino Men and Boys*, with A. Hurtado and E. Fergus (Routledge, 2011). Dr. Noguera appears as a regular commentator on educational issues on CNN, National Public Radio, and other national news outlets. From 2009 to 2012 he served as a trustee for the State University of New York (SUNY) as an appointee of the governor. He serves on the boards of numerous national and local organizations including the Economic Policy Institute, the Young Women's Leadership Institute, The After-School Corporation, and *The Nation* magazine.

Margary Martin is a visiting assistant professor at Brown University. Her research focuses on the ways in which education policies and reforms influence the schooling experiences and individual academic trajectories of youth in underserved communities.

Index